HIKING TRAILS 2
South-Central Vancouver Island and the Gulf Islands

Shawnigan Lake, Cobble Hill, Duncan and the
Cowichan Valley, Ladysmith, Cedar, Yellow Point, Nanaimo,
the Gulf Islands, Oceanside, Port Alberni and
west to Long Beach

Revised and expanded by Richard K. Blier

NINTH EDITION, 2010

VANCOUVER ISLAND TRAILS
INFORMATION SOCIETY (VITIS)

Dear Jean,
Here's to many more adventures with you & Lewis!

Merry Christmas!

Marissa
xoxo

2017

Ninth edition copyright © 2010
Vancouver Island Trails Information
Society

Original copyright © 1973; Outdoor
Club of Victoria Trails Information
Society. Revised and/or reprinted 1978,
1982, 1988, 1993, 2000, 2007. Society
name change, 1993, to Vancouver Island
Trails Information Society.

Illustrations
Judy Trousdell

Cover photo
Joyce Folbigg
Atop Mt. Norman, South Pender Island

Photos
Credits for other photos are shown
with photo

Book design
Frances Hunter, Beacon Hill
Communications Group Inc.

Maps
Map revisions by Richard K. Blier.
Final map production by
Jim Bisakowski, BookDesign.ca.

**Library and Archives Canada Cataloguing
in Publication**

Hiking trails 2 : south-central Vancouver
Island and the Gulf Islands / compiled
and edited by Richard K. Blier. —9th ed.
Previously publ. under title: Hiking trails II.

ISBN 978-0-9697667-7-3

1. Trails—British Columbia—Vancouver
Island—Guidebooks. 2. Trails—British
Columbia—Gulf Islands—Guidebooks.
3. Hiking—British Columbia—Vancouver
Island—Guidebooks. 4. Hiking—British
Columbia—Gulf Islands—Guidebooks.
5. Vancouver Island (B.C.)—Guidebooks.
6. Gulf Islands (B.C.)—Guidebooks. I. Blier,
Richard K., 1952- II. Vancouver Island Trails
Information Society

GV199.44.C22V35 2009 796.5109711'2
C2009-905570-8

*Printed and bound in Canada by Friesens,
Altona, Manitoba. Distributed by Orca Book
Publishers, Victoria, BC*

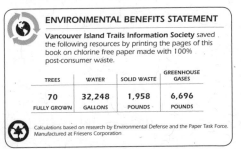

ENVIRONMENTAL BENEFITS STATEMENT

Vancouver Island Trails Information Society saved the following resources by printing the pages of this book on chlorine free paper made with 100% post-consumer waste.

TREES	WATER	SOLID WASTE	GREENHOUSE GASES
70 FULLY GROWN	32,248 GALLONS	1,958 POUNDS	6,696 POUNDS

Calculations based on research by Environmental Defense and the Paper Task Force. Manufactured at Friesens Corporation

Vancouver Island Trails Information Society (VITIS)

web page: www.hikingtrailsbooks.com
e-mail: trails@hikingtrailsbooks.com
telephone: Victoria area 250-474-5043

toll free: 1-866-598-0003
fax: Victoria area 250-474-4577
toll free fax: 1-888-258-4213

Contents

General Map of South-Central Vancouver Island and the Gulf Islands

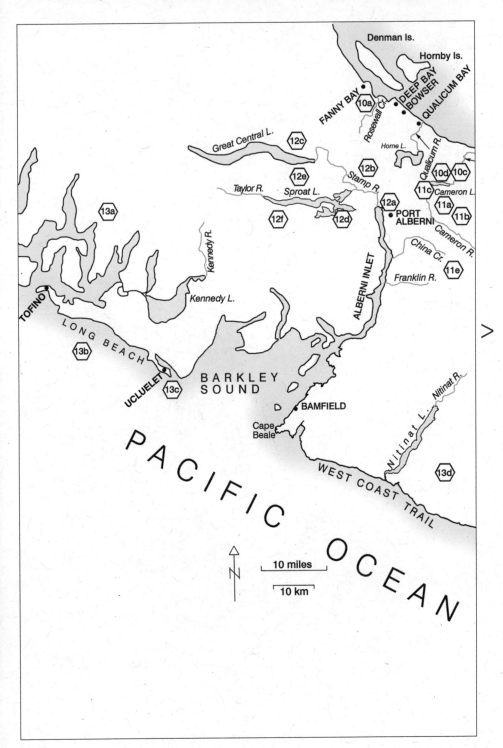

General Map of South-Central Vancouver Island and the Gulf Islands

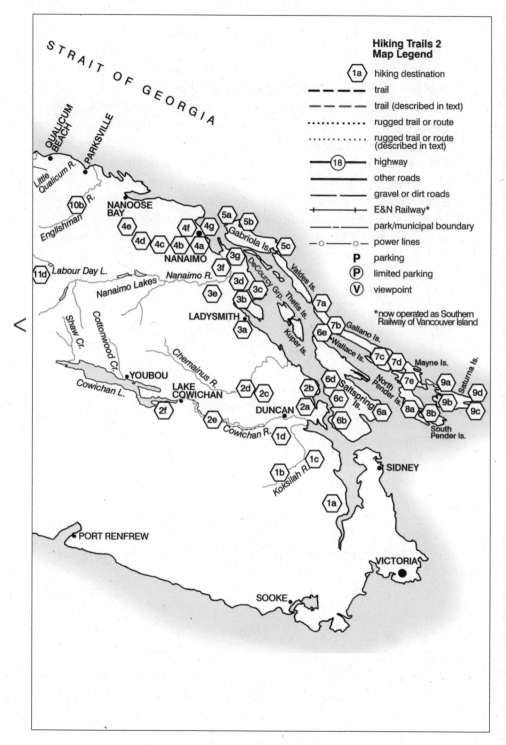

**Hiking Trails 2
Map Legend**

1a — hiking destination
— — — trail
— — — trail (described in text)
· · · · · · rugged trail or route
· · · · · · rugged trail or route (described in text)
—18— highway
—— other roads
— — gravel or dirt roads
+—+—+ E&N Railway*
—o—o— power lines
P parking
Ⓟ limited parking
Ⓥ viewpoint

*now operated as Southern Railway of Vancouver Island

STRAIT OF GEORGIA

QUALICUM BEACH
PARKSVILLE
Little Qualicum R.
Englishman R.
NANOOSE BAY
Labour Day L.
Nanaimo Lakes
Nanaimo R.
NANAIMO
Gabriola Is.
DeCourcy Grp.
Valdes Is.
Thetis Is.
Kuper Is.
LADYSMITH
Shaw Cr.
Cottonwood Cr.
Cowichan L.
YOUBOU
LAKE COWICHAN
Chemainus R.
DUNCAN
Cowichan R.
Koksilah R.
Galiano Is.
Wallace Is.
Mayne Is.
Saturna Is.
North Pender Is.
Saltspring Is.
South Pender Is.
SIDNEY
VICTORIA
PORT RENFREW
SOOKE

7

Editor's Note

Welcome to the Ninth Edition of *Hiking Trails 2: South-Central Vancouver Island*. Most of the hikes described are on clearly defined trails within relatively easy reach of Victoria. Areas included are Shawnigan Lake, Cobble Hill, Duncan, the Cowichan Valley, Ladysmith, Cedar, Yellow Point, Nanaimo, the Gulf Islands, Oceanside (including Parksville, Qualicum Beach, Qualicum Bay, Bowser, Deep Bay and Fanny Bay), Port Alberni and Highway 4 to the West Coast and Long Beach. New trails and routes have been added and existing material has been updated and expanded.

Readers familiar with the last edition of *Hiking Trails II* will notice that a few hikes are now missing from the book. Areas affected include Hill 60, Bald Mountain, Mount Sutton, Heather Mountain, Shaw Valley, Lomas Lake and the Nanaimo Lakes/Green Mountain area. These deletions are partly due to the "no public access at any time" policy that now applies to many private forestlands on southern Vancouver Island.

Other hiking destinations were removed owing to deactivated or impassable roads, obliteration of trails by logging, landslides or washouts. Many closures are for public safety and liability reasons. Should this situation change at any point, hopefully some of these hikes will return in a future edition of *Hiking Trails 2*. In the meantime, periodically check the Vancouver Island Trails Information Society's (VITIS) website at www.hikingtrailsbooks.com for updates.

Even one hiker can impact fragile wilderness areas. Practise no-trace camping, carry out all litter and treat the forests and trails with respect. Continued co-operation among local communities, industry, regional, municipal and provincial governments, private property owners, user-groups and individuals will help ensure lasting public access.

Whether you plan to revisit a favourite trail or head off to a new hiking destination, *Hiking Trails 2* is the place to start your adventure.

Richard K. Blier

Maps

Hiking Trails 2 includes a variety of maps. There are numerous regional access and individual maps for many featured hiking destinations. Not every hike has its own map, but in these cases we direct readers to our Additional Information heading, under which they will find sources of detailed guides. Trails highlighted in red on the maps are mentioned in the text. Note that this book's maps are not all at the same scale and toilet facilities and picnic tables are not shown. These are termed "park facilities" and will usually be found near main parking areas. The map legend is on the General Map on page 7.

Some *Hiking Trails 2* maps are based on the 1:50,000 (2 cm = 1 km) National Topographical Series (NTS). These contour (topographical) maps are printed in blue and grey, with overlays for trails and other features. These maps have been reproduced with the permission of Natural Resources Canada 2010, courtesy of the Centre for Topographic Information: 92B/11 Sidney, 92B/12 Shawnigan Lake, 92B/13 Duncan, 92B/14 Mayne Island, 92C/16 Cowichan Lake, 92F/2 Alberni Inlet and 92F/7 Horne Lake (1:50,000 scale).

This book's maps clearly differentiate between trails and routes. Wilderness hiking destinations are identified in the text. Remote trails and routes should only be used by experienced hikers or groups led by a knowledgeable leader.

The maps in this book are not substitutes for the NTS maps or other detailed guides. Use *Hiking Trails 2* in conjunction with relevant maps and highway guides that cover the region you intend to visit.

Maps are available from:

www.canmap.com *Canadian Cartographics*
www.cloverpoint.com *Clover Point Cartographics*
www.publications.gov.bc.ca *Crown Publications*
www.nrcan.gc.ca *Natural Resources Canada*
www.itmb.com *International Travel Maps*
www.islandblue.com *Island Blue Print*
1-800-665-2513 (toll-free) *Nanaimo Maps and Charts*
www.backroadmapbooks.com *Mussio Ventures' Vancouver Island Backroad Mapbook*
www.robinsonsoutdoors.com *Robinson's Outdoor Store*

Every effort has been made to ensure the accuracy of the maps within Hiking Trails 2. Should you spot any glaring omissions or discrepancies please send your updates to the Vancouver Island Trails Information Society (VITIS) at www.hikingtrailsbooks.com *or e-mail at* trails@hikingtrailsbooks.com. *Hike updates are periodically posted on the VITIS website.*

How to Use This Book

Hiking Trails 2: South-Central Vancouver Island and the Gulf Islands is divided into 13 chapters, based on geographical regions. There are over 60 featured hikes and short listings of many nearby hiking destinations. The book's map legend is on the General Map, page 7. The following brief definitions are used to describe levels of trail difficulty:

Easy: The trail is generally level with little or no elevation gain or hills. The trail's surface may be paved, boardwalk, gravel, chip or dirt. Chances of losing your way are slim.

Moderate: These trails may be muddy and uneven, with roots and branches, elevation changes, creek crossings and some steep hills. Unmarked junctions could be confusing. The trails may not be suitable for children or inexperienced hikers.

Strenuous: On these trails expect frequent elevation changes and long, steep hills. You may encounter slick logs, blowdowns and tricky creek crossings. Trails may be narrow, rough and uneven. These routes are prone to slippery, muddy conditions and are often less maintained and sometimes overgrown. Along many sections, staying on course is often problematic. These trails traverse difficult, more remote terrain and usually are not suitable for most children or inexperienced hikers.

Distances: Wherever possible one-way (or loop) hiking distances are noted. Occasionally average hiking times are listed. These are subjective and travel times will depend on an individual's pace, degree of fitness, the trail's condition, the weather and the time of year. Use these ratings as general guides only.

Highlights: Look here for a summary of what the hike offers and what scenic highlights you will discover in the area.

Access: This is where to find concise directions to area trailheads.

Cautions: Important information on specific trail hazards; potential problem spots; localized conditions and other things to watch out for and know prior to your hike are listed.

Hike Description: Featured hikes are described and shown in red on accompanying maps.

Worth Noting: Here are hints to help ensure your hike is enjoyable and safe. Included are facts on plants, animals, birds and landforms; information on the area's background and history; any local regulations and restrictions.

Nearby: This section briefly mentions any notable hiking destinations close to the featured area and describes how to get there.

Additional Information: This is where to find further information and area updates, maps, current applicable fees and seasonal closures. Pertinent area National Topographical Series (NTS) maps (scale 1:50,000) are listed.

Hints and Cautions

Hiking Trails 2 contains basic instructions for finding area trailheads. We do not include details on equipment and food; that is part of your pre-trip preparations. There are numerous sources of information available. Pre-trip planning is essential, especially if you are contemplating a full day's hike or travelling to a more isolated area. Our maps differentiate between trails and routes. Wilderness hiking destinations are clearly identified in the text. Remote trails and routes should only be attempted by experienced hikers or groups led by a knowledgeable leader.

Hiking

- *Trails*: For the benefit of newcomers to hiking, a trail is a distinctly defined way built and improved by humans, or an obvious path travelled regularly by animals. The most popular trails are easy to follow, receive regular upkeep and are signposted. Trails may be flagged with tape or ribbons or marked with cairns. The condition of many trails depends on the season, localized weather and amount of upkeep.

  Routes traverse rougher, more difficult terrain and are much harder to follow. Bad washouts and windfalls may impede progress.

- *Coastal hiking*: Be alert when hiking on beaches, tidal shelves or near headlands and surge channels. Unexpected or unusually large, rogue waves or a series of big waves may sweep in without warning. Hikers have been swept off rocks. Keep children and pets under close scrutiny and safely away from the surf. Be aware also of the danger posed by tsunami waves. These earthquake-induced giant surges can sweep inland for many kilometres. On most shoreline hikes an accurate knowledge of area tides is essential. Storms and steady winds may increase the heights of predicted high water. Tidal information is available at www.waterlevels. gc.ca.

- *Off-season hiking*: Be extra careful when hiking in the rainy off-season or after periods of extended heavy precipitation. Creeks and rivers may suddenly rise and washout, leaving a raging torrent where, previously, hikers faced only an easy wade across. Trails that traverse low-lying areas are prone to flooding and may be rendered impass-able for a time. During severe thunderstorms, lightning poses a serious threat to hikers. Take shelter immediately and avoid high ground and tall trees. Learn what the local weather has been like where you in-tend to hike and what the predicted trend will be. Gear up for adverse conditions and do not hesitate to turn back if things deteriorate.

- *Do not hike alone*: The wise hiker travels with a friend in case of an ac-cident. Leave information on your plans with someone who is reliable and include your expected time of return. Remember that searches in our rough terrain are difficult and expensive. Extra food, even on day hikes, may come in handy in case of delays.

- *Staying found*: Topographical maps and aerial photographs are useful adjuncts to the descriptions in this book. A compass—with knowledge of how to use it—is also useful since you can lose direction easily, even on a trail. Many hikers carry GPS units or cell phones. Remember these devices may not work in steep, mountainous terrain, deep valleys, or in other regions that are out of range.

- *Do not litter*: Conscientious hikers carry out all their litter on day trips and longer hikes. In many remote yet frequently visited areas there are no sanitation facilities, so be considerate of other trail users. Do not chop blazes into trees, as these scars are unsightly and lead to infection by various pests and diseases. Take nothing and leave only your foot-prints.

- *Fires*: Ideally you should build no fires except in an emergency. Be care-ful with any fire. Be aware of and follow seasonal fire regulations and closures. Clear at least a 1 m area from flammable materials around your fire and do not build a fire within at least 3 m of any log, bush or tree. Above all, put fires thoroughly out! Pour water on the fire afterwards and stir through the ashes to be certain there are no hot spots left which could flare up. Outdoor enthusiasts who still smoke should do so only at rest stops, never when hiking. Always make sure any cigarettes and matches are completely extinguished. Carry out your butts.

    Report fires at once to local authorities; do not assume someone else already has done so. Fires to reduce slash after logging are sometimes purposely set and are normally confined and patrolled. To report forest fires contact 1-800-663-5555 or dial 911.

The rugged beauty of Vancouver Island's West Coast Trail. RICHARD K. BLIER

- *Gear up properly*: Strong, sturdy footwear is recommended, as trails can be muddy, steep or rough. A small daypack is useful for lunch, matches, maps, camera, extra sweater, rainwear and other essentials, but weight should be kept to a minimum. Spare warm clothing is as vital as carrying water and extra food.

- *Parking and security*: For ease of access to trails like the Cowichan River Trail or the Trans-Canada Trail, it is prudent to travel to the trailheads in two vehicles and leave one at either end of the trail. This makes your return home a lot quicker and easier. Arrange to hike with some friends or an organized club or group. Park only in designated areas. If parking on the roadside, check for any restrictions. Do not block private driveways, access or fire roads or private property. Obey any posted notices.

  Lock your vehicle. Keep valuables out of sight or in your car's trunk. Trailhead theft is a growing problem at some locales. Many communities work together with local law enforcement agencies to monitor area forests under the Wilderness Watch or Observe, Record and Report programs.

- *Private property*: Respect all posted notices or signs and always ask permission before crossing private land. Do not damage anything and report any incidents you may witness.

- *Hunting season*: Do not risk being mistaken by hunters for a wild animal. Wear bright clothing. Stay away from hunting areas. Some hikers prefer to avoid the forests during the hunting season.

Wilderness Hiking

- When choosing a route for approaching an unfamiliar mountain, remember that unlogged ridges are easier to negotiate than valleys or draws. In central Vancouver Island, south and west-facing slopes below 1220 m are less bushy than those facing north and east. Above that elevation the reverse is true.

- Douglas-fir forests are clearer to walk through than western red cedar, yellow cedar and hemlock. From afar you can identify cedar by its yellow and green foliage. Avoid slopes with many dead, standing trees; they let in the light and make it bushy underfoot.

- Logging roads and bodies of water moving downstream usually lead out. Cross-country scrambling is difficult, so you should stay on trails unless you are absolutely certain where you are going. As you proceed, glance back often. Because mountainous terrain looks quite different when facing the other way, this will help you recognize features for your return. Every landmark noticed and remembered from the ascent will help.

- Deer and elk trails often are the best routes along valley floors and up the timbered ridges to the sub-alpine zone. Avoid the bottoms of V-shaped valleys and make for the ridges instead. Flat-bottomed valleys often have good game trails beside the creek or up on a flat bench 30 m or so above the water.

- Going up a mountain, all the ridges converge towards the summit, which is consequently hard to miss. But coming down, it is very easy in cloud to pick the wrong ridge and perhaps come down in the wrong valley. An altimeter is a worthwhile addition to the essential map and compass. On the descent, when the ridge suddenly divides, knowledge of your altitude should enable you to pinpoint your position accurately and pick the right route. In worsening weather, the barometer is probably falling and the altimeter may read high. A change of one kilopascal in barometric pressure represents about a 90 m error in altitude.

- If you scramble or climb on rocks, practise climbing down as well as up. A person ought to be able to climb down anything he or she can climb up, but few find this easy.

Hiking Health

- *Water*: Carry your own supply of drinking water and distrust water from creeks and lakes. Even in the wilderness the risk of water contamination is high. If you must use creek or lake water, boil, filter or treat it. This is the best precaution against giardiasis (beaver fever), a parasitic infection of the intestines spread by animal and human waste.

- *Hyperthermia*: This rapid rising of the body temperature (the opposite of hypothermia) is often caused by overexertion in hot, humid weather. Always wear a hat when hiking on sunny days and drink lots of fluids. Wear protective, loose fitting clothing and increase your salt intake.

- *Hypothermia*: Be aware of the dangers of hypothermia, a rapid lowering of the body temperature. Hikers exposed to the elements should learn to recognize early symptoms that include numbness in the extremities and shivering. Take immediate steps to get out of the wind and rain and to warm up by drying off, adding a layer of clothing and breaking for a snack or hot beverage. Advanced stages of hypothermia may be fatal.

- *First Aid*: Be sure that you have a first aid kit along. Many people are severely allergic to insect bites and poisonous plants. Carry insect repellent, antihistamine and your own prescription antidotes for any reactions.

- *Swimmer's Itch*: This allergic skin irritation is caused by microscopic parasites found in many west coast ponds and lakes. Tiny surface-dwelling larvae (mistaking humans for ducks and birds) accidentally enter a swimmer's skin. These organisms rapidly die off but their intrusion can cause rashes. Upon emerging from the water, bathers will first notice a tingling feeling on the skin and then red spots develop. Hours later, these will enlarge and start to itch. Individual reactions will vary. Symptoms may persist for 4 or 5 days, sometimes longer.

  Incidents are highest over the summer months when beaches are busiest. Worst swimming times are late in the day, especially after incoming winds have blown the parasites into shallow water. Avoid infested areas and look for posted advisories. Enter the water from a boat or dock rather than shoreline shallows. Towel off or shower (if possible) after coming out of the water.

- *Lyme Disease*: Some ticks found in BC carry the organism that causes Lyme Disease. Symptoms include muscle and joint pain, feverish headaches and fatigue or weakness in the facial muscles. A bull's-eye rash often develops. Paralysis starting in the legs and feet may occur in severe cases.

  Should you find a tick carefully use tweezers or forceps to gently remove the whole body by steadily lifting straight up. Be sure to extract any mouth parts that may be beneath the skin. Do not squeeze the tick as you remove it. Use of grease, gasoline or burning cigarettes and matches to remove the tick will not work and will increase the chance of infection. When the tick has been removed disinfect the bite site. For deeply imbedded ticks see a doctor.

  To avoid ticks stay on trails and do not bushwhack through tall grass or wooded areas. Tuck shirts in at the waistline and secure pant legs in socks or boots. Use an effective insect repellent. Wear light coloured clothing and check your clothing, body and scalp carefully.

- *Cryptococcal Disease*: In 1999, the air-borne fungus Cryptococcus gattii was identified in some trees and soils on Vancouver Island, notably along the island's east coast. These spores can attack the respiratory system creating symptoms akin to pneumonia. The fungus may also

Sturdy bridges along the Trans-Canada (Cowichan Valley) Trail now span the Cowichan River. Richard K. Blier

harm the nervous system. Persons over 60 years of age and domestic pets are most susceptible. In rare cases, death may result.

- *Hantavirus*: Hantavirus Pulmonary Syndrome is a flu-like illness that has been traced to rodents, especially deer mice. Infected animals spread the virus in their droppings, urine or saliva, the dust of which is then inhaled by people. Avoid disturbing mice nests and territories, particularly in and around old cabins. Cases of HPS remain extremely rare in BC.

Flora and Fauna

- *Plants*: Leave wild flowers where you find them; they seldom last long when picked, and uprooted specimens rarely can be transplanted to city gardens. Remember it is illegal to pick any park flowers. You may encounter the common stinging nettle or devil's club; poison oak is rare.

- *Wild animals*: Black bears, cougars and wolves are rarely seen and there are no poisonous snakes or established grizzly populations on Vancouver Island or the Gulf Islands. Sporadic grizzly bear sightings occur on northern Vancouver Island, where the distance required for the animals to swim over from the mainland is relatively short. When travelling trails in bear or cougar country look for telltale droppings or fresh tracks and avoid the area. Talk loudly or attach a bell to a backpack to alert animals of your presence. Watch for posted advisories.

Black bears: Bears are incredibly quick runners and are excellent tree-climbers. Always give these animals a wide berth. If you are approached, act big and make lots of noise. Avoid eye contact and slowly back away. Be particularly alert when hiking near berry patches, streams and rivers. Hang food securely away from camp, never in your tent.

Cougars: If you encounter a cougar do not panic and do not run. Make loud noises. Never turn your back or crouch. Give the animal an escape route. Gather up and protect children, who may be mistaken for prey. Face the animal, maintain eye contact and make yourself look bigger by standing tall, spreading your arms or waving branches. Cougars are powerful, agile predators. If attacked, fight back any way possible.

Ecological Reserves

These fragile areas of Crown Land are administered by BC Parks under the BC Ecological Reserves Program. The reserves are set aside for scientific research, outdoor classroom use and to preserve rare and endangered native plants or animals. BC Parks stresses the fact that reserves are not parks. In most cases, you require a Park Permit to do studies. Public use (e.g. hiking) is discouraged in ecological reserves. For those who are interested in what a reserve has to offer, it is better to arrange a guided tour at the appropriate time of year.

Vancouver Island Forest Lands

Multiple use of forestlands is now recognized, with recreation playing an important part in tree harvesting plans. Ownership of most forestlands is public Crown Land but some regions on Vancouver Island's east side (E & N Railway Grant) are privately owned. These may be closed to all public access. The bulk of public forests, and some private land, is under Tree Farm Licence (TFL) administered by the BC Forest Service. In recent years many private holdings have been removed from the TFLs. Area logging companies and the BCFS have developed select user-maintained camping and picnicking sites, but camping in non-designated areas is usually restricted.

Municipal Forest Reserves

Many community and municipality-based tracts of land and forest are dedicated to industry, recreation and forestry education. These areas of active and inactive logging roads and woodlots are also used by hikers, mountain bikers and horse riders. Motorized vehicles and fires are prohibited. Seasonal fire closures often restrict public access. This book features several Duncan area hikes that lie within the North Cowichan Municipal Forest (5000 ha). Created in 1946, the NCMF is one of North America's largest. If you visit a Municipal Forest, use designated access points, obey any posted notices and respect adjacent private property.

Forest Road Travel

Most trails described in *Hiking Trails 2* are reached along paved roads and highways. In some cases though, accessing more remote trailheads requires gravel forestry or logging road travel. The condition of Vancouver Island gravel roads varies seasonally and with the amount of maintenance received.

- *Logging roads*: Vancouver Island logging roads may be classified as "open", with travel allowed at all times; "restricted", with access limited to non-working hours on weekdays (normally from about 5:00 or 6:00 pm to 6:00 am) and around-the-clock on weekends and holidays; or "closed" at all times. When logging is completed many side roads and some mainlines are deactivated and bridges removed in compliance with Forestry and Fisheries guidelines.

- *Access restrictions*: Active logging, increased security due to the threat of vandalism, potential fire risk and public safety concerns are factors that restrict public access in certain regions. Some logging companies limit entry to weekends and holidays. Contract loggers may work on holidays and weekends forcing periodic road closures. Obey all signs and posted notices; a gate may be left open for logging trucks but locked later. Most logging trucks are in radio contact with each other and are not expecting unannounced traffic in unauthorized areas.

Access may be restricted on some roads during times of high fire hazard, even when BC Forest Service closures are not in effect. These limitations may change frequently without notice. A check a day or two in advance of a trip is worthwhile. Try to obtain available road and access updates from BC Forest Service offices, area logging companies or locals.

Some information may be available at:

BC Forest Service South Island Forest District (Port Alberni)
    www.for.gov.bc.ca/dsi
Island Timberlands
    www.islandtimberlands.com
TimberWest
    www.timberwest.com

Western Forest Products
    www.westernforest.com
West Island Woodlands Community Advisory Group
    www.westernforest.com/wiwag

- *Road safety*: On logging roads that are open travellers often share the routes with industrial traffic. Always yield to loaded trucks, particularly on narrow roads and when trucks are travelling downhill. This may require backing rapidly to a turn-off. When a logging truck is approaching, pull well over to the side of the road and wait until it passes. Trucks often travel in pairs, so don't be in a hurry to pull back onto the road after one has passed. You may have to wait for a company vehicle (the driver will be in radio contact with other industrial traffic) and follow it, pulling over when it does. Always travel with your headlights on, especially when the roads are dusty.

Private Logging Company or Tree Farm Licence Lands

Our Hiking Trails books do not normally advocate travel on private lands. If one wants to do so one naturally must seek permission and follow the rules of the landowner. Many traditional destinations have recently become less accessible due to new regulations laid down by some of the forest companies on private lands. Roads now are blocked by locked gates but sometimes it is difficult to identify and locate the landowner. Where known, the hiker should plan ahead by consulting the relevant company websites for information, visiting their offices or telephoning. (See Forest Road Travel on the previous page.) Some work sites are more receptive to public inquires while others may be too busy to volunteer to be helpful. Be polite but persistent.

In some cases, membership in an organization, such as the Federation of BC Mountain Clubs, may assist with access, particularly when the trip is an organized one. Trip leaders should bear this in mind when inquiring. This may help meet requirements such as liability insurance if this is needed. It behooves hikers to cooperate by reporting fires and suspected vandalism; license numbers may prove useful.

Be sure to check with the VITIS website where we try to include updates to trails and access where this information has been made available to us. But this site is only as good as hikers (or companies or organizations) make it by providing us with information. We will load such information onto the site usually hours after we receive it via our website.

Private logging companies claim to consider safety to be of paramount concern, but are also concerned with fires and vandalism. These are the main reason for their rules. Naturally, profits are of concern to shareholder driven companies. Rules of the road on private lands are similar to those on public lands except perhaps that in the former case they apply to a greater degree. Western Forest Products (WFP) has a general open road policy and with the usual precautions tends to welcome the public. Unfortunately some of the other major companies are more protective of their holdings and the utmost care should be taken to ensure there are no excuses for them to regret permitting public access.

Trucks on large operations, particularly on private roads, are often radio controlled, but there are many variations of this so scanners cannot be relied upon. On private roads, at least, truck drivers will assume that all vehicles travelling on them are radio equipped.

Gravel roads can be slippery and treacherous, particularly under adverse weather conditions, and to drivers unfamiliar with them. Drive slowly at all times; maximum speed on WFP roads currently is 60 km and most roads are speed controlled as posted. Deactivated roads may be trenched but not well marked. Many accidents on forest roads are between public vehicles, not with experienced company drivers. Yield at all times to working vehicles; be prepared to pull over and stop. Travel with lights on. Pullouts may only hold one vehicle; watch for work vehicles travelling in groups. Some logging trucks are much wider than those designed for public roads and are much longer so passing on corners and bridges can be extremely hazardous. The logs at the end of a load may destroy cars parked or pulled over at corners. Logging trucks may weigh as much a 135 tons and cannot stop easily.

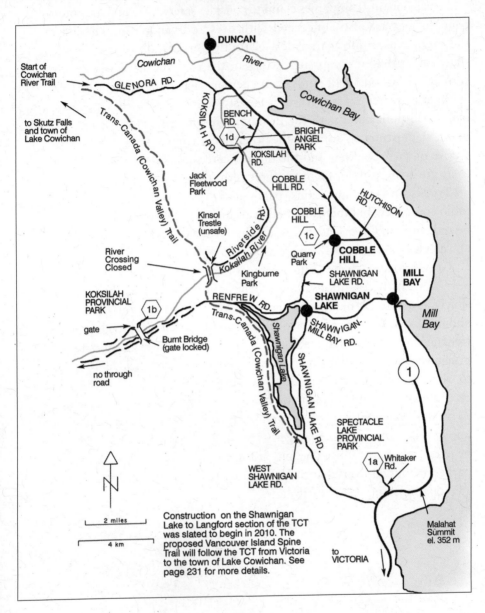

Start of
Cowichan
River Trail

to Skutz Falls
and town of
Lake Cowichan

Cowichan   *River*

GLENORA RD.

DUNCAN

Cowichan Bay

Trans-Canada (Cowichan Valley) Trail

KOKSILAH RD.

BENCH
RD.

1d

KOKSILAH
RD.

BRIGHT
ANGEL
PARK

Jack
Fleetwood
Park

Kinsol
Trestle
(unsafe)

Riverside Rd.

Koksilah River

COBBLE
HILL RD.

COBBLE
HILL

1c

HUTCHISON
RD.

River
Crossing
Closed

Kingburne
Park

Quarry
Park

**COBBLE
HILL**

SHAWNIGAN
LAKE RD.

**MILL
BAY**

KOKSILAH
PROVINCIAL
PARK

1b

gate

RENFREW RD.

Trans-Canada (Cowichan Valley) Trail

Shawnigan Lake

**SHAWNIGAN
LAKE**

SHAWNIGAN-
MILL BAY RD.

*Mill
Bay*

Burnt Bridge
(gate locked)

no through
road

SHAWNIGAN LAKE RD.

1

SPECTACLE
LAKE
PROVINCIAL
PARK

1a   Whitaker
Rd.

N

2 miles

4 km

WEST
SHAWNIGAN
LAKE RD.

Malahat
Summit
el. 352 m

to
VICTORIA

Construction on the Shawnigan
Lake to Langford section of the TCT
was slated to begin in 2010. The
proposed Vancouver Island Spine
Trail will follow the TCT from Victoria
to the town of Lake Cowichan. See
page 231 for more details.

1

Shawnigan Lake and Cobble Hill

1a. Spectacle Lake Provincial Park Maps M1, M1A

DIFFICULTY/DISTANCE Easy to moderate/2 km loop

HIGHLIGHTS Spectacle Lake Provincial Park (67 ha), high on the Malahat Ridge about 30 km northwest of Victoria, offers year round hiking. A scenic loop trail meanders through forest and wetlands to circle spring-fed Spectacle Lake. The day-use beach is popular with swimmers.

ACCESS From Victoria, travel north on Highway 1 (Trans-Canada) and continue about 0.8 km past the south Shawnigan Lake cutoff to Whitaker Road. For travellers driving north from Victoria, there is a left-turn lane on the highway. Swing left (west) onto Whitaker Road and follow the signs to the parking lot. At the first junction turn left, then continue another 1 km and turn right onto the gravel access road. Sections of the trail on Spectacle Lake's east side are wheelchair-accessible.

CAUTIONS
- Use extreme care when turning left off Highway 1 onto Whitaker Road.
- Many confusing old roads, paths and game trails branch off Spectacle Lake's loop trail and lead onto private land. Stay on designated park trails to avoid losing your way.
- Use caution when hiking near the bluffs on the lake's east side.
- Swimmers should be aware there are leeches in Spectacle Lake.

HIKE DESCRIPTION The loop trail at Spectacle Lake Provincial Park begins at the parking lot and you can travel in either direction. The lake's west side has more hills. Wooden bridges span numerous creeks and

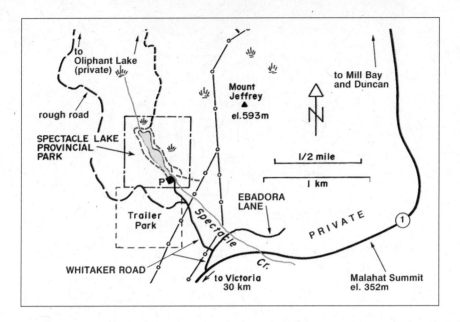

marshy areas. The trail runs through forest and wetlands and circles Spectacle Lake. The lake is so named because its shape resembles a pair of spectacles. Near a significant small alder blowdown near the lake's north end, the trail reverses direction and follows on the opposite shore back to the parking area. Allow about 1 hour to complete the loop.

WORTH NOTING
- The rare Mountain Quail may be seen along the power line.
- In the summer, treat yourself to some of the area's wild strawberries.
- Spectacle Lake is one of only a few southern Vancouver Island lakes where anglers fish for Eastern Brook trout. The lake is stocked.
- No camping is permitted at this day-use-only park.
- The water pump near the beach and picnic area is seasonally shut off.
- When the weather stays cold enough, Spectacle Lake is one of the best spots near Victoria for outdoor ice skating.

NEARBY   Opportunities exist for hikes along old roads, trails and routes to Oliphant Lake, Mount Jeffrey (593 m) and Mount Wood (616 m). The latter is the highest point on the Malahat Ridge. These regions are situated on private land. Contact local hiking groups for information on guided hikes. Logging has obliterated many of the area's old trails and routes.

www.env.gov.bc.ca/bcparks (BC Parks)
www.cvrd.bc.ca/parks (Cowichan Valley Regional District)
Refer to map NTS 92B/12 (1:50,000)

1b. Koksilah River Provincial Park Maps M1, M1B

DIFFICULTY/DISTANCE Easy to moderate/0.3 km to 3.5 km, one way

HIGHLIGHTS Koksilah River Provincial Park (210 ha in three sections), west of Shawnigan Lake village, is a great place for hiking, swimming and fishing. Though largely undeveloped, the park is a favourite
with hikers and other outdoor enthusiasts. Numerous trails snake
alongside the Koksilah River to waterfalls, huge trees, deep gorges and
canyons. The historic Kinsol Trestle along the Trans-Canada (Cowichan
Valley) Trail is close by.

ACCESS

To Koksilah River Provincial Park From the junction of Renfrew Road
and West Shawnigan Lake Road follow Renfrew Road west for about
5 km to the parking area near Burnt Bridge.

To the Trans-Canada Trail and Kinsol Trestle (south end) From the
junction of Renfrew Road and West Shawnigan Lake Road, take Renfrew
Road west for about 2 km to Glen Eagles Road. Turn right (north) for
0.5 km. Turn right onto Shelby Road and look for the parking area, to the
left. There is also limited parking available where the Trans-Canada Trail
crosses Renfrew Road.

To the Trans-Canada Trail and Kinsol Trestle (north end) From
Koksilah Road head south about 8.5 km on Riverside Road and watch for
a tiny parking area on the left. (See map on page 26.)

CAUTIONS
- At the Koksilah River crossing, the Trans-Canada Trail's Kinsol Trestle
  remains closed at this time, pending its restoration and rebuild. Trail
  users must temporarily detour 7 km around this missing link via the
  Kinsol Trestle Bypass Trail, which follows gravel roads and a challenging route on the Koksilah River's north side.
- BC Parks warns the Kinsol Trestle Bypass Trail has received minimal
  maintenance in recent years. Sections of the route are subject to flooding. The Bypass Trail is not suitable for mountain bikers or horse riders.

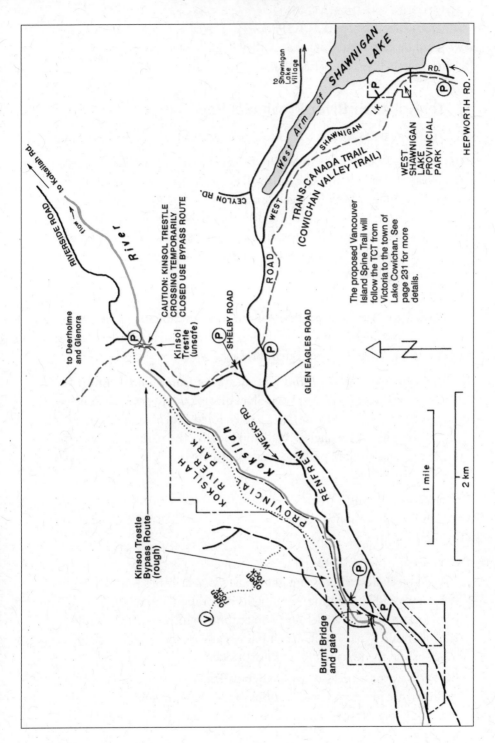

HIKE DESCRIPTIONS   From the Burnt Bridge area hikers can explore a number of old forestry roads and riverside trails. These routes are also very popular with mountain bikers. Side trails are everywhere.

The rugged Kinsol Trestle Bypass Trail runs 3.5 km east along the Koksilah River's north side. It connects to the Trans-Canada (Cowichan Valley) Trail, at the trestle's north end, near Riverside Road. The northeastern section of the Bypass Trail was originally called the Jack Fleetwood Trail, after a local historian who lived beside the Koksilah River. He donated the original land for Bright Angel Provincial Park.

Also on the Koksilah River's north side, an old logging road leads 2 km northeast to an area of clay cut cliffs on the left. A rough, primitive trail leaves the road here and climbs steeply through mostly open, rocky terrain to some rock bluffs. The fine view here includes southern Vancouver Island and the Gulf Islands.

WORTH NOTING

- The steel gate on Burnt Bridge is permanently locked to prevent vehicle access. The span is named after earlier wooden bridges that were destroyed by set fires.
- The park is open all year.
- No campfires or motorized vehicles are permitted.
- Bring your own water supply. Boil, treat or filter all river and creek water.

THE KINSOL TRESTLE, completed by 1920, is Canada's largest remaining wooden trestle. The spectacular span is 38 m high, 187.2 m long and dates back to the era of rail logging. The rail line, instrumental in opening up the Cowichan Valley's early forest industry, was eventually abandoned in 1979. The Kinsol name is a shortened form of King Solomon Mines, which once operated nearby. The Kinsol Trestle is unsafe to cross due to its age, deterioration and lack of maintenance. Over the years, a couple of set fires further weakened the structure.

In the fall of 2008 the Cowichan Valley Regional District, through a non-profit society, initiated a major fundraising campaign to save and restore the historic Kinsol Trestle. With adequate funds raised from the 2-year plan, it was estimated the restoration work would take another year to complete. At the time of this writing, the closed Koksilah River crossing remained the missing link along the Trans-Canada (Cowichan Valley) Trail. For project reports and updates contact the CVRD.

The Kinsol Trestle is Canada's largest remaining wooden trestle. RICHARD K. BLIER

NEARBY *Trans-Canada (Cowichan Valley) Trail (TCT/CVT)* The Trans-Canada Trail follows the abandoned right-of-way for the CNR's Galloping Goose rail line—from Shawnigan Lake to the Town of Lake Cowichan. This section of the Trans-Canada Trail is also called the Cowichan Valley Trail, part of a 140 km corridor linking various Vancouver Island communities. Seven restored trestles are highlights along the route.

From the Shelby Road parking area, hike 15 minutes north to the Kinsol Trestle. It is also possible to hike south to West Shawnigan Lake Provincial Park, just north of Hepworth Road, and continue another 7 km to the Sooke Lake Road trailhead. Limited parking is also available where the trail crosses Renfrew Road.

From the Kinsol Trestle's north end on Riverside Road, the trestle is a five-minute walk away. The TCT/CVT extends north to Cowichan River Provincial Park near Glenora and then turns west to Lake Cowichan. See page 56. The planned Vancouver Island Spine Trail will follow parts of the TCT/CVT. See page 231 or visit www.vispine.ca for more details.

ADDITIONAL INFORMATION
www.env.gov.bc.ca/bcparks (BC Parks)
www.cvrd.bc.ca/parks (Cowichan Valley Regional District)
www.trailsbc.ca or www.tctrail.ca (Trans-Canada Trail)
Refer to map NTS 92B/12 (1:50,000)

1c. Cobble Hill   Maps M1, M1C

DIFFICULTY/DISTANCE Easy to strenuous/0.3 km to 2 km, one way

HIGHLIGHTS Cobble Hill, situated within the Vancouver Island Forest Reserve, has a variety of trails to explore. Steep trails climb to the Cobble Hill summit. Others meander through a mixed coniferous and deciduous forest. It is easy to create your own loop hike and there are great opportunities for bird watching, wildlife viewing and nature appreciation.

ACCESS
To eastern trailhead at Quarry Wilderness Park From Highway 1 (Trans-Canada) follow Hutchison Road west to the Shawnigan Lake Road/Cobble Hill Road junction. Keep straight ahead on Empress Avenue and cross the railway tracks. Then make an immediate right to the main parking area at Quarry Wilderness Park. See Nearby on page 32.

Map M1C   Cobble Hill

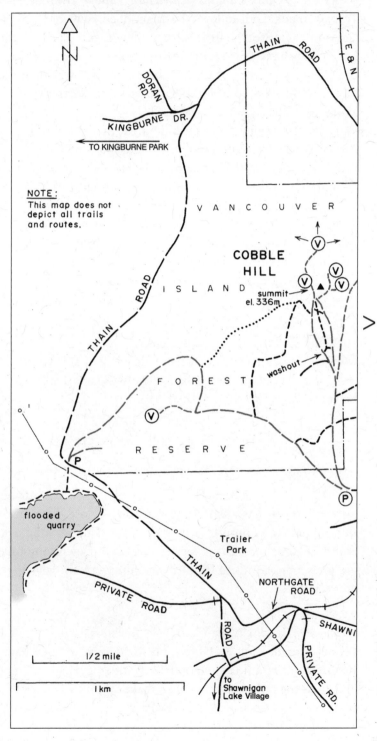

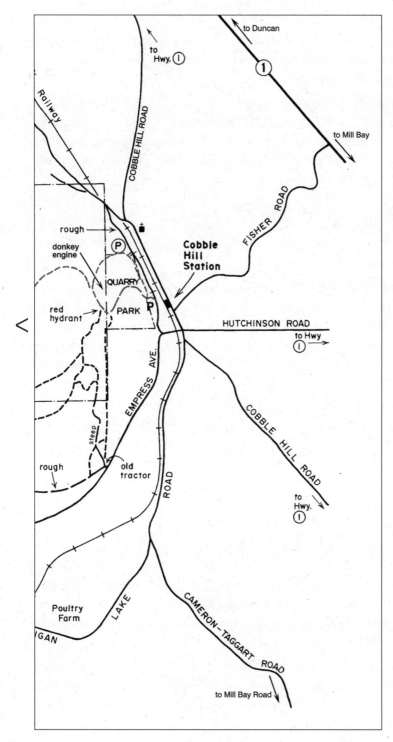

To southern trailhead on the Forestry Road   Alternately, take Empress Avenue 0.7 km from the Shawnigan Lake Road cutoff to the rough BC Forest Service access road, on the right. A sturdy, high-slung vehicle may be required on the forestry road to reach the southern parking spot, about 0.5 km from Empress Avenue.

To western trailhead on Thain Road   The west side approach, next to a flooded quarry, is off Thain Road. From Shawnigan Lake Road, take Northgate, which becomes Thain Road, and soon after passing under the power lines, watch for the parking area to the right, on north side of the road, next to an arbutus grove.

CAUTIONS

- Carry adequate water.
- A trail goes around the quarry, which is located on private property. Please stay outside the fencing.

HIKE DESCRIPTION   Choose from a number of trailheads and routes in the Cobble Hill area. Trails generally get steeper, halfway up to the summit. At the Cobble Hill summit (336 m) trees have grown up to partially obscure the stunning views of the Cowichan Valley, Saltspring Island and the Saanich Peninsula. A hike to the top is still well worth the effort.

WORTH NOTING

- The quarry area is a prime bird watching area. Look for migratory and resident birds. The quarry perimeter offers excellent views of the Cobble Hill summit. Cobble Hill forests are home to squirrels, raccoons, deer—even wandering black bears or cougar.
- Members of area riding clubs and horse riders created many Cobble Hill trails. Most routes are unmarked. Please remember to share the trails.

NEARBY

Quarry Wilderness Park   (9.3 ha) is the eastern gateway to Cobble Hill trails. Here, at the site of a former quarry, are several Cobble Hill trailheads. An old donkey engine and picnic tables are located a short distance from the main parking lot.

Kingburne Park   (5.9 ha), situated alongside the boisterous Koksilah River, was once the location of the Bonanza Ranch (29.5 ha), a homestead dating back to the early 1900s. From Highway 1 (Trans-Canada) turn

Island sunset.   JOYCE FOLBIGG

west onto Cobble Hill Road. Travel 2 km and swing right (west) onto Thain Road. Cross the railway tracks and take Thain Road another 2 km to Kingburne Road. Turn right (west) and follow Kingburne Road to Gray Lane. Turn right (west) to the parking area and turnaround at the bottom of the hill. Rough trails from here lead down to the Koksilah River.

ADDITIONAL INFORMATION
www.cvrd.bc.ca/parks (Cowichan Valley Regional District)
Refer to map NTS 92B/12 (1:50,000)

1d. Bright Angel Provincial Park   Maps M1, M1D

DIFFICULTY/DISTANCE   Easy/0.5 km to 1.2 km, one way

HIGHLIGHTS   Bright Angel Provincial Park (18.5 ha) features over 5 km of wooded trails that wind through one of the last stands of old growth forest along the Koksilah River bottomlands. A lofty suspension foot-bridge links two sections of the park.

ACCESS   On Highway 1 (Trans-Canada) north of Cobble Hill and Mill Bay, and around 3 km north of the Cowichan Bay Road intersection,

Map M1D   Bright Angel

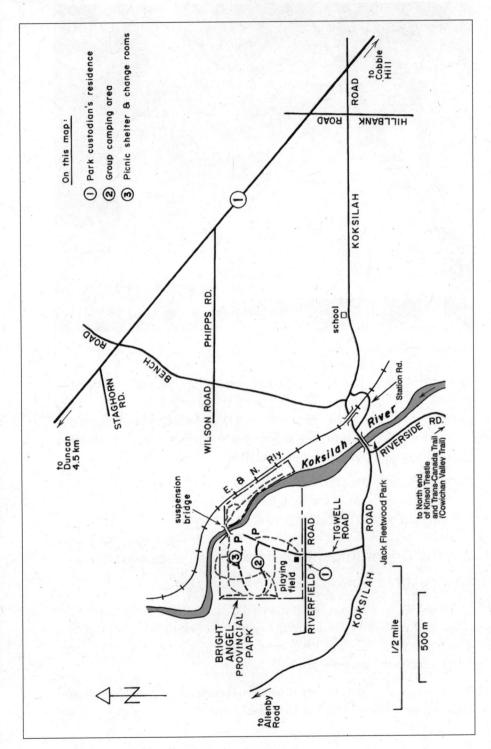

On this map:

① Park custodian's residence
② Group camping area
③ Picnic shelter & change rooms

to Cobble Hill

HILLBANK ROAD

KOKSILAH ROAD

school

PHIPPS RD.

BENCH ROAD

STAGHORN RD.

WILSON ROAD

to Duncan 4.5 km

E. & N. Rly.

Koksilah River

Station Rd.

RIVERSIDE RD.

to North end of Kinsol Trestle and Trans-Canada Trail (Cowichan Valley Trail)

Jack Fleetwood Park

suspension bridge

③ P
P ②

playing field

RIVERFIELD ROAD

TIGWELL ROAD

KOKSILAH ROAD

①

BRIGHT ANGEL PROVINCIAL PARK

to Allenby Road

N

1/2 mile

500 m

watch for the Bright Angel Park signpost. Turn west onto Koksilah Road. Another 3 km or so will bring you to the park, at the corner of Tigwell and Riverfield roads. Bench Road offers alternate access to Koksilah Road.

CAUTIONS

- Keep children under close scrutiny and away from steep banks or the riverbanks.
- The E & N rail line skirts the park's east side. Stay off the tracks.

HIKE DESCRIPTIONS

Koksilah River Walk   Easy/0.5 km, one way. The most popular hike at Bright Angel Park heads from the parking area to the Koksilah River suspension bridge. Take your time crossing the river and enjoy this highlight of the park. On the Koksilah River's east side, turn south and follow delightful riverside trails about 0.5 km to the park boundary.

Forest Hike   Easy/1.2 km, one way. Numerous trails criss-cross the forests on the park's west side. From the parking area hike west, then choose any of the side trails that lead south to the playing field. It is easy to create your own loop hike. As you travel through the mixed forest, try and identify as many trees and plants as you can.

WORTH NOTING

- There are numerous resting benches along the trails.
- Large Douglas-fir and red cedar, mixed with bigleaf maple and grand fir dominate the forests at Bright Angel Park.
- Visit the park at Easter when the forest floor explodes with a seasonal display of fawn lilies.
- Near the Koksilah River watch for Belted Kingfisher, Great Blue Heron and mergansers. Scan the skies for eagles, hawks and other birds of prey.
- Swimming is possible at the gravel beach below the suspension bridge.
- The park is open daily from dawn to dusk all year.

IN 1958, WILLIAM JOHN HARDY (JACK) FLEETWOOD and his wife Mabel donated about 4 ha of bottomland near the Koksilah River as a park. Jack believed a guardian angel watched over him, hence the park's name. Bright Angel Park was created in 1967, through a South Cowichan Centennial Committee project. Over the years it has grown to its current size. The Jack Fleetwood Memorial Park commemorates this local historian and is also situated along the Koksilah River, south of Bright Angel Park, near the Koksilah Road bridge.

NEARBY *Kinsol Trestle* The north end of the Kinsol Trestle, on the Trans-Canada (Cowichan Valley) Trail (TCT/CVT), is reached via Riverside Road. On your way to Bright Angel Park along Koksilah Road, cross the Koksilah River bridge and make an immediate left turn onto Riverside Road. Continue 8.5 km to the parking area for the TCT. See map on page 26.

ADDITIONAL INFORMATION
www.env.gov.bc.ca/bcparks (BC Parks)
www.cvrd.bc.ca/parks (Cowichan Valley Regional District)
Refer to map NTS 92B/12 (1:50,000)

BRIGHT ANGEL PARK is a "Class C" Provincial Park. That means there is no government funding. Revenues are generated through volunteer efforts and donations. Since 2001, the Cowichan Valley Regional District has administered the park. Facilities include a campground, barbecue pit, picnic area and fitness trail. For current information on fees and reservations contact the park custodian at 250-746-4762 or the CVRD.

Delicate mosses highlight the forest canopy at Bright Angel Park. RICHARD K. BLIER

2

Duncan and the Cowichan Valley

2a. Mount Tzouhalem   Maps M2, M2A

DIFFICULTY/DISTANCE   Easy to strenuous/0.3 km to 4.5 km, one way

HIGHLIGHTS   Mount Tzouhalem (483 m) and its craggy bluffs are Duncan landmarks. Here, hikers can explore over 4.5 km of North Cowichan Municipal Forest Reserve roads. A myriad of unofficial trails and mountain bike routes proliferate Mount Tzouhalem's forests. Many roads and trails access spectacular viewpoints near the mountain bluffs. One short, easy and very popular trail leads to the Mount Tzouhalem Ecological Reserve.

ACCESS
Via Kaspa Road   In Duncan, turn east from Highway 1 (Trans-Canada) onto Trunk Road, which becomes Tzouhalem Road. At the 2-km mark, swing left (northeast) onto Maple Bay Road. Travel another 3 km to the gate of "The Properties" subdivision. Follow Kingsview a little under 1.5 km to its end, then take Chippewa Road, past Haida Road, to Kaspa Road. Look for the Mount Tzouhalem Ecological Reserve signposts. Bear left to the end of Kaspa Road. Continue down the narrow, paved road and park close to the water tower, near a locked gate.

SECONDARY ACCESS
Via Nevilane Drive   Mount Tzouhalem may be reached from its east side via power line and forestry roads. From MacKenzie Drive or Marine Crescent follow Nevilane Drive to its end. No parking is allowed at the turnaround and locked gate. Leave your vehicle further back along the

Map M2 Duncan and the Cowichan Valley

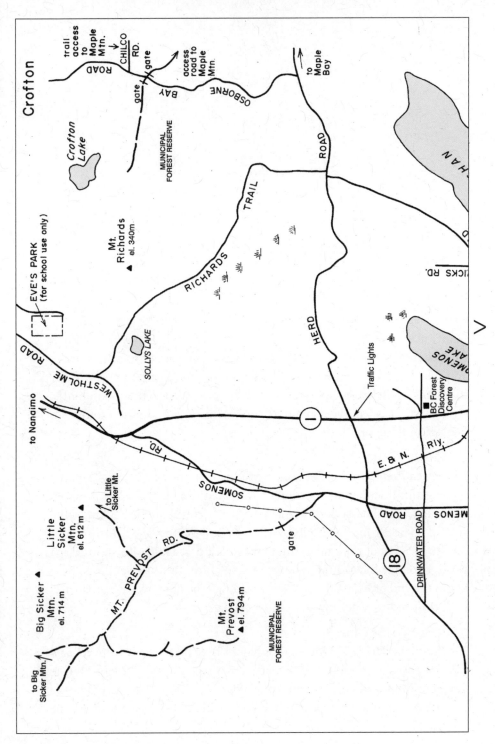

Map M2 Duncan and the Cowichan Valley

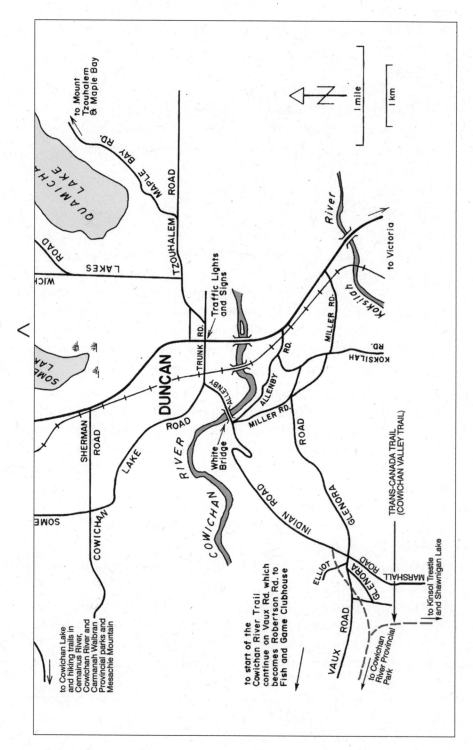

road. Hike beyond the gate and take the right fork. This road eventually links to Branch B. This alternate access is recommended only for hikers who know the area well.

CAUTIONS

- There are many confusing old roads, side trails, routes and mountain bike paths on Mount Tzouhalem. Signage is incomplete. It is easy to lose your way. Travel with someone familiar with the area.
- Exercise extreme caution when hiking near the Mount Tzouhalem bluffs.
- The cliffs are NOT suitable for rock climbing.
- Carry adequate water.

HIKE DESCRIPTIONS

Mount Tzouhalem Ecological Reserve   Easy/0.3 km, one way: From the water tower parking area follow the Ecological Reserve signs and head generally west to the fence surrounding the reserve. Please stay outside the fence to avoid damaging the soil and flowers. To extend your hike, follow the fence and continue uphill to the southeast. Several viewpoints take in Duncan, Mount Prevost and the Cowichan Valley. Beyond the viewpoints the trail peters out into a route.

Mount Tzouhalem Loop   Moderate/4.5 km loop: From the parking area near the water tower take Tzouhalem Mainline about 1 km to the Branch B junction. Swing left (east) onto Branch B and follow a serpentine course through the forest to where the road eventually rejoins Tzouhalem Mainline, closer to the Mount Tzouhalem summit. Turn right (west) onto Tzouhalem Mainline to return to the parking area. Alternatively, take Tzouhalem Mainline first and then Branch B back to the start. Either way, expect to encounter many confusing side roads, trails and bike paths en route.

The White Cross   Moderate/2.5 km, one way: From the water tower parking area hike along Tzouhalem Mainline, past the Branch B cutoff. Hike southwest another 0.5 km to a branch road that angles off on the flat to the right. Keep left, up the hill, to stay on Tzouhalem Mainline. At the next major road junction, the mainline turns left and heads southeast to hook into Branch B. Keep to the road straight ahead and ignore any roads and side trails to the left. Hike due south to the base of a steep, rugged washout. From here a cliffside route cuts west over open, rocky outcrops and through stands of arbutus and Garry Oak to the White Cross. Look

Cross on Mt. Tzouhalem. JOYCE FOLBIGG

A WOODEN CROSS, on Mount Tzouhalem's southwest summit, was erected in 1976. In the early 1990s, a white iron cross replaced the original. To celebrate Easter, the Sisters of Saint Ann would make a Good Friday pilgrimage from their convent and school below, following the Stations of the Cross up the steep mountainside. That tradition continues. Every Good Friday hikers of all ages meet in the Saint Ann's Church parking lot to begin a reflective ascent to the White Cross.

Since 1979, when the Sisters of Saint Ann donated the land, the non-profit society, Vancouver Island Providence Community Association (VIPCA) has operated the organic Providence Farm on the site as a centre for horticultural therapy, vocational training and community programs. The farm is named after Sister Mary Providence, founder of the former school. In September 2009, at Providence Farm's 30th Anniversary, the Sisters of Saint Ann officially conveyed the administration of Providence Farm to VIPCA. Contact www.providence.bc.ca for more information.

for marker ribbons and stay clear of the sheer rock faces and bluffs you will skirt en route; the cliffs are extremely dangerous. Should you tackle the climb up the washout, you will discover more stunning viewpoints that overlook the Cowichan River estuary.

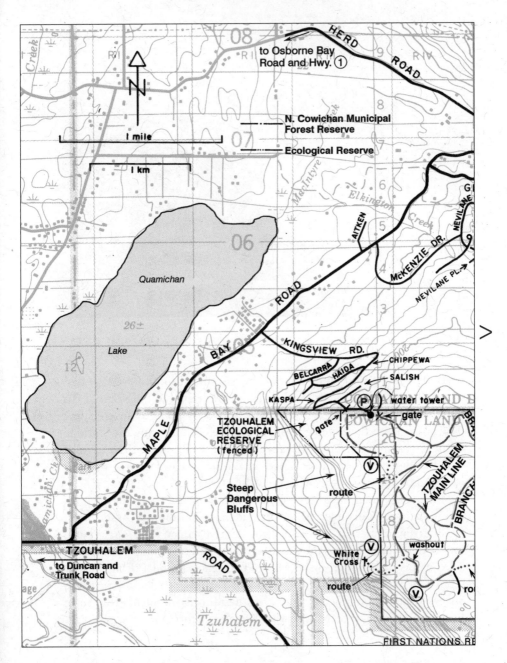

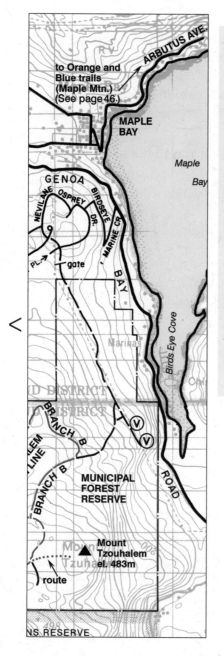

TZOUHALEM, OF THE COWICHAN TRIBE, lived from about 1800 to 1850. He was not a hereditary chief. Born with an abnormally large head, he was only three when his mother and younger brother were seized by a Haida raiding party and thrown out of a canoe to drown in Sansum Narrows. Tzouhalem led the 1844 attack on Fort Victoria. The clash happened shortly after some natives allegedly killed a number of oxen near the fort. Roderick Finlayson, Chief Factor of Fort Victoria for the Hudson's Bay Company, defused the confrontation.

Many colourful, yet erroneous accounts about Tzouhalem have appeared. Some confuse him with a character known as Tsoqelem, an outlaw from the 1840s. Charles Lillard's book, *Seven Shillings A Year*, gives an accurate sketch of Tzouhalem's life. The high-cliffed mountain, west of Genoa Bay, now bears Tzouhalem's name.

- The Mount Tzouhalem Ecological Reserve (17 ha) is one of BC's best examples of a Garry Oak woodland. In the spring, wildflowers colour the landscape. Visit the area in late April and early May to observe the showiest display. Seasonal guided tours of the reserve are available through local groups. Remember to stay outside the Ecological Reserve fence to avoid damaging the soil and flowers. Read about these reserves on page 18.
- The majority of Mount Tzouhalem roads are inside a Municipal Forest Reserve. See page 18.
- The actual Mount Tzouhalem summit is within a First Nations Reserve. Please do not trespass.
- No camping, overnight parking, fires or motorized vehicles permitted.

NEARBY   Maple Mountain. See below.

ADDITIONAL INFORMATION
www.northcowichan.bc.ca (Municipality of North Cowichan)
Refer to map NTS 92B/13 Duncan (1:50,000)

2b. Maple Mountain   Maps M2, M2B

DIFFICULTY/DISTANCE   Easy to strenuous/2.6 km to 5.1 km, one way

HIGHLIGHTS   Maple Mountain, within the Municipality of North Cowichan's Forest Reserve, is 16 km northeast of Duncan. There is an excellent colour-coded trail system with five official routes totalling 14 km in length. With several access points, hikes range from easy forest walks to more strenuous climbs suited for experienced hikers. Most routes feature great viewpoints. The trails follow established trails and old roads.

ACCESS
Via Chilco Road   This northern trailhead accesses the north end of both the Blue and Yellow trails. From Highway 1 (Trans-Canada) at the Highway 18 junction, north of Duncan, turn right onto Herd Road and drive east to Osborne Bay Road. Make a left (north) onto Osborne Bay Road and travel 3.5 km to Chilco Road. Swing right and follow Chilco Road 0.5 km to a limited parking area near a locked gate.

Via Osborne Bay Road/Maple Mountain Main   Maple Mountain Main accesses the Green Trail lower down, and up at the Main Viewpoint turn-

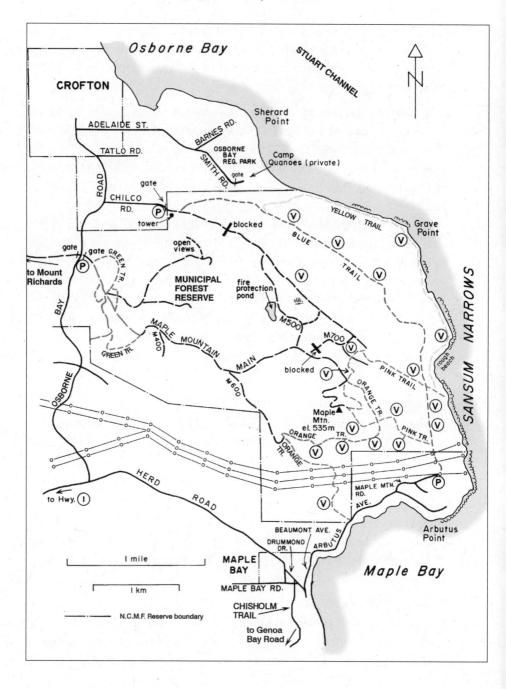

around, the Orange and Pink trails. From Highway 1 (Trans-Canada) at the Highway 18 junction, north of Duncan, turn right onto Herd Road and drive east to Osborne Bay Road. Make a left (north) onto Osborne Bay Road and travel just under 3 km to the main entrance to Maple Mountain. Limited parking space is available outside the locked gate.

Via Arbutus Avenue/Maple Mountain Road This access to Maple Mountain leads to the southern trailheads for the Orange and Blue trails and, via the Blue Trail, the Pink and Yellow trails. In Maple Bay stay on Maple Bay Road, drop down the hill to Beaumont Avenue and turn left to pass the pub. Beaumont Avenue becomes Arbutus Avenue and swings right (east).

About 1 km from Maple Bay Road watch for a tiny trail sign, on the left, that marks the Orange Trail's southern trailhead. If you see a roadside hydrant, you have gone too far. Parking is virtually nonexistent on Arbutus Avenue. Stay on Arbutus Avenue, turn left onto Maple Mountain road and continue to the end of the road, about 2.5 km from Maple Bay Road. There is a turnaround and small limited parking area near the markers for the Blue Trail. Remember to allow room for other visitors to turn around and do not block driveways.

CAUTIONS

- Visitors use the Maple Mountain trails at their own risk.
- The Maple Mountain gate on Osborne Bay Road, at the bottom of Maple Mountain Main, is permanently locked to prevent any vehicular traffic, but you may still hike up.
- Maple Mountain is subject to seasonal fire closures. Be prepared when hiking as weather conditions can deteriorate quickly.
- Trail signage is incomplete. Watch for colour-coded markers or ribbons on trees. A profusion of unmarked old roads and trails exists on Maple Mountain. If you chose to explore off the designated trails, be sure to travel with someone familiar with the area.
- Carry adequate water.
- Exercise extreme care when hiking near cliff edges and bluffs.
- Some trail creek crossings are via wooden bridges, which can become dangerously slick in wet weather. Use caution when traversing these areas.

Chocolate lilies.   JOYCE FOLBIGG

HIKE DESCRIPTIONS

The Blue Trail   Strenuous/5.1 km, one way: From Chilco Road hike past the municipal water tower and follow the old logging road uphill to the signposted Blue Trail cutoff. Straight ahead the logging road leads to a fire protection pond and the spur roads that connect with Maple Mountain Main, Maple Mountain's primary access route.

Cut left onto the Blue Trail at the signpost. After a km or so you will reach the trail junction, on the left, at the Yellow Trail's north end. The Blue Trail continues straight ahead and climbs to spectacular viewpoints on Maple Mountain's east side. These include Sansum Narrows and Saltspring Island. The Blue Trail is steep most of the way. Expect tricky log crossings en route. The highest point is at the trail's northern end. Further south the Blue Trail links up twice with the Pink Trail. Allow about 2.5 hours hiking time one way from Chilco Road to the Blue Trail's south end at Maple Mountain Road.

The Yellow Trail   Strenuous/4 km, one way: From the Chilco Road trailhead, hike past the water tower to the cutoff for the Blue Trail. After a km or so, watch for the Yellow Trail turnoff, on the left. This challenging trail follows a serpentine route along the Stuart Channel shoreline. There are steep grades, many twists and turns, gullies, log crossings and muddy, slippery sections. Expect lots of up and down hiking. Grave Point is a popular destination. The Yellow Trail connects to the Pink Trail just east of the latter's intersection with the Blue Trail. The Yellow Trail takes a little over 2 hours hiking time to travel.

The Green Trail   Easy/2.6 km loop: From the parking area on Osborne Bay Road, near the locked gate at the bottom of Maple Mountain Main, walk 0.5 km up the mainline to where the Green Trail intersects the road. This path, the reserve's easiest, winds through the lower forest on old roads and trails. Give yourself a little over an hour to complete a loop hike.

The Main Viewpoint   Strenuous/4.7 km, one way: From the locked gate on Osborne Bay Road hike Maple Mountain Main for 4.7 km to the Main Viewpoint, near the turnaround at the end of the road. The mainline is half gravel, half pavement. Part way up the steep ascent, Branch M600 cuts off to the southeast to meet up with the Orange Trail, north of the powerlines. The Orange Trail's north end trailhead is located near the turnaround at the end of Maple Mountain Main.

The Main Viewpoint looks out over Stuart Channel. Watch for the Crofton/Vesuvius ferry. Clear days offer great vistas of northern Saltspring, Kuper and Secretary islands. Some visitors hike from the turnaround up the ditched road on the right, to the communication tower near Maple Mountain's summit (505 m). The Pink Trail meets the road just east of the summit. From the top of Maple Mountain you will see Genoa Bay, Mount Tzouhalem, Maple Bay, Birds Eye Cove and Cowichan Bay.

The Orange Trail   Moderate/3.2 km, one way: From its northern trailhead at the Main Viewpoint turnaround, the Orange Trail heads southeast to some of Maple Mountain's best viewpoints. The trail is steep and rocky at the start but eventually it levels out. The trail crosses the Pink Trail due east of the Maple Mountain summit. There are magnificent views east over Sansum Narrows to Saltspring Island and southeast towards Burgoyne Bay and Mount Maxwell. One lookout faces south towards Maple Bay and Birds Eye Cove, which is well named as the small island shows up as the eye in a bird's head.

The Orange Trail swings west to more viewpoints, including one that overlooks Quamichan and Somenos lakes. About two-thirds of the way along the Orange Trail, the route swings sharply to the south. The next old road to the right, Branch M600, goes northwest and hooks up with Maple Mountain Main. The Orange Trail zig-zags south and begins a sharp descent to the power lines. Hike south under the transmission lines to the final drop to Arbutus Avenue. Allow just under 2 hours to hike from the Main Viewpoint to Arbutus Avenue.

The Pink Trail Strenuous/3.7 km, one way: The Pink Trail, with the greatest elevation changes, is the most strenuous route on Maple Mountain. The Main Viewpoint is at the Pink Trail's halfway point. From here a mostly downhill hike will take you north, then southeast to intersect the Blue Trail and then meet the south end of the Yellow Trail. The Pink Trail extends down to Sansum Narrows. Be wary near the narrows as fluctuating currents here are treacherous.

The southern section of the Pink Trail climbs from the Maple Mountain Main turnaround almost to the Maple Mountain summit and then swings east and intersects the Orange Trail. The trail turns south at the 300 m mark and then plunges down through the forest to meet the Blue Trail just north of the transmission lines near the Maple Mountain Road trailhead. Watch for a side trail to a bonus viewpoint. The Pink Trail takes a little over 2 hours to hike.

WORTH NOTING

- Spring and summer flowers abound on Maple Mountain's open bluffs.
- Please tread lightly to prevent damage to sensitive vegetation and soil.
- Lookouts are not marked. Look for natural openings to the rock bluffs.
- No camping, overnight parking, fires or motorized vehicles permitted.
- Read more about Municipal Forest Reserves on page 18.

NEARBY

Mount Richards Part of the North Cowichan Municipal Forest Reserve, Mount Richards may be accessed via the gated road on the west side of Osborne Bay Road, directly opposite the main Maple Mountain Park entrance. Park on the east side of Osborne Bay Road, at the bottom of Maple Mountain Main. No formal trails exist, but hikers, mountain bikers and horse riders have used this area and its road and trail networks for years. Closer to Mount Richard's 340 m summit, the higher bluffs are known for their spring wildflowers. Lower down are several viewpoints that look out towards the Sicker mountains and Mount Prevost.

ADDITIONAL INFORMATION

www.northcowichan.bc.ca (Municipality of North Cowichan)
Refer to map NTS 92B/13 Duncan (1: 50,000)

2c. Mount Prevost   Maps M2, M2C

DIFFICULTY/DISTANCE   Moderate/0.3 km to 0.5 km, one way

HIGHLIGHTS   The high cliffs of Mount Prevost's twin peaks give Duncan a distinctive landmark. The old trail, built in 1929 to erect the War Memorial, is now a forestry road. You can drive almost all the way to the top of Mount Prevost, but be aware that the roads up are usually rough. From the parking area, short, very steep trails lead to some of the Cowichan Valley's most spectacular viewpoints. The mountain's lower forest is criss-crossed with old roads, trails and routes worth investigating.

ACCESS   From Highway 1 (Trans-Canada) north of Duncan, follow Highway 18 west 1.3 km toward the town of Lake Cowichan. Turn right (north) onto Somenos Road, continue another 0.7 km to Mount Prevost Road and turn left. After 0.5 km the gravel begins. For the summit trails, keep left at the fork about 4 km from Somenos Road. To the right is Plantation Road, a Little Sicker Mountain access route.

At a forest clearing 1 km away, make a sharp left and head south on Prevost Mainline. If you continue west onto Mines Road you will reach BC Tel Road, a forestry road that goes to Big Sicker Mountain. Prevost Mainline climbs and winds south to a limited parking area, 7.3 km from Somenos Road.

CAUTIONS

- Mount Prevost Road and Prevost Mainline are steep, narrow, gravel forestry roads within a working Municipal Forest Reserve. Watch for and yield to all logging trucks and industrial traffic. Use your headlights. Public access may be restricted due to active logging or fire closures.
- Area forestry roads are seasonally passable in a regular car but a vehicle with ample clearance is preferred.
- Exercise extreme caution near the sheer bluffs at the War Memorial and the cliff faces at the old forestry lookout site. Keep away from the edges; there are no barricades. Never leave children unattended.
- Carry adequate water.
- There are no facilities and no formally developed trails. Visitors hike area trails at their own risk.

HIKE DESCRIPTIONS

War Memorial   Moderate/0.5 km, one way: From the parking area keep

Map M2C   Mount Prevost

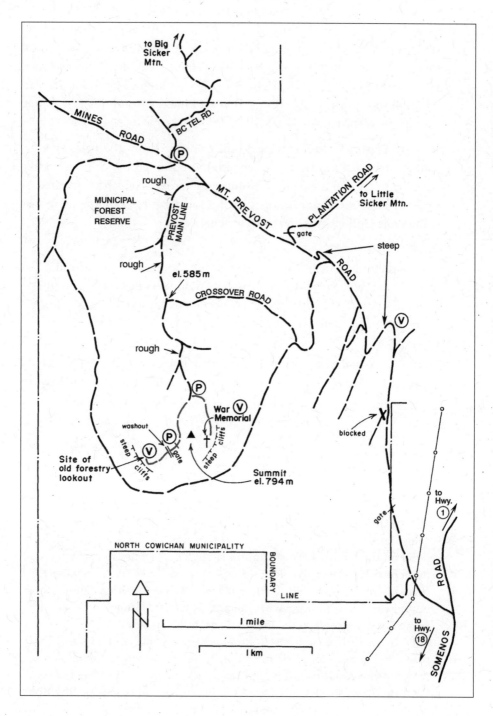

left onto a rough, steep old road that serves as a trail to the War Memorial. This washed-out road is blocked at the bottom. Although only a relatively short hike, the abrupt incline of the grade makes the going somewhat tough. The open rock areas en route may be very slippery in wet weather. Hikers are rewarded for their efforts with a striking vista of the Duncan area and the Gulf Islands. Mount Prevost's main summit (794 m) is due west of the War Memorial.

Forestry Lookout Moderate/0.3 km, one way: From the parking area, walk or drive 0.4 km west to a second, more limited parking area. Hike past a gate and up a rugged washout and across an open rocky area to emerge at the second summit, site of a former forestry lookout. Views include the Gulf Islands and the Cowichan Valley.

WORTH NOTING

- Rare yellow avalanche lilies grow near the Mount Prevost summits. These delicate flowers still survive here despite overuse on the mountain. Please tread lightly in these regions to avoid trampling fragile vegetation and soil structure.
- Paragliders and hang gliders regularly use Mount Prevost's southern summit. When wind conditions are right, these fearless flyers launch themselves off the precipice and soar down to the distant fields below.
- Time your visit to coincide with good weather so you can enjoy the viewpoints at their best.
- The War Memorial is within a protected 45 ha wilderness park.
- Learn more about Municipal Forest Reserves on page 18.

NETWORKS OF HIKING, WALKING, cycling, mountain biking and equestrian trails snake through the lower forest on Mount Prevost's east side. Those familiar with the area can work their way all the way up to the low point on the Mount Prevost summit ridge. These trails are reachable via numerous branch roads along Mount Prevost Road. This includes the first side road on the left, barricaded by a cement barrier. One hiking option for those familiar with the area is to take Crossover Road and rejoin the main road up the mountain at the 585 m level.

Paths in the lower forest follow mostly unmarked overgrown old roads and game trails that meander through shady forests and across small creeks. Visitors will find pleasant hiking, especially on a hot day. Over the years these trails were established by hiking groups, the Boy Scouts, municipal foresters, mountain bikers and horse riders.

Big and Little Sicker Mountain Areas   Located within North Cowichan's Municipal Forest, there are no established trails here but there are plenty of old roads and informal routes to explore. The region has a rich mining history. The Lenora and Tyee mines operated nearby from 1895 to 1907 and produced copper, gold and silver.

Access as for Mount Prevost, via Somenos and Mount Prevost roads. Plantation Road, 4 km from the bottom of Mount Prevost Road, goes to Little Sicker Mountain. BC Tel Road, off Mines Road, is a further 1.5 km west and leads to Big Sicker Mountain.

Grace Road   This part of North Cowichan's Municipal Forest features short trails to a Chemainus River canyon and a picturesque Banon Creek waterfall. A Boy Scout day-use area is nearby. From Highway 1 (Trans-Canada) north of Duncan, turn west onto Mount Sicker Road and drive 2 km to unmarked Grace Road. Turn right (north) and follow Grace Road 4 km to a limited parking area. Access is also possible via Cranko Road, further west.

ADDITIONAL INFORMATION
www.northcowichan.bc.ca (Municipality of North Cowichan)
Refer to map NTS 92B/13 Duncan (1:50,000)

On Mount Prevost a hiker gazes east toward Cowichan Bay and Mount Tzouhalem.   RICHARD K. BLIER

2d. Chemainus River Provincial Park   Maps M2, M2D

DIFFICULTY/DISTANCE   Easy to moderate/1.5 km, one way

HIGHLIGHTS   Chemainus River Provincial Park (128 ha) features woodland trails that lead through a second growth forest alongside the Chemainus River. These forests are habitat for a variety of wildlife, including bears, wolves, cougar, deer and Roosevelt elk.

ACCESS   From Highway 1 (Trans-Canada) north of Duncan, turn west onto Highway 18 (Lake Cowichan Highway) and travel 6.8 km west. Turn right (north) onto Hillcrest Payne Road, a seasonally rough gravel road that leads a further 6 km to the park.

CAUTIONS
- This day-use park has no facilities. Trails are undeveloped.
- Carry some water. Boil, treat or filter all river and creek water.
- Parking is extremely limited and turning a larger vehicle around can be problematic.
- Hillcrest Payne Road may be unsuitable for long, low-slung vehicles. Logging trucks frequent this road. Drive defensively.

HIKE DESCRIPTION   From the parking areas, short trails extend 0.5 km up and downriver to swimming holes and fishing areas along the picturesque Chemainus River. The riverside trails extend beyond the park boundaries.

WORTH NOTING   On summer weekends this area is over-used and congested. At these times, parking spots are non-existent.

NEARBY   Mount Prevost and Big and Little Sicker mountains may be reached via a rough road which branches off Hillcrest Payne Road, on the right, just beyond the BC Hydro substation. For details on access via Mount Prevost, see page 50.

ADDITIONAL INFORMATION
www.env.gov.bc.ca/bcparks (BC Parks)
www.cvrd.bc.ca/parks (Cowichan Valley Regional District)
Refer to map NTS 92B/13 (1:50,000)

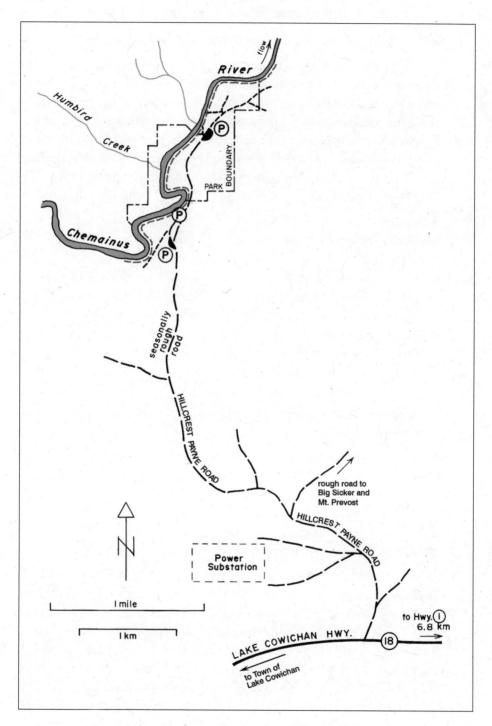

2e. Cowichan River Provincial Park   Maps M2, M2E

DIFFICULTY/DISTANCE   Easy to moderate/1.4 km to 10 km, one way

HIGHLIGHTS   Cowichan River Provincial Park (1414 ha) is a spectacular recreation corridor that stretches over 30 km along the Cowichan River. Anywhere from Glenora, just south of Duncan, to the town of Lake Cowichan, you might encounter hikers, wildlife viewers, naturalists, picnickers, swimmers, paddlers, campers or anglers. Visitors will find a serviced campground and a variety of trails along the Cowichan River. The popular Cowichan River (Footpath) Trail extends from Glenora to Skutz Falls. The Trans-Canada (Cowichan Valley) Trail (TCT/CVT) intersects the park.

CAUTIONS
- Hikers should gear up adequately and be prepared for capricious weather.
- Exercise extreme caution when walking or hiking near riverside cliffs, dropoffs and overhanging banks. Never leave children or pets unattended. Wooden boardwalks may be slippery.
- The Cowichan River has changeable water levels and treacherous currents. Swimmers, tubers and paddlers beware.
- Carry adequate water. Boil, treat or filter all river and creek water. BC Parks recommends treating all pumped water.
- Campfires are allowed only at designated park campsites and may be seasonally restricted.

SOUTHEAST ACCESS TO COWICHAN RIVER TRAIL   From Highway 1 (Trans-Canada), south of Duncan, turn west onto Miller Road and then left onto Glenora Road. Near the Glenora Community Hall take Vaux Road, which becomes Robertson Road, and continue to the Cowichan River Trail, close to the Cowichan Fish and Game Association clubhouse. The Trans-Canada (Cowichan Valley) Trail is nearby.

HIKE DESCRIPTIONS

Holt Creek Loop   Easy/2.4 km loop: From the Glenora trailhead, follow the Cowichan River Trail about 1 km to Holt Creek, close to the restored Holt Creek Trestle along the Trans-Canada (Cowichan Valley) Trail. Turn right (north) before the bridge onto a well-worn path and swing back along the river to the starting point. Parts of the route are known as the Angler's Trail as they access popular Cowichan River casting spots. This area is criss-crossed with side trails. The riverside paths are uneven. Watch for protruding roots and slippery, muddy sections.

Cowichan River Trail—Glenora to Skutz Falls   Moderate/10 km, one way: From the Glenora trailhead the Cowichan River Trail heads west to Holt Creek and winds along the Cowichan River's south side. Picnicking spots and river access points are plentiful. The route traverses low-lying river bottomlands prone to seasonal flooding. If necessary, detour around these areas via the TCT. There are a few challenging steep sections. The more severe switchbacks are near Marie Canyon and Skutz Falls. Many unmarked, unimproved side trails exist. Watch for trail markers to stay on course. Allow about 6.5 hours hiking time, one way.

MIDDLE ACCESS

To Stoltz Pool Campground, Marie Canyon and Skutz Falls   At the Highway 1/Highway 18 intersection, north of Duncan, turn west onto Highway 18. Travel just over 15 km to the Highway 18 Connector and swing left. At Cowichan Lake Road turn left (east) again and follow the park signs via Stoltz Road to Riverbottom Road. Turn right and head 2.5 km west to Marie Canyon, 5 km to Skutz Falls. Turn left at Riverbottom Road and continue another 1.5 km east to the entrance of the Stoltz Pool Campground.

HIKE DESCRIPTION

Stoltz Pool Loop   Easy/1.4 km loop: From the main parking area at the Stoltz Pool Campground, head south to the river and wheelchair-accessible picnic area. The Stoltz Pool picnic area features a grove of

DURING THE 1960S, the Cowichan Fish and Game Association, with help from the provincial government, industry and interested individuals, developed the Cowichan River Trail. Also known as the Cowichan River Footpath, its construction involved hundreds of hours of volunteer labour. These work parties were organized through local environmental organizations, outdoor groups and hiking clubs. A suspension footbridge once linked two sections of the trail near Skutz Falls. In 1986 this span was removed and replaced by the existing Forestry Road bridge.

Over the years, logging, water extraction, development and overuse have posed threats to the Cowichan River's wilderness character and its fish and wildlife values. The creation of Cowichan River Provincial Park helped preserve the region's natural environment for public recreation and enjoyment. A year later, in 1996, the Cowichan River was designated a BC Heritage River.

Map M2E Cowichan River (down-river)

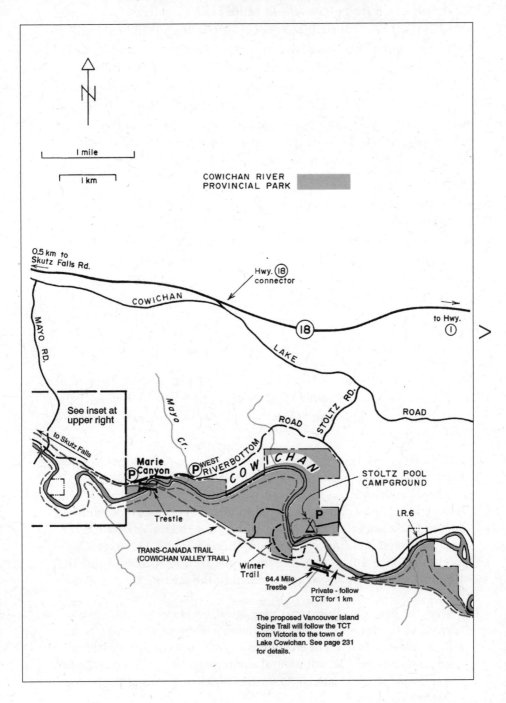

N

I mile

I km

COWICHAN RIVER
PROVINCIAL PARK

0.5 km to
Skutz Falls Rd.

Hwy. ⑱
connector

COWICHAN

LAKE

⑱

to Hwy.
①

MAYO RD.

Mayo Cr.

See inset at
upper right

to Skutz Falls

STOLTZ RD.

ROAD

ROAD

Marie
P Canyon

P WEST
RIVERBOTTOM

C O W I C H A N

STOLTZ POOL
CAMPGROUND

P

Trestle

I.R.6

TRANS-CANADA TRAIL
(COWICHAN VALLEY TRAIL)

Winter
Trail

64.4 Mile
Trestle

Private - follow
TCT for 1 km

The proposed Vancouver Island
Spine Trail will follow the TCT
from Victoria to the town of
Lake Cowichan. See page 231
for details.

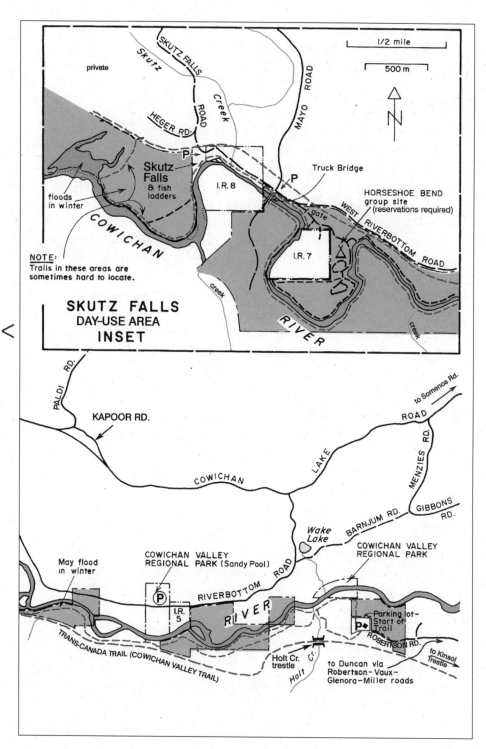

bigleaf maple trees that fringe the river. Nearby is the Burma Star Memorial Cairn that commemorates an Allied WWII offensive in East Asia. The trail continues along the river for about 1 km and then swings back through second-growth upland forest north of the campsites to the parking area.

WEST ACCESS

To Skutz Falls, Cowichan River Trail and Marie Canyon From the Highway 1/Highway 18 junction, north of Duncan, drive 18.7 km west on Highway 18 and turn left (south) onto Skutz Falls Road. Make an immediate left and head east (back in the direction you came) on Cowichan Lake Road. At Mayo Road turn right (south) to Riverbottom Road, the Cowichan River and Skutz Falls. BC Parks recommends the paved Mayo Road access rather than the rougher Skutz Falls Road, which is 3 km of gravel road. At Riverbottom Road, turn right and proceed west to the Skutz Falls parking area.

For Marie Canyon turn left at the Mayo Road/Riverbottom Road junction. The first side road on the right is the gated access road to the BC Parks Horseshoe Bend group camping area. From Mayo Road via Riverbottom Road, it is just under 2.5 km to the Marie Canyon day-use area.

HIKE DESCRIPTION

Skutz Falls Loop Moderate/8 km loop: The Skutz Falls Loop crosses the Cowichan River via the Forestry Road bridge near Skutz Falls and the 66 Mile Trestle closer to Marie Canyon. Expect steep sections and switchbacks near Marie Canyon. Hikers can travel in either direction and on both sides of the river. There is a profusion of side trails along the route. Watch for trail markers. The views from the trestle and Marie Canyon are stunning. Many visitors incorporate the TCT/CVT as part of their loop hike.

WORTH NOTING

- Skutz Falls, where the Cowichan River churns through a rocky chute, is a park highlight. The name "Skutz" is taken from the First Nations word, "Skwetz", meaning falls. The banks of the river near the Skutz Falls salmon ladders are great places to view spawning fall salmon. Remember to stay off the fishways; they are dangerous to climb or walk on.

- The park's forests are predominantly bigleaf maple and alder. The colourful bigleaf maple trees create a spectacular forest backdrop in the fall. There are scattered stands of Garry oak all the way from Glenora

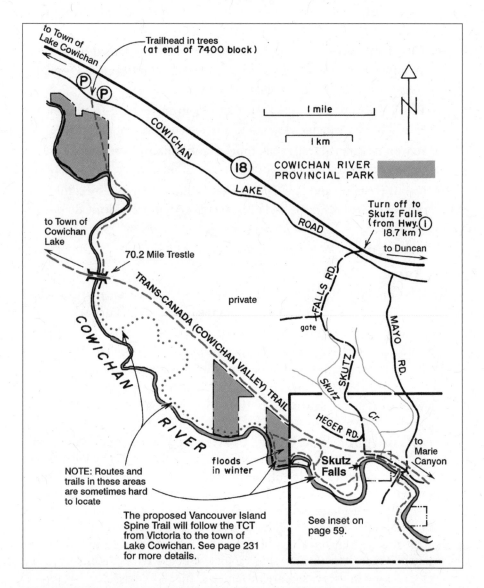

THE PARK'S STOLTZ POOL CAMPGROUND is open all year, but services are limited in the off-season, November – mid-May. The campsite features 43 vehicle sites, 4 walk-in campsites and a group camping area. A second group camping area, Horseshoe Bend, is located farther upstream, toward Skutz Falls. Other campground amenities include pit toilets, fire rings, picnic tables, pumped water and a boat launch for cartop boats. The park's Skutz Falls Campground is closed indefinitely. For current campsite information, including details on seasonal closures, fees and reservations, visit BC Parks at www.env.gov.bc.ca/bcparks.

to the Skutz Falls area. The grove adjacent Horseshoe Bend is the one furthest west.

- The park is habitat to a variety of animals including squirrels, raccoons, mink, river otters, deer, Roosevelt elk, black bear and cougar. Over 200 species of birds have been documented.
- The day-use areas at Skutz Falls, Marie Canyon, 66 Mile Trestle and Stoltz Pool have picnic tables, information shelters and pit toilets.
- Stay on designated trails at all times to minimize soil erosion and vegetation damage. Please do not litter.
- Private property and First Nations land abut the park. Respect the privacy of area residents and obey any posted notices. Please do not trespass.
- Motorized vehicles are prohibited.

NEARBY

Trans-Canada (Cowichan Valley) Trail   The Trans-Canada (Cowichan Valley) Trail cuts through Cowichan River Provincial Park via the abandoned right-of-way for the CNR's Galloping Goose rail line. Extending from Shawnigan Lake to the town of Lake Cowichan this 140 km multi-use corridor links various Vancouver Island communities. Seven restored trestles are route highlights. The trail stays away from the Cowichan River to run mainly through second growth upland forest.

PARTS OF THE ORIGINAL COWICHAN RIVER (FOOTPATH) TRAIL still exist west of Skutz Falls. Other sections have been obliterated by logging or succumbed to the whims of the Cowichan River's churning currents. Lack of maintenance and clearing, seasonal flooding and resultant riverbank erosion, winter storms and blowdowns have all combined to make the remaining trail hard to locate. Even local anglers, familiar with the uneven terrain, sometimes become misplaced in the river bottomlands. The thickets and tangles of dense riverside underbrush that abound in these areas are extremely difficult to navigate.

Hikers wishing to explore anywhere west of Skutz Falls are best to travel 10 km along the TCT/CVT and seek out river access points along the way. The old footpath is most distinct near the 70.2 Mile Trestle, where a well-worn path runs north to Cowichan Lake Road, in the 7400 block. You can also turn south along the river until the trail becomes less obvious. From the trestle, the TCT/CVT continues west to the corner of Comiaken Avenue and Pine Street in the town of Lake Cowichan. Allow 3.5 to 4 hours hiking time from Skutz Falls west to Lake Cowichan.

Hikers, horse riders and mountain bikers share the trail. The TCT/CVT can be accessed at many spots in the park. For more details on the TCT see page 29. The planned Vancouver Island Spine Trail will follow part of the TCT/CVT. See page 231 for more details or visit www.vispine.ca.

ADDITIONAL INFORMATION
www.env.gov.bc.ca/bcparks (BC Parks)
www.cvrd.bc.ca/parks (Cowichan Valley Regional District)
www.trailsbc.ca or www.tctrail.ca (Trans-Canada Trail)
Refer to maps NTS 92B/13 and 92C/16 (1:50,000)

2f. Mesachie Mountain   Maps M2, M2F

DIFFICULTY/DISTANCE   Moderate/2 km, one way

HIGHLIGHTS   Mesachie Mountain is one of the Cowichan Valley's hidden gems. Well-established trails climb to superb viewpoints overlooking Cowichan, Mesachie and Bear lakes and surrounding mountains.

ACCESS   From the Town of Lake Cowichan follow South Shore Road 6 km west to Mesachie Lake and turn right (north) onto Forestry Road. Go past the houses and the access road to Mesachie Lake. Cross the bridge and drive to the Cowichan Lake Forestry Research Station sign, boundary fence and gate. Look for a small parking area, on the right, just outside the fence.

CAUTIONS
• Be sure to park your vehicle OUTSIDE the research station fence. Otherwise you run the risk of returning to find your vehicle stuck behind a locked gate.
• Logging has affected some trails. In these areas, hike along the logging roads.
• Public access on the main research station property is not permitted. Read and obey any posted notices.

HIKE DESCRIPTION   At the east end of the parking area is a gated road and fence with an opening for hikers. Walk northeast about 0.5 km down the road and watch for a trail on the right, which goes up a hill. At a fork 10 m in, cut left onto a narrow trail to a steep, washed-out logging road. Climb to a large stump (look for ribbons) on the right. Take the trail beside the stump and head up toward the mossy, open hill. It is hard to get lost on the obvious, well-trodden trails. Pick your own special

Map M2F   Mesachie Mountain

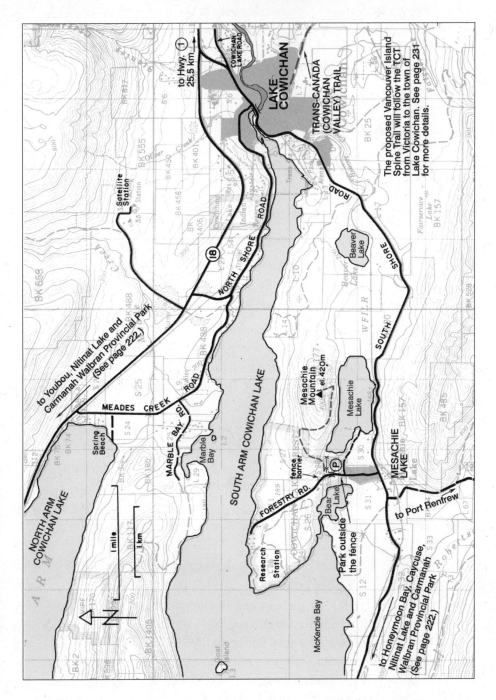

View over Cowichan Lake to Mesachie Mountain and the Research Station in the centre. ERIC BURKLE

viewpoint at the Mesachie Mountain summit. Allow about an hour's hiking time to the summit, one way.

WORTH NOTING   In early summer, Mesachie Mountain's open areas explode with bright wildflowers and showy manzanita.

NEARBY   There are interesting groomed trails along the road within the fence for viewing huge stumps and trees. Information panels describe forest ecology. This area, on the east side of Forestry Road, is not within the main grounds of the research station and permission to enter is not required. Hiking or walking anywhere on the research station property west of Forestry Road is not allowed.

ADDITIONAL INFORMATION
www.for.gov.bc.ca/hre (Cowichan Lake Forest Research Station)
Refer to NTS 92C/16 (1:50,000)

3

Ladysmith, Cedar and Yellow Point

3a. Holland Creek Trail

(Refer to a detailed Ladysmith road map.)

DIFFICULTY/DISTANCE   Easy to strenuous/5.8 km loop

HIGHLIGHTS   Delightful Holland Creek Trail runs along both banks of Ladysmith's picturesque Holland Creek. The trail goes from sea level, up the Holland Creek Valley to the hydro lines, west of town. The viewing of Crystal Falls is a hike highlight. There is choice of trail access points. Several additional Ladysmith hiking areas are nearby; some are linked to the Holland Creek Trail. An excellent trail map is available at www. ladysmith.ca.

ACCESS

Via Holland Creek Park   There are two main trailheads for the Holland Creek Trail, both near large parking areas. To reach the first, at Holland Creek Park, turn west from Highway 1 (Trans-Canada) onto Davis Road, near Ladysmith's Coronation Mall, at the Davis Road/Chemainus Road traffic lights. Continue up the hill on Davis Road and through the subdivision. At Dogwood Drive, turn right and drive down the hill to the parking area at Holland Creek Park, on the left, next to Holland Creek.

Via Methuen Street   The second main trailhead is at the corner of 6th Avenue and Methuen Street. Access as above for the Holland Creek Park. Continue on Dogwood Drive, go up the hill to Methuen Street and bear left (west) to 6th Avenue and the trailhead. If you are coming into Ladysmith on Highway 1 from the north, turn right at the traffic lights onto 1st Avenue and continue to Methuen Street. Note that from the east

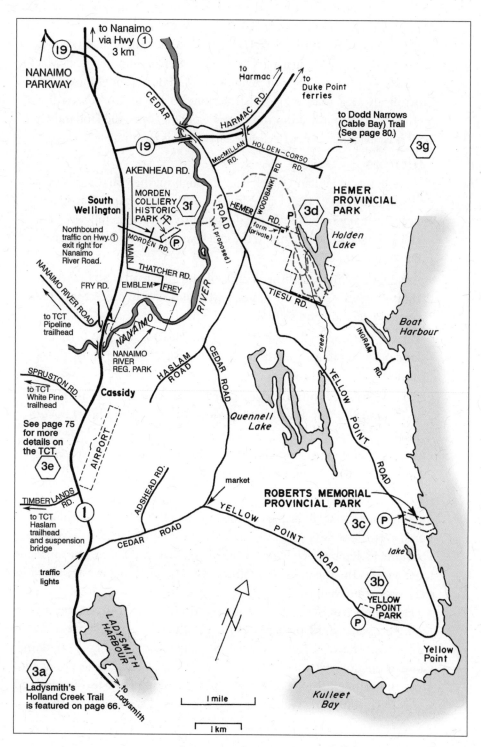

to Nanaimo
via Hwy ①
3 km

⑲

NANAIMO
PARKWAY

to Harmac

to Duke Point
ferries

to Dodd Narrows
(Cable Bay) Trail
(See page 80.)

3g

CEDAR

HARMAC RD.

⑲

MacMILLAN RD.

HOLDEN-CORSO RD.

AKENHEAD RD.

South
Wellington

MORDEN
COLLIERY
HISTORIC
PARK

3f

HEMER RD.

WOODBANK RD.

P

3d

HEMER
PROVINCIAL
PARK

ROAD (proposed)

farm
(private)

Holden
Lake

Northbound
traffic on Hwy.①
exit right for
Nanaimo
River Road.

MORDEN RD.

P

MAIN

THATCHER RD.

TIESU RD.

creek

NANAIMO RIVER ROAD

FRY RD.

EMBLEM FREY

RIVER

Boat
Harbour

to TCT
Pipeline
trailhead

NANAIMO

NANAIMO
RIVER
REG. PARK

HASLAM ROAD

CEDAR ROAD

INGRAM RD.

YELLOW POINT ROAD

SPRUSTON RD.

to TCT
White Pine
trailhead

Cassidy

AIRPORT

Quennell
Lake

See page 75
for more
details on
the TCT.

3e

market

ROBERTS MEMORIAL
PROVINCIAL PARK

TIMBERLANDS RD.

①

ADSHEAD RD.

YELLOW

POINT

3c

P

to TCT
Haslam
trailhead
and suspension
bridge

CEDAR ROAD

ROAD

lake

traffic
lights

3b

YELLOW
POINT
PARK

LADYSMITH HARBOUR

P

Yellow
Point

3a

to Ladysmith

Ladysmith's
Holland Creek Trail
is featured on page 66.

I mile

Kulleet
Bay

1 km

end of Methuen Street and 1st Avenue you can take a trail that links to Transfer Beach Park via a tunnel under Highway 1.

A secondary Holland Creek Trail entry point is situated at Davis Road Park, on Davis Road, just past Dogwood Drive. Another is at Mackie Road Park, reached via 6th Avenue and Malone and Mackie roads. Consult an area road map for directions to the trailheads. From the Methuen Street trailhead to the Upper Colliery Dam, the Holland Creek Trail is wheelchair accessible. Some assistance is required.

CAUTIONS

- Water levels in Holland Creek vary throughout the year. Rapids exist year round near Crystal Falls. Sections of the creek valley, particularly near the many rocky bluffs, are dangerously steep. Carefully supervise children when hiking close to the creek and near overhanging creek banks and cliff edges.
- Area trails follow established paths, old logging roads and hydro line right-of-ways. Keep to the designated routes to help protect the area's fragile vegetation and soils.
- Parts of the loop trails near Stocking and Heart lakes cross private land. Stay on official trails and do not trespass. Obey any posted notices.
- No camping, fires or motorized vehicles are allowed. Bikes are permitted on the Stocking and Heart Lake loops and on the Rotary Lookout Trail.
- Stay away from the creek in the fall to avoid disturbing the spawning salmon. Be alert for black bears.

HIKE DESCRIPTION With several trailheads to start from, visitors may choose to hike all or part of the Holland Creek Trail. On the creek's north side the trail is well groomed and provides relatively easy hiking. From the Holland Creek Park trailhead on Dogwood Drive, one option is to go east on the short, lower loop that winds along the forested creek to the Coronation Mall.

Hike west from the parking area and head upstream on the upper loop. Part way up the path passes the Methuen Street and Mackie Road trailheads. The trail swings south and then skirts two colliery dams. Close to the Rotary Lookout Trail at the Holland Creek Trail's upper end, cross the wooden bridge and swing north to loop back to the Holland Creek Park trailhead. Watch for trail markers. The trail running south

Yellow Skunk Cabbage or Yellow Arum.   RICHARD K. BLIER

from the bridge leads to the hydro lines. From here the Heart Lake and Stocking Lake loops are accessible.

From the wooden bridge, the Holland Creek Trail changes its nature and goes from an easy, generally smooth path to a more rugged, strenuous trail that traverses uneven terrain and rises and falls in twists and turns along Holland Creek's south bank. The best viewpoint of Crystal Falls is on this side of the creek, just north of the lower colliery dam. The complete Holland Creek Loop is 5.8 km in length and requires about 2 hours hiking time to complete.

WORTH NOTING

- The closest trailhead to Crystal Falls is on Mackie Road. Locals refer to this cascade simply as "The Falls".
- Ladysmith area trails are colour coded to help rescuers pinpoint the location of any hikers who require assistance.
- Benches, bridges and information signposts are situated along many trails.
- The Holland Creek weirs, dating from the turn of the 20th Century, held back creek waters and created reservoirs. Holland Creek has three

colliery dams. The water reserves were used for coal washing at Transfer Beach. In the 1920s, a logging railway ran 4 km up the Holland Creek Valley.

- In the mid-1990s, a crew working on highway widening uncovered an old sandstone culvert dating back to 1908. This relic of an earlier era now marks the Holland Creek Trail's lowest point, near Ladysmith Harbour.

- Stocking Lake is a source of Ladysmith's drinking water.

NEARBY   Ladysmith has created many other hiking trails and walks within its boundaries, including several that are accessed from the Holland Creek Trail. Many of these trails traverse the more rugged terrain in behind Ladysmith. Be sure to carry adequate water, warm clothes and some food. Wear sturdy footwear. Raingear is an extra precaution against changeable weather.

Heart Lake Loop   Moderate to strenuous/6.4 km loop: The most direct access to the Heart Lake Loop is via the Mackie Road trailhead and the upper Holland Creek Trail. Alternately, from Davis Road Park, follow the route markers along the power line trail. The Heart Lake Loop offers one of Ladysmith's most impressive viewpoints. The vista includes Ladysmith, Ladysmith Harbour and the Gulf Islands. However, to reach the scenic lookout requires a strenuous climb on one of the area's steepest trails. The most arduous grade is near the power lines and begins as a set of stone steps. There are a couple of resting benches on the way up to Heart Lake. The trail climbs to the viewpoint and then loops around the lake. At a signpost south of Heart Lake, turn west over private land and pass a swamp. Eventually the trail roughens as it begins its abrupt descent to a bridge. At Holland Creek the ground flattens out a little more. Hike east to reach the upper end of the Holland Creek Trail or follow the hydro line trail to Davis Road Park. Allow 2 hours to complete the loop.

Stocking Lake Loop   Moderate to strenuous/9.3 km loop: Access is via Davis Road Park, the Holland Creek Trail or the Heart Lake Loop. From the Davis Road Park trailhead the first part of the trail turns south and offers easy hiking over relatively flat ground. After 1 km the route steepens as it climbs past a water reservoir. The trail zigzags up to a couple of great viewpoints, both with benches, east of Stocking Lake. The going gets easier on the approach to Stocking Lake, where the path splits to skirt both sides of the lake. Cut north and follow the steepest part of the Heart

Lake Loop down to the stone steps, near the power lines. Turn right (east) and hike back to Davis Road Park. Alternatively swing left (west) at the bottom of the Heart Lake hill and follow the signposts to the upper end of the Holland Creek Trail and the Mackie Road trailhead. Allow 2 hours, 45 minutes to complete the loop.

Rotary Lookout Trail   Easy/1.2 km, one way: Access is from the Mackie Road trailhead. From the parking area, a short path connects to the Holland Creek Trail. Head south (upstream) past two dams to the wooden bridge at the Holland Creek Trail's top end. The Rotary Lookout Trail begins nearby and leads to a Ladysmith Harbour lookout and picnic site.

Marine Walk   Easy/1 km, one way: From Transfer Beach Park this trail runs north through a wooded area and parallels the Ladysmith waterfront to the Government Wharf. The trail turns east to Highway 1, close to the 1st Avenue intersection and traffic lights.

Estuary Trail   Easy/0.3 km, one way: Accessed on King Road, off Chemainus Road, on Highway 1's east side, this trail along Ladysmith Harbour is a local favourite. At low tide it is possible to walk north along the beach to Transfer Beach Park.

ADDITIONAL INFORMATION
www.ladysmith.ca (Town of Ladysmith)
Refer to NTS 92/13 (1:50,000)

3b. Yellow Point Park   Map M3

DIFFICULTY/DISTANCE   Easy/2 km, one way

HIGHLIGHTS   A variety of trails wind through Yellow Point Park (51.4 ha), near Yellow Point. It is easy to create your own loop hike as many of the paths interconnect. The park is a perfect destination for woodland walks, nature appreciation, birdwatching and wildlife viewing.

ACCESS   On Highway 1 (Trans-Canada) south of Nanaimo, take the southern Cedar Road cutoff and travel 3 km to the first Yellow Point Road junction, near the market. (Yellow Point Road also meets Cedar Road farther north, near Tiesu Road and Hemer Provincial Park.) From Cedar Road turn east onto Yellow Point Road and drive another 4.2 km. Watch for the signposted Yellow Point Park entrance and parking area, on the left. Yellow Point Road is also accessible via the northern Cedar Road turnoff on Highway 1. This alternate way to the park is 11 km in length.

CAUTIONS
- There are numerous unmarked trails and bridle paths in this area.
- Stay on the main trails and take care not to trample fragile park vegetation and soil.
- Carry your own water. Wear sturdy footwear.

HIKE DESCRIPTION From the parking area several trails lead off into the second-growth forest. Create your own loop hike along the variety of trails that criss-cross the park. Some intersections are marked; others are not. Most trails have flat, easy sections, but you will encounter uneven terrain and some hills.

WORTH NOTING
- This park is a great place for birdwatchers. Look for owls, hawks, woodpeckers, jays and eagles.
- Delicate seasonal wildflowers, such as camas, brighten the forest floor in the spring.
- Facilities include an information signpost, picnic tables and toilets.

NEARBY Roberts Memorial Provincial Park. See below.

ADDITIONAL INFORMATION
www.cvrd.bc.ca (Cowichan Valley Regional District)
www.rdn.bc.ca (Regional District of Nanaimo)
Refer to NTS 92G/4 (1:50,000)

3c. Roberts Memorial Provincial Park   Map M3

DIFFICULTY/DISTANCE Easy/1 km, one way

HIGHLIGHTS Roberts Memorial Provincial Park (14 ha), about 13 km south of Nanaimo, features an easy trail that descends to a beautiful sandstone beach on Stuart Channel. This day-use park has excellent opportunities for viewing wildlife and marine mammals.

ACCESS As for Yellow Point Park, from Highway 1 (Trans-Canada) take the southern Cedar Road cutoff and continue 3 km to Yellow Point Road. This point is also accessible from the northern Cedar Road highway junction. Turn east onto Yellow Point Road at the market and travel another 9 km to the signposted park entrance and parking area, on the right.

CAUTIONS

- Please stay within park boundaries, respect adjacent private property and obey any posted notices.
- Bring adequate water.
- Carry out all your litter.
- No motorized vehicles, fires or camping allowed.

HIKE DESCRIPTION   From the parking area a well-defined trail drops down through a predominantly second growth Douglas-fir forest to the rocky beach fronting Stuart Channel. The beach consists of a series of sandstone ledges. Allow about 15 minutes to hike down to the beach, longer to hike back uphill to the parking area.

WORTH NOTING

- California and Steller sea lions haul out on the beach's sandstone ledges to bask in the summer sun. Seals may be spotted in Stuart channel.
- Watch for eagles, other birds of prey, Great Blue Herons, gulls and a diversity of waterbirds.
- In 1980, in memory of her husband and daughter, Mrs. May Vaughn Roberts donated the parkland to the province.
- Facilities include a tiny picnic area near the beach. Pit toilets are located at either end of the trail.

NEARBY   Yellow Point Park. See page 71.

ADDITIONAL INFORMATION
www.env.gov.bc.ca/bcparks (BC Parks)
Refer to NTS 92G/4 (1:50,000)

3d. Hemer Provincial Park   Map M3

DIFFICULTY/DISTANCE   Easy/1 km, one way

HIGHLIGHTS   Hemer Provincial Park (93 ha) has 11 km of easy, connecting trails. Delightful forested paths lead to Holden Lake or to the park's more open marshlands. Create your own loop hike or take a simple walk in the woods. This day-use destination is great for birdwatching and wildlife viewing.

ACCESS

Cedar Road from the north   In the Cedar area, south of Nanaimo, take the northern Cedar Road cutoff on Highway 1 (Trans-Canada) and travel south for 5 km to Hemer Road.

Cedar Road from the south   Take the southern Cedar Road turnoff from Highway 1 and continue 9 km north to Hemer Road. Turn east onto Hemer Road and follow the signposts for 1.5 km to the end of the road at the Hemer Provincial Park parking area. Parking is limited.

CAUTIONS

- Hemer Provincial Park is located in a rural farm region surrounded by private property. Please respect the privacy of area residents.
- Stay on the trails to avoid damaging sensitive plants and fragile soil structure.
- There is no public access from the park's eastern boundary to Boat Harbour.

HIKE DESCRIPTION   Several inviting trails, mostly unmarked, snake out from the parking area, but it is hard to get lost. The well-maintained trails are easy to figure out. A popular destination about 1 km from the parking area is the viewing platform that overlooks a large marshland. Another intriguing trail runs along Holden Lake. Here the mixed coniferous and deciduous forest of primary bigleaf maple, alder and Douglas-fir is thicker than the forest surrounding the park's wetlands.

WORTH NOTING

- At the marshland viewing platform look for birds of prey and other bird species overhead. Scan the wetland waters for ducks, swans, and even beavers.
- Listen and watch for pileated woodpeckers in the park's shady forests.
- Hikers, bikers and horse riders are welcome. No motorized vehicles are allowed.

- Facilities include benches along some trails and a picnic area. The pit toilets are just up the main trail from the parking area.
- Anglers will find seasonal trout fishing in Holden Lake. There is good lakeshore access.
- In 1981, John and Violet Hemer donated Hemer Provincial Park to the people of BC. They are the grandchildren of the Hemers who originally purchased the land. They have life occupancy of their property including the continued farming of the park's cleared portion (6.5 ha). Park trails follow old roads, one of which was once the railway grade from Boat Harbour to Departure Bay. It was along this route that coal was shipped to tidewater from mines south of Nanaimo.

NEARBY The eastern section of the Morden Colliery Trail extends from the park to Cedar Road. See page 79.

ADDITIONAL INFORMATION
www.env.gov.bc.ca/bcparks (BC Parks)
Refer to NTS 92G/ 4 (1:50,000)

3e. Trans-Canada Trail
(Ladysmith/Nanaimo area) · Maps M3, M4

DIFFICULTY/DISTANCE Moderate/1 km to 5 km, one way

HIGHLIGHTS The Trans-Canada Trail (TCT) is a work-in-progress for the Regional District of Nanaimo (RDN), its partners and countless trail volunteers. When completed, this part of Canada's multi-use corridor will stretch from the Cowichan Valley, through Ladysmith, all the way north to the City of Nanaimo. The TCT's north and south sections are currently severed at the Nanaimo River, but still offer several access points and plenty of scenic highlights. The trail is a favourite destination for hikers, joggers, walkers, cyclists and equestrians.

CAUTIONS
- Carry ample water. Bring extra food, warm clothing and raingear. Be ready for changeable weather.
- There is no trail bridge over the Nanaimo River. The RDN does not recommend hikers try swimming or wading the river.
- The TCT passes through the habitat of black bear, cougar and other wildlife. Be alert while hiking.

- Many parts of the trail are rough and still under development. Be prepared for steep hills, rocky sections and lots of up and down hiking. Wear sturdy footwear.
- En route are numerous old roads, trails and side paths. Improved trail signage is ongoing but remains incomplete in some sections. Watch for trail markers. Parts of the trail cut across private timberlands or abut private land. To ensure permission for continued public access along these right-of-ways please stay on official routes and respect these areas. Do not trespass.
- No motorized vehicles, camping or fires are allowed.
- Park safely at the trailheads. Stay clear of other potential traffic. Do not block gates. Secure your vehicle and remove all valuables.

ACCESS

To the TCT South End via Timberlands Road   From Highway 1 (Trans-Canada) in Cassidy, near the Nanaimo Airport, turn west at the traffic lights onto Timberlands Road. Drive just under 2.5 km to the Rondalyn Resort. Swing south to a gravel pit near the start of a gated industrial road. Park at the roadside and follow the rough logging road 1 km around the gravel pit's south side. Watch for TCT markers. Logging trucks sometimes use the trailhead access road so be careful walking in this area.

Via Spruston Road   From Highway 1 (Trans-Canada) in Cassidy, on the north side of Haslam Creek near the Nanaimo Airport, turn west onto Spruston Road and drive to the trailhead at the end of the road.

HIKE DESCRIPTIONS (TCT SOUTH END)

The Haslam Creek Trail   Moderate/3.8 km, one way: From the logging road trailhead, the Haslam Creek Trail heads north along the gravel pit's west side. A trail highlight is 1 km away—the Haslam Creek suspension bridge, opened in 2003. The majestic span is 48 m in length and 18 m high. The view of the Haslam Creek gorge is particularly impressive when the creek is running high.

From the suspension bridge the trail parallels Haslam Creek's north side. At the top of a steep grade is a viewpoint. The Haslam Creek Trail ends at serene Timberland Lake, a perfect place for a picnic. Beyond here the TCT is called the White Pine Trail.

The White Pine Trail   Moderate/3.2 km, one way: This section of the TCT extends north from Timberland Lake to Spruston Road. The route follows mainly old logging roads through logged areas and climbs a ridge

The Nanaimo River is beautiful at any time of the year. RICHARD K. BLIER

near Crystal Lake to a viewpoint. East of McKay Lake the trail reaches the Spruston Road trailhead. Expect muddy and marshy sections.

Darryl's Way   Moderate/1 km, one way: From the Spruston Road trailhead it is possible to extend your TCT hike another 1 km north along Darryl's Way. This short trail begins at Spruston Road and goes to the Nanaimo River and the site of a future bridge and trail crossing.

ACCESS

To the TCT North End via Nanaimo River Road From Highway 1 (Trans-Canada) in Cassidy, on the north side of the Nanaimo River highway bridge, take the Nanaimo River Road cutoff. Please note that travellers driving north on Highway 1 will turn right off the highway. Follow Nanaimo River Road west for approximately 9 km, past White Rapids Road, to the TCT trailhead, marked by what the RDN describes as "two large blue waterline vent pipes beside the road." The actual trailhead markers are quite small and easy to miss.

Via the Extension region The Extension trailhead is reached along Bramley Road, near the volunteer firehall. Along Nanaimo River Road, 4 km west of Highway 1, turn north on White Rapids Road to Godfrey Road. Turn left (northwest) to Bramley Road. Swing left (west) here to the trailhead. Some trail rerouting has taken place in the Extension region. Watch for and follow trail markers.

HIKE DESCRIPTIONS (TCT NORTH END)

The Pipeline Trail Moderate/4 km, one way: From Nanaimo River Road the Pipeline Trail heads generally northeast through a second growth forest to the community of Errington, once a coal mining centre. The trail negotiates undulating terrain alongside a water pipeline, hence its name. From Errington the TCT continues north and is called the Extension Ridge Trail. Consider exploring the TCT on the Nanaimo River Road's south side. From the road the trail twists 1.5 km south down to the Nanaimo River and the location of a future bridge.

Extension Ridge (The Abyss) Trail Moderate/5 km, one way: From the Extension area the trail abruptly ascends the Extension Ridge. The forest here, interspersed with small clearcuts, is mainly Douglas-fir, Garry oak and arbutus. The ridge offers several breath-taking views of Mount Benson and the Strait of Georgia seascape and its island archipelago. One of many trail features is The Abyss, an earthquake fissure marked by a long, deep, shadowy crevice that slices across a rocky meadow. There are several such fractures along this trail; the Abyss is the largest. The trail ends on Harewood Mines Road, near the Hydro lines. Trails from here connect to Nanaimo's Colliery Dam Park and many other area parks and trails.

WORTH NOTING

- The White Pine Trail is named after a species of tree that grew among Douglas-fir in this area. Most of the large pines were logged years ago.
- Extension Ridge is popular with mountain bikers.

- Pay parking is available at the Rondalyn Resort.

NEARBY   Morden Colliery Trail and Colliery Dam Park. See below and page 84.

ADDITIONAL INFORMATION
www.nanaimo.ca (City of Nanaimo)
www.rdn.bc.ca (Regional District of Nanaimo)
www.trailsbc.ca or www.tctrail.ca (Trans-Canada Trail)
Refer to NTS 92G/4 (1:50,000)

3f. Morden Colliery Trail   Map M3

DIFFICULTY/DISTANCE   Easy/1.2 km to 2.2 km, one way

HIGHLIGHTS   The Morden Colliery Trail is a work-in-progress for the Regional District of Nanaimo (RDN). Two existing sections of the trail follow an old railway right-of-way that once connected South Wellington coal mines with the ships moored at Boat Harbour.

ACCESS
To the Morden Road trailhead   On Highway 1 (Trans-Canada) north of Ladysmith, turn east at the traffic lights onto Morden Road and continue to the four-way-stop at Akenhead Road. Keep straight ahead down the hill to where the road seems to end at three driveways. Take the middle one to Morden Colliery Historic Provincial Park, the parking lot and day use picnic area. The Morden Colliery Trail begins nearby.

To the Cedar Road trailhead   The trailhead for the Morden Colliery Trail's eastern section is off Cedar Road, near the shopping centre, between MacMillan and Hemer roads. Look for a small trail signpost near a limited parking area.

CAUTIONS   The trail's middle link from the Nanaimo River to Cedar Road has yet to be completed.

HIKE DESCRIPTION   The Morden Colliery Trail's western section begins at Morden Colliery Historic Provincial Park, crosses two branches of Thatcher Creek and ends 1.2 km away at the Nanaimo River. Until a footbridge here spans the gap, it is necessary to pick up the trail's eastern section on Cedar Road (near the shopping centre). From Cedar Road the trail stretches 2.2 km through forest and residential areas to Hemer Provincial Park. See page 74.

MORDEN COLLIERY HISTORIC PROVINCIAL PARK (4 ha) features an old reinforced concrete coal tipple that dates back almost a century to 1912. It was built by the Pacific Coal Company for their Morden Coal Mine. This is the last remaining tipple on Vancouver Island. For public safety, a fence surrounds the site. This day-use park is undeveloped.

Among the RDN's concerns in future planning of the Morden Colliery Trail are the Nanaimo River crossing and the trail's proximity to ball fields and private farmland. As funds allow, the RDN purchases any available land and creates routes through negotiated easements, access ways and covenants. When finished, the trail will be around 6.5 km long.

WORTH NOTING
- Hikers, bikers and horse riders are welcome.
- No motorized vehicles are allowed.

NEARBY *Nanaimo River Regional Park* (56 ha), along the banks of the Nanaimo River, was established for public recreation and to protect valuable fish habitat. There are two access points along Highway 19. One is immediately north of the Nanaimo River bridge, via Fry Road. The second is via Morden, Main, Thatcher East, Emblem and Frey roads. The regional park is currently undeveloped. A rough anglers trail exists on the Nanaimo River's north side.

ADDITIONAL INFORMATION
www.env.gov.bc.ca/bcparks (BC Parks)
www.rdn.bc.ca (Regional District of Nanaimo)
Refer to NTS 92G/4 (1:50,000)

3g. Dodd Narrows (Cable Bay) Nature Trail
Maps M3, M3G

DIFFICULTY/DISTANCE Moderate/2 km to Cable Bay, one way; 3 km to Dodd Narrows, one way

HIGHLIGHTS The Dodd Narrows (Cable Bay) Nature Trail, south of Nanaimo, leads to spectacular seascapes and a rugged sandstone beach on Northumberland Channel. From Cable Bay a shoreline trail winds its way to Dodd Narrows, infamous for its turbulent, reversing currents. This region is known for its wildlife viewing and the trail can be hiked at any time of the year.

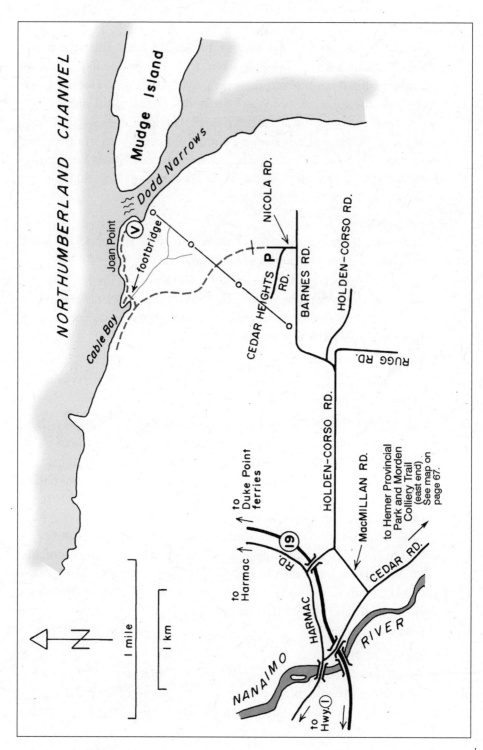

ACCESS On Highway 1 (Trans-Canada) south of Nanaimo, take either the north or south Cedar Road turnoff and stay on Cedar Road to MacMillan Road. The distance to MacMillan Road from the north, via the Nanaimo River bridge, is 4 km; from the south, 10 km. Follow MacMillan Road 0.5 km and then turn right (east) onto Holden-Corso Road (near the corner store). Watch for Dodd Narrows Trail signs.

Halfway to the trailhead, at Rugg Road, Holden-Corso Road makes a sharp left, climbs a hill and swings right. At this point keep straight ahead onto Barnes Road and continue east to the signposted Nicola Road turn, a little under 4 km from Cedar Road. Take Nicola Road north for 0.5 km to the Dodd Narrows Trail parking area.

CAUTIONS
- Hikers use the trail at their own risk. Seaside rocks are slippery at low tide. Exercise caution. Supervise children closely.
- Expect some steep grades. These are harder to hike on the way out since the trail back to the parking lot runs mostly uphill. Several old roads and trails intersect the route. To avoid confusion, stay on the main trail to avoid becoming lost.
- Carry adequate water.
- Please stay on the main trail, respect adjacent private property and comply with posted notices.

HIKE DESCRIPTION From the parking area the Dodd Narrows (Cable Bay) Trail goes under the power lines and enters the second growth forest. Gates prevent motorized vehicles from entering. Next, the trail begins a steady descent to Cable Bay and its sandstone beach. Allow about half an hour to reach the shoreline. At Cable Bay, swing right (east) where the trail branches and cross the footbridge.

To reach Dodd Narrows, 30 minutes away from Cable Bay, simply take the 1 km trail along the picturesque Northumberland Channel shoreline to the Joan Point lighthouse and Dodd Narrows. From here you can see the Gulf Islands to the south, Gabriola Island and the bluffs to the north, and Mudge Island. As with most coastline trails, expect some up and down hiking.

WORTH NOTING
- Eagles congregate near Northumberland Channel each December. Nesting seabirds and birds of prey are common over the summer.
- From mid-October to March, the log booms near the Harmac mill site

A boater negotiates the often-turbulent waters of Dodd Narrows. RICHARD K. BLIER

are home to thousands of sea lions. You may even spot passing killer whales.

- There are no facilities. No camping or fires allowed.
- The Dodd Narrows (Cable Bay) Nature Trail was created as a co-operative effort of the City of Nanaimo, Harmac Pacific and MacMillan Bloedel.

NEARBY Hemer Provincial Park. See page 74.

ADDITIONAL INFORMATION
www.nanaimo.ca (City of Nanaimo)
Refer to NTS map 92G/4 (1:50,000)

DODD NARROWS offers visitors a close look at the power of the ocean. At maximum flow, powerful currents surge through the constricted channel between Vancouver Island and Mudge Island. These flows may reach speeds of up to eight knots, creating hazardous water conditions for boaters. The Canadian Hydrographic Service at www.waterlevels.gc.ca provides information for calculating times of peak tidal flows. Dodd Narrows was named after Captain Charles Dodd, who commanded the Hudson's Bay Company steamer *Beaver* from 1843 to 1852.

4

Nanaimo

4a. Colliery Dam Park   Map M4

DIFFICULTY/DISTANCE   Easy/1 hour loop

HIGHLIGHTS   Colliery Dam Park (28 ha) features two quiet, artificial lakes bordered by over 2.5 km of scenic trails. Opportunities to observe a wide variety of bird and wildlife are many.

ACCESS

Via Nanaimo Lakes Road   In Nanaimo, take Wakesiah Avenue south to Nanaimo Lakes Road. Turn right (southwest) and watch for a small parking lot on the left.

Via Wakesiah Avenue   In Nanaimo, take Wakesiah Avenue and cross Nanaimo Lakes Road to the corner of Wakesiah Avenue and Sixth Street. A small parking area and trailhead are close by.

Via the Nanaimo Parkway   Turn east off the Nanaimo Parkway (Highway 19) at the Fifth Street traffic lights (Exit 16). At Wakesiah Road, turn right and continue to Nanaimo Lakes Road. Swing right (southwest) and look for the parking lot, to the left.

CAUTIONS   Secure your vehicle and leave no valuables behind.

HIKE DESCRIPTION   From the trailheads you can hike a figure-eight around the lakes via well-groomed trails and bridges. Allow about an hour to complete a lake loop.

WORTH NOTING
- Both the upper and lower lakes are periodically stocked with trout. The park is a favourite angling destination. Summer swimming is a popular pastime.

- The dam once provided fresh water to the Nanaimo waterfront's #1 Coal Mine.
- In the fall the forest canopy provides a colourful backdrop of vine maples and other deciduous trees.
- Common wildlife in the lakes includes muskrats, mergansers, geese, ducks and other waterfowl. Raccoon, deer and grouse inhabit the forests. Scan the skies for Bald Eagles, hawks and other birds of prey.

NEARBY The Morrell Nature Sanctuary is near Colliery Dam Park. The sanctuary is along Nanaimo Lakes Road, west of the Nanaimo Parkway overpass. See below. The Nanaimo Parkway Trail and the Trans-Canada Trail follow the same route through Colliery Dam Park's east side. These multi-use corridors link many Nanaimo parks and trails. See map on page 86.

ADDITIONAL INFORMATION
www.nanaimo.ca (City of Nanaimo)
Refer to NTS 92 G/4 (1:50,000)

4b. Morrell Nature Sanctuary   Map M4

DIFFICULTY/DISTANCE   Easy/3 km loop

HIGHLIGHTS The Morrell Nature Sanctuary (111 ha) features 11.5 km of trails through a mainly second growth Douglas-fir and western red cedar forest. The diverse vegetation along the wetland trails is amazing and includes ferns, shrubs and aquatic plants. Create your own woodland loop hike to scenic lookouts, a beaver pond and Morrell Lake.

ACCESS

Via Nanaimo Lakes Road   In Nanaimo, take Nanaimo Lakes Road and head southwest to pass the DND Base and Colliery Dam Park. Drive under the Nanaimo Parkway and immediately look for Dogwood Road and the sanctuary entrance signpost, on the right. Follow the signs to the parking lot.

Via the Nanaimo Parkway   If you arrive via the Nanaimo Parkway (Highway 19), turn east onto Fifth Street at the Exit 16 traffic lights. Continue 1 km and turn right onto Wakesiah Avenue. At the next corner, swing right onto Nanaimo Lakes Road. From here it is about 1 km to the sanctuary. A loop trail near the parking area is wheelchair accessible.

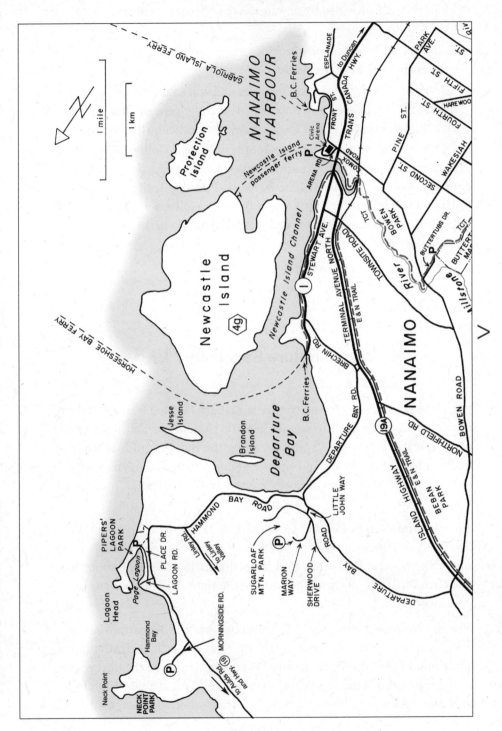

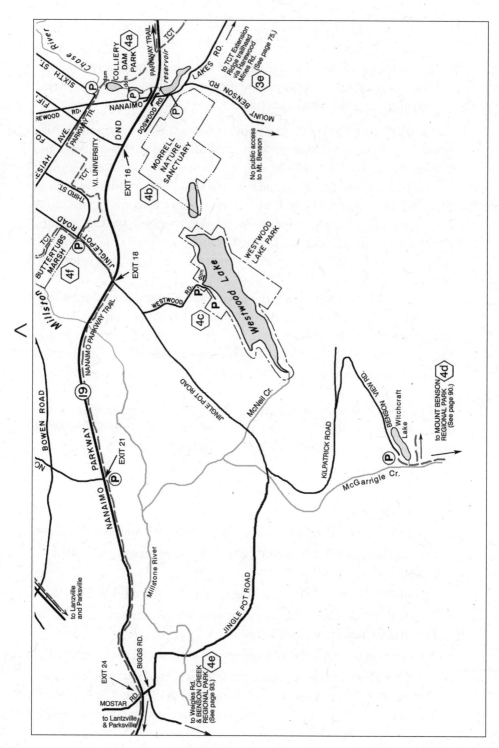

CAUTIONS

- Stay on existing trails at all times to protect sensitive plants and soil structure.
- Numerous unmarked side trails extend out beyond sanctuary boundaries and onto and through private property. Please avoid these areas and obey any posted notices.

HIKE DESCRIPTION A very popular Morrell Nature Sanctuary hike is the 3 km loop to a beaver pond via the Rocky Knoll, Beaver Pond and Tranquility trails. The route snakes through a tranquil second growth forest that abounds with birds and other wildlife. The networks of trails at Morrell Nature Sanctuary access great viewpoints. Two are located along a 1 km path that circles the beaver pond. Another high vantage point is along the 0.4 km Lookout Trail, which branches off the Tranquility Trail. Allow about 1.5 hours to complete the loop and extra time to explore and observe.

To get to Morrell Lake from the beaver pond, hike a few minutes west along the fire road, then cut onto the short trail that leads to Morrell Lake's southeast end. Extend your hike by continuing another 1 km to the other end of Morrell Lake. You can take a trail that winds through the shady forest, away from the lake, or follow another that hugs the lake's serpentine shoreline.

The Yew Loop Trail, next to the parking area, is wheelchair accessible and takes about 30 minutes to walk. Information signposts provide details on the types of trees that grow at trailside.

WORTH NOTING

- Watch for beaver in the pond and lake and blacktail deer in the surrounding forest.
- The sanctuary is open from dawn to dusk and offers year round hiking.
- Guided tours and Woods Room Nature House programs are offered seasonally.
- Pit toilets are situated at the parking area and at Morrell Lake.
- A wide dirt road circles the sanctuary and acts as a fire access route. Bicycles are permitted on this road.
- A rough trail connects the sanctuary with Westwood Lake.
- In 1973 William Morrell donated the sanctuary land to the BC Land Commission. The Nature Trust of BC now owns the site. The Morrell Sanctuary Society for Environmental Education manages the sanctuary.

NEARBY Colliery Dam Park and the Trans-Canada Trail are 1 km to the east, along Nanaimo Lakes Road. See map on page 87.

ADDITIONAL INFORMATION
www.morrell.bc.ca (Morrell Sanctuary Society)
Refer to NTS 92G/4 (1:50,000)

4c. Westwood Lake Park   Map M4

DIFFICULTY/DISTANCE   Easy/6 km loop

HIGHLIGHTS   Westwood Lake Park (120 ha) is the perfect destination for anyone who enjoys a loop hike, and the park is within easy striking distance of downtown Nanaimo. The park's many trails have something for everyone, whether you enjoy hiking, birdwatching, wildlife viewing, nature appreciation, photography, or simply getting away for awhile.

ACCESS   From the Nanaimo Parkway (Highway 19), turn west onto Jingle Pot Road at the Exit 18 traffic lights and continue past Calder Road to Westwood Road. Turn left (south) and travel another 0.7 km to the end of the Westwood Road and the ample parking area near the beach and picnic area. It is possible to reach Westwood Lake from the north end of Jingle Pot Road by turning west from the Nanaimo Parkway at the Exit 24 traffic lights.

CAUTIONS
- Stay on designated park trails at all times. Side paths are many and these generally lead onto private property. Please avoid these areas and respect the privacy of the landowners adjacent to Westwood Lake Park.
- Carry adequate water.
- No overnight parking, camping fires or motorized vehicles allowed. Secure your vehicle and leave no valuables behind.

HIKE DESCRIPTION   Hikers may choose from a number of park trails. The most popular one winds 6 km around Westwood Lake's perimeter. Whichever direction you hike this trail, remember to keep the lake in sight to stay on course. Most of the route is flat and follows a well-maintained bark mulch trail. The only elevation gain is at the lake's east end. Allow about 2 hours to complete the loop.

WORTH NOTING
- The rocky bluff (30 m) at Westwood Lake's east end offers fine views of

the lake and Mount Benson. This hill is often referred to as Westwood Knoll. From this area a 15 minute side trail runs northeast to the end of Calder Road. There is no parking at this trailhead.

- Hikers, joggers, walkers, picnickers, swimmers, canoeists and anglers use Westwood Lake Park. Summer is the busiest season.
- Westwood Lake (92 ha) is stocked regularly with trout. There is a boat ramp. Electric motors only.
- Watch for deer and raccoon in the forest; ducks and geese on the lake.
- Visit the park in the spring to see the wildflowers in bloom.
- A rough trail connects to the Morell Nature Sanctuary.

NEARBY   Mount Benson Regional Park. See below.

ADDITIONAL INFORMATION
www.nanaimo.ca (City of Nanaimo)
Refer to NTS 92G/4 (1:50,000)

4d. Mount Benson Regional Park   Map M4

DIFFICULTY/DISTANCE   Strenuous/4 hours, one way

HIGHLIGHTS   Mount Benson Regional Park (212 ha) offers some of Nanaimo's best viewpoints. Perched on Mount Benson's southeast flank, the park is reached via steep, strenuous trails. Those who tackle the well-travelled trails to the top are rewarded with outstanding views at the Mount Benson summit (1006 m). The climb is well worth the effort. Many visitors consider Mount Benson one of Vancouver Island's premier hiking destinations.

ACCESS   The only official access to Mount Benson Regional Park is from the Witchcraft Lake trailhead. From the Nanaimo Parkway (Highway 19), turn west onto Jingle Pot Road at the Exit 18 traffic lights, continue to Kilpatrick Road, and turn left. Bear right onto Benson View Road to the trailhead, near Witchcraft Lake's west end. It is also possible to reach Kilpatrick Road from the north end of Jingle Pot Road by turning west from the Nanaimo Parkway at the Exit 24 traffic lights.

CAUTIONS
- Park trails are steep and rough. Wear adequate, sturdy footgear.
- Hikers should be relatively fit. Hiking times will vary. Carry ample water, extra food, warm clothes and raingear.

- Mount Benson is laced with old roads and trails. Please keep to the designated trails. If you are wary of travelling in unfamiliar terrain, travel with someone who knows the region.
- Secure your vehicle and leave no valuables behind.

HIKE DESCRIPTION From the parking area, the trail skirts Witchcraft Lake's west end and then turns south to cross a small footbridge and then begins an almost steady ascent. At a fork, you can take the steeper trail straight ahead that passes close to McGarrigle Creek. The left trail is a bit longer and not quite as steep. It turns southeast, then southwest and rejoins the other path farther up the slope. An open rock outcrop and viewpoint along the left trail is a good spot to rest awhile.

About halfway up Mount Benson, a side trail leads to a popular viewpoint. Beyond this viewpoint access, the terrain levels out slightly and then the trail meets an old logging road and follows it west for approximately 0.5 km. At a signpost, the summit trail cuts south once more and continues its serpentine climb to the top. Expect countless old roads, mountain bike routes and long-established side paths along the way. Watch for and follow the summit markers to stay on the designated routes.

The spectacular 360 degree panorama gazes out onto Westwood Lake, Nanaimo, Duncan, the Strait of Georgia and the Gulf Islands, Vancouver

View from Mount Benson to Westwood Lake, Nanaimo and Newcastle Island. ERIC BURKLE

and Mount Baker, in Washington State. It is easy to identify many prominent peaks among Vancouver Island's central mountains: Mount Arrowsmith, Mount Moriarty, Mount Washington and others. Choose a clear day for your hike to ensure optimum viewing.

WORTH NOTING

- Area forests consist of second growth trees, interspersed with open, rocky outcrops and small bluffs.
- The Mount Benson summit area is the headwaters for Nanaimo's Millstone River. McGarrigle Creek, west of Mount Benson Park trails, runs down to Witchcraft Lake.
- Mountain bikers use park trails. In the winter, snowshoeing and cross-country skiing are popular area pastimes.
- Area signage is incomplete. Most major trail junctions and turnoffs are signposted. The Regional District of Nanaimo continues to improve trail marking.
- The two trails that start at Witchcraft Lake cross private land belonging to the Vancouver Island University Woodlot. Public access is permitted. Via either steep route it is about 1.5 km to the park boundary, which is just above the ruins of a cabin. Both trails are tricky to negotiate in wet weather due to area runoff, adverse drainage and the steepness of the terrain. A plan for a relocated, better main trail up from Witchcraft Lake to the park boundary is under development.
- Mount Benson Regional Park was created in 2006 through the combined efforts of the Regional District of Nanaimo and the Nanaimo Area Land Trust. Become involved in the park's planning process by adding your concerns and suggestions to an online survey. Contact the RDN or NALT for details.

NEARBY   Westwood Lake Park. See page 89.

ADDITIONAL INFORMATION

www.nanaimo.ca (City of Nanaimo)
www.nalt.bc.ca (Nanaimo Area Land Trust)
www.rdn.bc.ca (Regional District of Nanaimo)
Refer to NTS 92G/4 and 92F/1 (1:50,000)

4e. Benson Creek Falls Regional Park   Map M4

DIFFICULTY/DISTANCE   Strenuous/2 hours, one way

HIGHLIGHTS   Benson Creek Falls Regional Park (22 ha) is a magical land of waterfalls, gurgling creeks and damp, lush ravines. The park features unimproved, challenging trails that pierce a thick forest on Mount Benson's northwest side. These rugged routes wind alongside Flynnfall and Benson creeks to several boisterous waterfalls, among them Ammonite Falls.

ACCESS   From the Nanaimo Parkway (Highway 19) turn west at the Jingle Pot/Mostar roads traffic lights (Exit 24). Almost immediately, swing right off Jingle Pot Road onto Biggs Road. Stay on Biggs Road to the junction with Doumont Road. From here, continue on Weigles Road for about 0.5 km to the roadside parking area. You can also reach Weigles Road from Doumont, via Metral Drive. Consult a Nanaimo street map for details. It is also possible to reach Biggs Road from the south end of Jingle Pot Road by turning west from the Nanaimo Parkway at the Exit 18 traffic lights.

CAUTIONS
- Trails at Benson Creek Regional Park are suitable for experienced hikers only.
- The Regional District of Nanaimo (RDN) warns that most trails at Benson Creek Regional Park are primitive and unmaintained. In the uneven terrain of the shadowy creek valleys, trails are overgrown, muddy, slippery and covered with roots and blowdown. These factors make hiking very difficult and tedious. Directional signage is non-existent. It is easy to get lost.

HIKE DESCRIPTION   From Weigles Road the trail goes 375 m south to the park boundary and continues another 250 m to an old east/west trail. A steep descent via switchbacks into the creek valleys begins nearby. Many of the interior park trails and routes are currently closed for public safety and environmental reasons. Safe, suitable water crossings, particularly at Flynnfall and Benson creeks, require expensive bridges. Hikers are contributing to erosion along the steep, unmaintained trails and in the valley bottoms. Until future park improvements are implemented, the RDN does not recommend these wilderness routes as being suitable for the general public or casual hikers. For the time being, Benson Creek Regional Park will remain one of Nanaimo's secret places.

- The name Ammonite Falls comes from a type of fossil that occurs in the region's sedimentary rocks. Shaped similar to a snail, ammonites were common in the ancient oceans 400 million years ago.
- The RDN leases the parkland on a long-term contract with the BC government.

NEARBY   Mount Benson Regional Park. See page 90.

ADDITIONAL INFORMATION
www.rdn.bc.ca (Regional District of Nanaimo)
Refer to NTS 92F/1 and 92G/4 (1:50,000)

4f. Buttertubs Marsh   Map M4

DIFFICULTY/DISTANCE   Easy/2.3 km loop

HIGHLIGHTS   Buttertubs Marsh (18.7 ha) is a popular destination for nature walks, birdwatching and wildlife viewing. This bird and wildlife sanctuary has over 4.5 km of well-maintained trails, many with benches, observation platforms and viewpoints. Visitors will find lots to see, starting at the interpretive signposts at the trailheads.

ACCESS
Via Bowen Road   In Nanaimo, take Bowen Road to Buttertubs Drive. Turn south onto Buttertubs Drive and continue to the road's end and the parking area on the marsh's north end.

Via the Nanaimo Parkway   For a southern access point on Jingle Pot Road, from the Nanaimo Parkway (Highway 19) swing east at the Exit 18 traffic lights onto Jingle Pot Road. Continue 0.5 km and then make a sharp left to stay on Jingle Pot Road. Watch for a parking area, just ahead on the left. If you end up on Third Street, you missed the turn. Sections of some trails at Buttertubs Marsh are wheelchair accessible.

CAUTIONS
- Parts of the trail around Buttertubs Marsh may be seasonally overgrown. Expect some potentially slippery sections in the off-season. Watch your step when hiking under wet conditions.
- Narrow gates at the trailheads prevent motorized vehicle entry.

HIKE DESCRIPTION   From the parking area choose from a number of relatively level trails to explore. Follow the trail that loops 2.3 km around the marsh. A leisurely circle hike takes about 45 minutes to an hour to complete, but you will want to allow more time to look around. Hike down the wide dyke that runs down the centre of the marsh and spend some time at the observation platform. This is an ideal spot to look for local and migratory birds.

WORTH NOTING
- The Millstone River runs along the sanctuary's northern boundary. In this area in particular, watch for muskrat, river otter, beaver and mink. The river's height is regulated to sustain water levels in the marsh, which improves habitat for a variety of wildlife.
- Many types of birds may be seen at Buttertubs Marsh. Look for hawks, ducks, geese, owls and woodpeckers.
- A row of mostly dead English red oaks lines the dyke and provides habitat for woodpeckers. These trees, planted years ago, have died as a result of high water.
- Buttertubs Marsh is a Conservation Area owned by the Nature Trust of BC and is managed in partnership with the City of Nanaimo, the provincial government and the Nanaimo Field Naturalists.

NEARBY The Nanaimo Parkway Trail and the Trans-Canada Trail (TCT) are accessed at the south end trailhead, off Jingle Pot Road. These trails follow the same route south to Colliery Dam Park. The TCT runs through Buttertubs Marsh's east side and heads north to Bowen Park. Both multi-use corridors connect numerous Nanaimo parks and trails. See map on page 87.

ADDITIONAL INFORMATION
www.nanaimo.ca (City of Nanaimo)
www.nalt.bc.ca (Nanaimo and Area Land Trust)
Refer to NTS 92G/4 (1:50,000)

4g. Newcastle Island Provincial Marine Park
Maps M4, M4G

DIFFICULTY/DISTANCE Easy to moderate/1.5 km, one way; up to 8 km loop

HIGHLIGHTS Newcastle Island Provincial Marine Park (336 ha) is located just offshore from Nanaimo. One of this park's charms is that the island has no cars and is accessible only by private boat or 10 minute

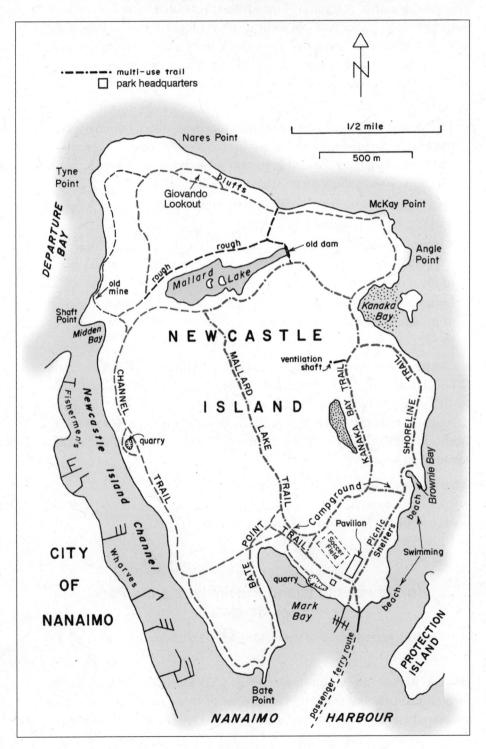

ride on a foot-passenger ferry. There are 22 km of well-marked, interconnecting trails to hike. Shoreline paths lead to sandstone cliffs, rocky points and pocket beaches. Inland routes snake through forests and past small lakes. Part of the island's east side is grassy and flat; the rest is wooded. Newcastle Island features many historic points of interest, many with information signposts. Creating your own memorable loop hike is easy.

ACCESS **Newcastle Island is reachable only by boat.** A seasonal passenger ferry makes regular runs to the park from Nanaimo's Maffeo-Sutton Park. From Highway 1 (Trans-Canada) in downtown Nanaimo, at the Comox Road/Terminal Avenue traffic lights, turn right (east) onto Front Street, then make an immediate left to the park, which is located behind the Civic Arena.

CAUTIONS

- Please keep to the main trails at all times to avoid damaging sensitive vegetation and soil structure.
- Dogs and pets must be kept leashed and off the beaches.
- Some Newcastle Island trails are multi-use. On these routes, be alert for bikers.
- Fires are permitted only in the fire rings at the camping areas. Burning driftwood is prohibited. Firewood is available from the Parks Operator. Campers should bring along a portable camp stove.
- Seasonal pumped water is available. Carry water with you when hiking.
- The island has a healthy raccoon population. These nocturnal bandits

Nanaimo and Vancouver Island as seen from Newcastle Island. ERIC BURKLE

wander the island so secure your food and camping supplies carefully. Food lockers are available at the designated camping areas. Promptly dispose of all garbage. Never feed wildlife.

HIKE DESCRIPTIONS Newcastle Island Provincial Marine Park offers a variety of hiking trails. You can follow one trail and complete a loop on a choice of return trails. Some popular park trails and destinations are described below.

Bate Point Trail Easy/1.5 km, one way: From the dock area the trail cuts left to pass a quarry and curves around Mark Bay to wind south to the point. Allow about 45 minutes to reach Bate Point.

Channel Trail Easy/3 km, one way: This hike begins at the dock area, turns toward Bate Point and swings west, then north to parallel Newcastle Island Channel, the waterway that separates Newcastle Island and Nanaimo. South of Midden Bay is an old quarry site. The trail eventually swings inland near Mallard Lake. Midden Bay provides excellent views of Nanaimo and the bustling Departure Bay water traffic. Allow 1.5 hours hiking time, one way.

NEWCASTLE ISLAND was named in 1849 when coal was discovered there. Coal mines at Tyne and Shaft points operated for over 30 years. A quarry provided sandstone for large buildings throughout North America, notably for the San Francisco Mint and the BC Penitentiary, and locally for the Nanaimo Court House. Another quarry, close to the ferry docks, produced stone used to make grinding wheels for pulp mills. Other island industries included a cannery and saltery. A First Nations settlement was situated at Midden Bay.

Newcastle Island ceased its commercial life in 1931 when the coal mining company sold the island to the Canadian Pacific Railway, who developed it for recreational use. The CPR built a change and bathhouse for swimmers, the pavilion, picnic shelters and many other amenities, which still exist. A company boat moored at the jetty and operated as a floating hotel offering moonlight cruises. Dancing was a regular fixture at the pavilion.

World War II decreased the island's popularity and it has since changed hands twice—to the City of Nanaimo and then to the BC provincial government. The pavilion was restored thanks to the Newcastle Island Society. It now combines a Visitor Information Center with a restaurant, a snack bar, gift shop and concession stand that rents recreational equipment. Pavilion rentals are available.

Mallard Lake Trail   Easy/2 km, one way: From the dock area the trail cuts left toward Bate Point and then, near the head of Mark Bay, runs north, right down the center of Newcastle Island. This multi-use trail traverses marshland and inland forest to Mallard Lake. Here you may spot mergansers, a variety of ducks or even beaver. An old dam is located at the lake's east end. This hike takes about 45 minutes to 1 hour, one way.

Kanaka Bay Trail   Easy/1.5 km, one way: This multi-use trail starts near the dock area, cuts left toward Bate Point, then swings off to the right (northeast) at a signposted trail junction near the playing field. The trail accesses a wetland and a side trail leads to an old coal mine ventilation shaft, over a century old and 119 m deep. The trail meets the Shoreline Trail at Kanaka Bay. Allow about 30 to 45 minutes hiking time, one way.

Shoreline Trail   Moderate/8 km loop. For an exceptional hike that circumnavigates Newcastle Island, start at the ferry dock and take the marked trail to the right that runs past the day-use picnic area and heads north to the beach at Brownie Bay and up to Kanaka Bay. Part of this route up to Kanaka Bay is a designated multi-use trail. You can shorten your hike and loop back to the ferry dock on one of the island's many interconnecting inland trails.

The Shoreline Trail requires a fair bit of up and down hiking, particularly near the many points of land. At McKay Point the trail turns due west to Giovando Lookout and Nares Point. At Tyne Point the trail swings south to pass an old mine site near Shaft Point and Midden Bay. At this point you will have hiked about 2.5 hours and 5 km. From Midden Bay, take either the Channel Trail or the inland Mallard Lake Trail back to the start near the dock. Allow approximately 4 hours hiking time to loop around the perimeter of Newcastle Island.

Giovando Lookout   Moderate/3 km to 4 km, one way. The Giovando Lookout on Newcastle Island's northern tip is a favourite day hike destination. To reach the viewpoint from the ferry dock take either the Shoreline, Mallard Lake or Channel Trail north to the Mallard Lake area. Continue north on a short inland path or follow a longer coastal trail to the Giovando Lookout, near Nares Point. Stay away from the edge of the bluffs. The viewpoint looks out across the Strait of Georgia over to the Mainland Mountains. Depending on the route you take, allow 1.5 to 2 hours hiking time, one way.

- The park's forests consist mainly of Garry oak, arbutus, dogwood and mature Douglas-fir. In the spring, Newcastle Island's Garry oak meadows are abloom with camas, lilies and other wildflowers. Tread lightly.
- Along the forested trails look for signs of rabbits, raccoons and deer. The latter like to linger near the campsites at dusk.
- Swimming is good near the ferry dock and at Kanaka Bay, but there are no lifeguards.

NEWCASTLE ISLAND PROVINCIAL MARINE PARK has 18 designated walk-in campsites, including group sites. The camping areas are approximately 500 m from the ferry dock. Other amenities include a playground, showers, large day-use and picnic area, interpretive signage and some wheelchair-accessible trails and toilets. Seasonal visitors programs are available. For current information on camping fees, group camping reservations, park regulations, mooring fees, rentals and ferry schedules, contact BC Parks.

NEARBY

Sugarloaf Mountain Park (1.5 ha) has a short, steep trail that climbs about 30 m via concrete steps and wooden stairs to a rocky viewpoint. Sunrises here can be spectacular. The viewpoint overlooks Departure Bay and the seascapes of the mainland mountains as well as Gabriola, Newcastle and Protection islands. The elevated view of Nanaimo and its western hills and mountains is equally impressive. Stay on designated paths to avoid trampling the delicate mosses near the summit.

To reach the park, in Nanaimo, at the Highway 19A junction with Brechin Road and Departure Bay Road, take Departure Bay Road north for 2 km to Hammond Bay Road. Keep left (west) on Departure Bay Road to Little John Way. Turn right, then make an immediate left on Sherwood Way. Turn right onto Marion Way to its end and limited roadside parking. Please do not block driveways. See map on page 86.

Linley Valley/Cottle Lake Park (445 ha) features a number of trails through the City of Nanaimo's last remaining large tract of natural habitat. Informal trails lead to Linley Lake and through wetlands, forest and meadows. Most of the uneven paths follow old logging roads. There are a few boardwalks in place. The trail on the lake's north side accesses the water at two spots. This sensitive area teems with wildlife and is extremely popular with birdwatchers.

Access as on page 100 for Sugarloaf Mountain Park. From Departure Bay Road take Hammond Bay Road to Linley Road and turn left to the parking area. The map on page 86 shows this access from Hammond Bay Road. There are several other points from which to reach the park and valley. Further details are available from the Nanaimo Area Land Trust at www.nalt.bc.ca.

Pipers' Lagoon Park (8 ha) and its tranquil ocean setting near Hammond Bay may be Nanaimo's best-kept secret. Trails lead to a beautiful lagoon and over an isthmus and through Garry oak and Douglas-fir to a rocky headland. The park is a great destination for a shoreline hike or a seaside picnic. Explore the spit at low tide to view intertidal life and shorebirds. The main trail runs through the forest to Lagoon Head. From this head-land you can see over the Strait of Georgia to the Coast Mountains. To the southeast are the Five Fingers, a group of tiny, offshore islands that are the breeding grounds for seagulls and cormorants. April and May bring the park's wildflowers. In early spring, spritely lilies adorn the headlands.

Access to Pipers' Lagoon Park is as above for Sugarloaf Mountain Park. See map on page 86. At the Departure Bay Road/Hammond Bay Road junction, turn right (northeast) onto Hammond Bay Road and continue 3 km to Lagoon Road. Turn right and make an immediate right from Lagoon Road onto Place Drive to the parking area. A grassy picnic area is close by.

In the early 1900s, Pipers' Lagoon was the site of a Japanese fishing village and a whaling station. Rowboat anglers used the nearby Shack Islands in the 1920s. A few of the old wooden shacks remain. Scour the second hand bookshops for Vi Henderson's out of print *Pipers' Lagoon*, which offers an excellent glimpse of the park and its history.

Neck Point Park (14.5 ha) is just north of Pipers' Lagoon Park. Numerous easy trails run through Neck Point Park and along seaside cliffs to shoreline picnic areas, small beaches and scenic lookouts. Many paths intersect each other. Most trails are well groomed and have boardwalks, interpretive signposts and benches, the latter with memorial plaques. The park viewpoints gaze out over the Strait of Georgia to the Coast Mountains. Nearby waters harbour sea otters, sea lions, seals and killer whales. Waterbird sightings are plentiful.

Neck Point's name comes from a point of land that is connected to the rest of the park at low tide. When the waters recede you can walk out across a gravel strand to a normally inaccessible stub of rock. Access as for Pipers' Lagoon Park. Continue a little over 1 km past Lagoon Road on Hammond Bay Road and watch for the Neck Point signposts. Turn right onto Morningside Road to the parking area. See map on page 86.

The Nanaimo Parkway Trail is a paved, 20 km multi-use trailway that parallels parts of Highway 19 and the Nanaimo Parkway. Hikers, walkers, joggers and bikers use the route as an alternate to commuting. When overtaking other trail users, be courteous and alert them of your presence. The Parkway Trail, with links to many Nanaimo parks, trails and lakes, is well marked and has convenient access points, maps, distance markers and painted route indicators. One section of the trail, between Harewood Mines Road and Jingle Pot Road, forms part of the Trans-Canada Trail. See map on page 87.

The E & N Trail, 8 km in length, follows an easy, paved path alongside the E & N rail line and parts of the Island Highway. The E & N is now operated as the Southern Railway of Vancouver Island, part of the Southern Railway of British Columbia. The E & N Trail's south end begins along the Trans-Canada Trail, near Bowen Park. The north end comes out on Wellington and Mostar roads, close to Long Lake. Consult a detailed Nanaimo road map for more information. This multi-use trail is popular with hikers, bikers and joggers and is a crucial link in the City of Nanaimo's trail system.

ADDITIONAL INFORMATION
www.env.gov.bc.ca/bcparks (BC Parks)
www.nanaimo.ca (City of Nanaimo)
www.nanaimoharbourferry.com (Nanaimo Harbour Ferry)
Refer to NTS 92G/4 (1:50,000)

Newcastle Island. ERIC BURKLE

5

Gabriola Island

5a. Descanso Bay Regional Park Map M5

DIFFICULTY/DISTANCE Easy/up to 1.5 km, one way

HIGHLIGHTS Descanso Bay Regional Park (16 ha) is a spectacular oceanfront park with networks of woodland trails and paths to explore. The park features three saltwater coves, water access points and a campground from which you can base and explore additional Gabriola Island hiking destinations.

ACCESS From Nanaimo, take BC Ferries to Gabriola Island. From the ferry terminal, keep straight ahead for 0.3 km to Taylor Bay Road. Turn left (north) onto Taylor Bay Road and follow the park signposts another 0.3 km to the park entrance road, on the left.

CAUTIONS
- Use extreme care when crossing Taylor Bay Road to the road's east side to access trails within Cox Community Park, directly opposite Descanso Bay Regional Park.
- The dilapidated farmhouse near the waterfront is closed to the public for safety reasons.
- Pumped water is available but it must be boiled, treated or filtered.

HIKE DESCRIPTION Descanso Bay offers a variety of easy hiking and walking paths and trails. Follow seaside trails at Descanso Bay to viewpoints that take in Nanaimo, Mount Benson, Northumberland Channel, and Protection and Newcastle islands. Explore the three shallow bays where the beach area has an intriguing sandstone shelf, best explored at low tide. This is the optimum time to walk out on the slanting rocks and explore a profusion of marine life, right at your feet.

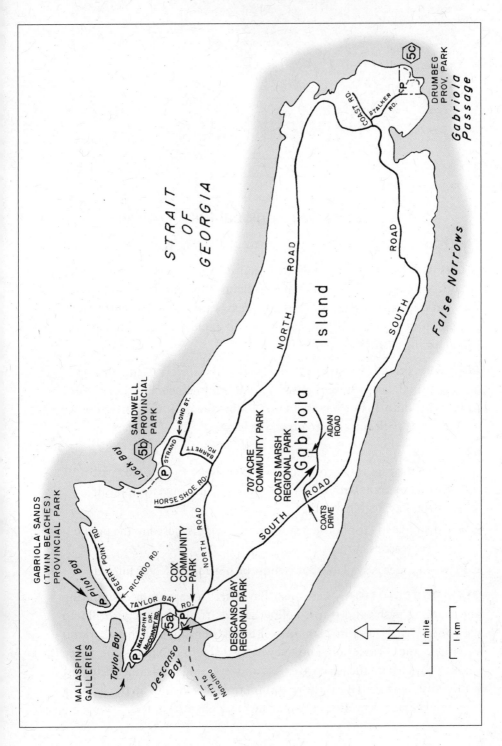

- The Descanso Bay forest consists mainly of second growth Douglas-fir, spruce and hemlock. At trailside look for Oregon grape and salal.
- Park facilities include 32 campsites, 2 day-use picnic areas, information kiosks, pit toilets and boat launch. Contact the Regional District of Nanaimo for current campground fees and regulations.

NEARBY

Cox Community Park (35.2 ha) is situated directly across from Descanso Bay Regional Park, on Taylor Bay Road's east side. Countless trails thread through this forested park, a popular destination for locals. Some of these well-established trails are also used as mountain biking routes.

Malaspina Galleries is a 100-metre-long sandstone cliff that resembles a petrified breaking wave. The shoreline here has been sculpted by centuries of rain, wind and waves. First Nations inhabitants considered the area a spiritual place. Access to a tiny parking space at the end of Malaspina Drive is via Taylor Bay Road. Please do not block driveways and respect the private property, which abuts the area.

Gabriola Sands Provincial Park (5.3 ha) features a narrow neck of land and two beautiful swimming beaches. One strand fronts Taylor Bay, to the west; the other, Pilot Bay, to the east. The area is also known as Twin Beaches. Short beach and shore walks are possible at this day-use park. Access is via Ricardo Road, off Taylor Bay Road. Ample parking is available at the bottom of the Ricardo Road hill.

Gabriola Sands Provincial Park, only 3 km from the ferry terminal, is well within walking distance. Many Gabriola Island visitors leave their cars behind in Nanaimo and journey over as foot passengers. From the park it is even possible to hike completely around the small peninsula at Gabriola Island's north end. Start your shore hike at Taylor Bay and return to Pilot Bay, or vice-versa. Optimum time for the peninsula hike is near low tide. Contact the Canadian Hydrographic Service at www.waterlevels.gc.ca for current tidal information.

Coats Marsh Regional Park (44 ha) protects a sensitive wetland and forest on Gabriola Island's south side. This is a popular birdwatching destination. Existing trails are rough and unimproved. Tread lightly when visiting this fragile area. Access is via South Road, Coats Drive and Aidan Road. Park at the end of Aidan Road.

707 Acre Community Park (286 ha) is a large tract of second growth forest intersected by a maze of old logging roads, trails and equestrian paths. The park is adjacent to Coats Marsh Regional Park. There are numerous access points along North and South roads, which skirt the community park's perimeter.

ADDITIONAL INFORMATION
www.bcferries.com (BC Ferries)
www.env.gov.bc.ca/bcparks (BC Parks)
www.rdn.bc.ca (Regional District of Nanaimo)
Refer to NTS 92G/4 (1:50,000)

5b. Sandwell Provincial Park, Gabriola Island   Map M5

DIFFICULTY/DISTANCE   Moderate/800 m, one way

HIGHLIGHTS   Sandwell Provincial Park (12 ha), about 5 km from the ferry terminal, is situated on Gabriola Island's northeast side. A short trail (just under 1 km in length and with a steep section) extends from the trailhead to sea level at Lock Bay. Here you will discover a beautiful sand and pebble ocean beach. The park is a great place for a hike, seaside picnic or leisurely beach walk.

ACCESS   From Nanaimo take the BC Ferry to Gabriola Island. From the Descanso Bay ferry terminal keep straight ahead for 0.7 km to the North Road/South Road junction, close to the post office. Swing left (east) onto North Road and travel another 2.3 km to Barrett Road. Turn left onto Barrett Road and then take Bond Street and Strand to a tiny turnaround and limited parking area at the end of the road. Watch for blue park signs on the way.

CAUTIONS
- The trail steepens abruptly on its approach to the beach. This section tends to be very slippery in wet weather. Wear sturdy footwear.
- Bring along adequate water.
- Within the park are fragile sand dunes and their sensitive ecosystems. Also present are First Nations archaeological sites and middens. Avoid completely or tread extremely lightly in these areas.
- A locked trailhead gate prevents motorized beach access. No overnight parking, camping or fires are allowed.

HIKE DESCRIPTION   From the trailhead, hike for about 5 minutes or so and watch for a side trail on the right. Take this trail to reach some

SPANISH NAVAL OFFICERS Galiano and Valdes circumnavigated Vancouver Island in 1792, aboard their tiny ships *Sutil* and *Mexicana*. They took shelter, near the end of one stormy day, in a small Gabriola Island cove. They named their anchorage Cala del Descanso, meaning "small bay of ease". Descanso Bay was their refuge.

The place name Malaspina honours an Italian, Captain Alexandro Malaspina. In 1791, in the service of Spain, he explored the west coast of what is now Vancouver Island. The name Gabriola is thought to have evolved from Punta Gaviota, which is Spanish for "cape seagull".

Evidence of more recent Gabriola Island history is visible as you arrive on the island. At the top of the hill on the right above the ferry landing is an abandoned quarry. Gabriola Island sandstone was used in the 1880s for the construction of the old federal Post Office and Customs House, situated at the corner of Victoria's Government and Wharf streets.

wooden stairs and a beach area. The main trail follows a dedicated beach access and soon starts to climb. En route to Lock Bay are old-growth trees and sandstone cliffs, directly at trailside. At a high point the trail suddenly makes a sharp descent to Lock Bay. The park's day-use picnic area overlooks the beach.

Along the expansive sandy beach at Lock Bay the Strait of Georgia seascapes are striking. Gaze north to see Forward Channel and the lighthouse on Entrance Island. A glance east over the Strait of Georgia reveals the Coast Mountains.

WORTH NOTING

- The marsh behind the beach is popular with birdwatchers.
- At low tide hikers often head east of the day-use picnic to seek out a First Nations petroglyph etched into the sandstone. Be sure to time your exploration with favourable tides; this part of the beach is cut off by rising tides. Gather relevant tide information from the Canadian Hydrographic Service at www.waterlevels.gc.ca.
- There are picnic tables, an information shelter and two pit toilets at the day-use picnic area at Lock Bay. Please carry out all your litter.

NEARBY Descanso Bay Regional Park. See page 103.

ADDITIONAL INFORMATION
www.bcferries.com (BC Ferries)
www.env.gov.bc.ca/bcparks (BC Parks)
Refer to NTS 92G/4 (1:50,000)

5c. Drumbeg Provincial Park, Gabriola Island   Map M5

DIFFICULTY/DISTANCE   Easy/1 km, one way

HIGHLIGHTS   Drumbeg Provincial Park (20 ha) is situated on Gabriola Island's southeast tip, about 15 km from the ferry terminal. Short, well-maintained trails lead to beautiful seascapes near Drumbeg Bay. This relatively protected bay is popular with swimmers and divers. The curving sand and pebble beach stretches about 1 km in length.

ACCESS   Take BC Ferries from Nanaimo to Gabriola Island. From the ferry terminal go straight ahead for 0.7 km to the North Road/South Road junction, near the post office. Keep straight ahead on South Road and continue 13.3 km to Coast Road. Turn east (right) onto Coast Road, then make another immediate right onto Stalker Road, which is gravel. Continue just under 1 km to the park entrance and bear left to the parking lot. Reaching Coast Road via North Road is a slightly longer route.

CAUTIONS

- Treacherous rip currents and surging waters in Gabriola Passage may reach up to eight knots. Exercise extreme caution when swimming in Drumbeg Bay and stay close to shore. There is no lifeguard on duty.
- No overnight parking, camping or fires are permitted at this day-use-only park.
- The park borders private property. Please stay within designated boundaries and obey any posted notices.

GIANT HOGWEED, an ornamental plant introduced from Asia, grows in Drumbeg Park. Watch for and avoid it at all times. The plant is suitably named and averages 4 m in height. In rare cases it can grow as high as 7 m. The darkish red/purple stems can reach 3–10 cm in diameter. The plant's hollow leaf stems are spotted and have bristles. Look for coarse, somewhat large white hairs at the base of the leaf stems. The leaves are like maples but 1–1.7 m in width and have hairs on their undersides. Giant Hogweed looks similar to cow parsley.

Touching this plant, followed by UV ray and sunlight exposure, creates painful skin blisters or burns that can last up to two days. Temporary and even permanent blindness may result from eye contact. Should you have an unfortunate encounter with the Giant Hogweed, immediately wash all affected areas, stay out of the direct sun and go for medical treatment.

HIKE DESCRIPTION   From the parking area and day-use area several trails lead to Gabriola Passage. Watch boat traffic from the sandstone shoreline of Drumbeg Bay beach where low tide exposes a sandstone shelf. Wander through meadows of Douglas-fir and Garry oaks to reach spectacular seascapes. One popular viewpoint looks out onto the mainland mountains, the Strait of Georgia, and Breakwater and Valdes islands.

WORTH NOTING
- Drumbeg Park is an excellent spot for wildlife viewing. You may see Bald Eagles, Black Oystercatchers, Great Blue Herons and a variety of gulls, ducks and other waterbirds. Foraging mink often scurry amid shoreline driftwood. Watch offshore waters for seals, sea lions and whales.
- Interpretive signposts describe the region's Garry oak ecosystems and marine intertidal zones.
- Resting benches are located along the trails. Other facilities include an information shelter, picnic tables and pit toilets.
- The late owner, Neil Stalker, donated the land to the province. The park is named after his ancestral home in Scotland.

NEARBY   Sandwell Provincial Park. See page 106.

ADDITIONAL INFORMATION
www.bcferries.com (BC Ferries)
www.env.gov.bc.ca/bcparks (BC Parks)
Refer to NTS 92G/4 (1:50,000)

6

Saltspring Island and Wallace Island

The Gulf Islands National Park Reserve

Some Gulf Island trails mentioned in *Hiking Trails 2* are within Parks Canada's Gulf Islands National Park Reserve (GINPR). In 1995, the Pacific Marine Heritage Legacy program began land procurement which in 2003 resulted in the creation of Canada's fifth smallest national park. The Gulf Islands National Park Reserve covers 35.4 square kilometres. The park, located in the southern section of the Strait of Georgia, is made up of 16 islands, over 30 reefs and islets, as well as their adjoining waters and intertidal zones. More information is available at www.pc.gc.ca/gulf.

The Gulf Islands   Map M6

Hiking Trails 2 describes many of the southern Gulf Island's most popular hiking spots and a few lesser-known hiking destinations. The context of this book does not allow inclusion of every single Gulf Island hike. Readers are directed to Charles Kahn's *Hiking the Gulf Islands*, a comprehensive guidebook dedicated exclusively to Gulf Island trails.

The Gulf Islands enjoy a unique Mediterranean-type climate that has produced some of Canada's rarest ecosystems. The Pacific Ocean's maritime influence results in some of the most moderate winter and summer temperatures in the country. In stark contrast to the wet weather in the rainforests of Vancouver Island's west coast, the effect of the Vancouver Island Mountain Range and the Olympic Mountain Range in Washington State is to cast a rain shadow over the Gulf Islands. This results in a much drier climate with some spots classified as deserts, with cacti to prove it.

These factors combine to create a temperate maritime climate with dry, warm summers and mild, damp winters. The Gulf Islands boast the longest frost-free season in Canada—around 275 days. Approximately 80 cm of precipitation falls mostly as rain, and generally over the fall and winter. Summer drought is the norm. On this book's cover photo, notice the dry, brown grass in the foreground.

This unique climate results in many unusual plants within the larger Coastal Douglas-fir bio-climatic zone. The dry, rocky slopes at higher elevations display open, grassy areas known as grass balds. Downslope are Garry oak meadows and woodlands that explode with colourful spring wildflowers. The Garry oak has an extremely limited range and is BC's only native oak. In the company of the oak you will often find the arbutus, also known as madrone or madrona. This is Canada's only broadleaf evergreen tree.

The Garry oak, arbutus and predominant Douglas-fir are all adapted to withstand the wildfires to which this region has been vulnerable for thousands of years. The local First Nations used this natural protection to their advantage, setting controlled fires to open up the forest. This, in turn, encouraged food plants such as camas to flourish. Today, fire remains a serious summer threat on the Gulf Islands.

GULF ISLAND NOTES

- Gulf Islanders are committed recyclers. Visitors can greatly help by taking out their litter with them.

- Do not light fires! Fire is a serious hazard on all the Gulf Islands. Smoking in park forests and along trails is strongly discouraged. If you smoke, do so only at rest stops. Ensure your cigarette is out and take the butts with you.

- Accommodation is limited on the smaller Gulf Islands. Bed-and-breakfast establishments are often booked months in advance, particularly on long weekends. Local campsites, including BC Park facilities, fill up quickly during fair weather. If you plan an overnight stay, make reservations well in advance or be sure to find a place to stay before the last evening ferry.

- Use extreme caution when descending any Gulf Island trails and slopes littered with fallen arbutus leaves. For slipperiness, they are August's equivalent to January's black ice.

- Be careful when walking down Gulf Island roads. Shoulders are narrow, many corners offer limited visibility and traffic can be heavy at times.

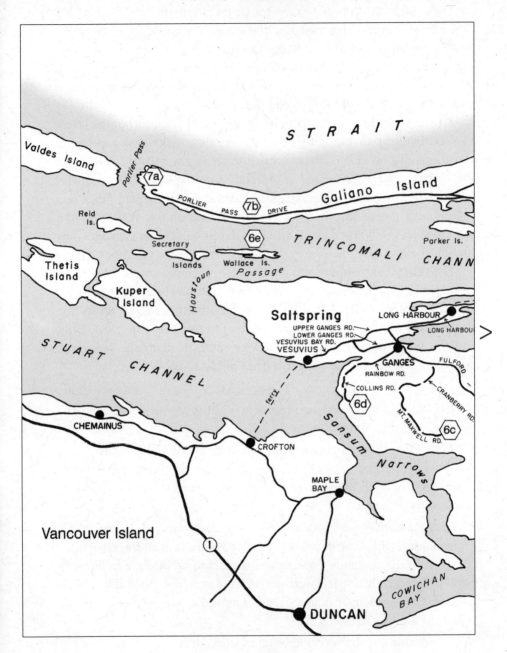

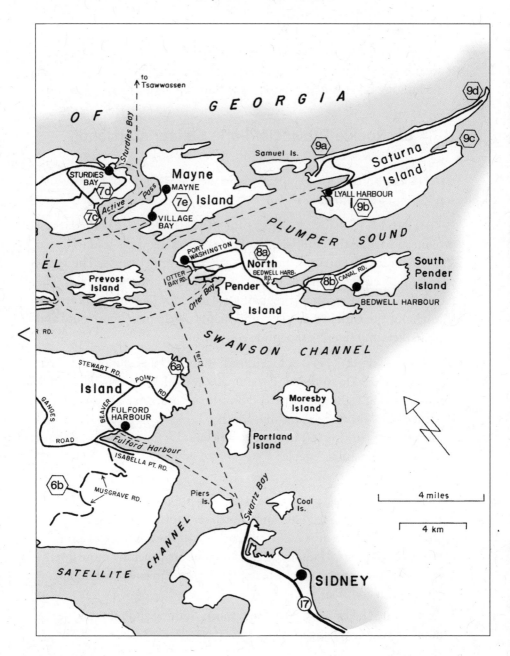

- There are many sheep and goats on the Gulf Islands. Keep all dogs and pets leashed.
- Hunters frequent some areas in the fall. Avoid hiking at these times or wear bright colours so you can be easily identified. On the Gulf Islands, no hunting is permitted in parks or within 400 m of a road.

6a. Ruckle Provincial Park, Saltspring Island
Maps M6, M6A

DIFFICULTY/DISTANCE Easy to moderate/0.6 km to 4.4 km, one way; 3.7 km to 4.3 km loops

HIGHLIGHTS Saltspring Island's Ruckle Park (486 ha) is the largest provincial park in the Gulf Islands. The park's many trails lead to ocean shoreline, rocky headlands, pocket beaches and quiet coves. The paths pass through cultivated fields, hedgerows, meadows and thick forests. The park's 15 km of interconnecting paths are ideal for loop hikes. Scattered throughout the park are detailed trail maps to help plan your route and trail markers and signposts to guide you on your way.

ACCESS Take BC Ferries to Fulford Harbour, then follow Fulford-Ganges Road 0.3 km to Beaver Point Road. At the Ruckle Provincial Park signpost, swing right onto Beaver Point Road and drive about 8 km to the gated park entrance. Continue another 1.3 km along the access road to the day-use parking lot, near the picnic area. A few of the easier park trails are wheelchair accessible.

CAUTIONS
- Parts of inland forest and coastal paths traverse uneven ground and may be rough with steep sections. Watch for protruding roots and rocks. Exercise care near rocky outcrops, on the headlands and along beach access paths. Trails above the shoreline are generally more level than ones closer to sea level where there is more up and down hiking. Wear sturdy footwear.
- On extended hikes carry extra food, warm clothing and raingear. Be aware of weather changes.
- Bring ample water.
- An active farm operates within the boundaries of Ruckle Provincial Park. No public access is permitted on the working farm. Please obey posted notices. Some trails around the farm's fenced perimeter have stiles.

- Build fires (when seasonally permitted) in fire rings only, at designated campsites and never on beaches. Use only provided firewood.
- Some park meadows are closed to help prevent the spread of carpet burweed, an invasive species.
- Bicycles are permitted on park roads only. Dogs must be leashed at all times. Some park trails are closed to dogs. Please obey all posted notices and stay on marked trails.

HIKE DESCRIPTIONS

Swanson Channel Viewpoints   Easy/0.6 km, one way: From the day-use parking lot near the picnic area, hike east and follow the signs to the Beaver Point viewpoint. Alternately, hike north about 350 m to the side path that accesses the next viewpoint on a jut of land between Beaver and Bear points. Both sites are great spots to see the bustling Swanson Channel boat and ferry traffic.

Beaver Point/Grandma's Bay Loop   Easy to moderate/3.7 km loop: From the day-use picnic area head east to Beaver Point where a side path accesses the viewpoint. Swing right (south) to pass the camping area and lighthouse. The trail winds through a Garry oak and arbutus forest and follows a ridge above the rocky outcrops near Grandma's Bay. A wooden staircase descends to the pocket beach. Turn right at the farm fence and hike north to the Heritage Farm and Orchard. Allot some time to view the historic site. At the nearby park access road, head east about 1 km to the picnic area.

Beaver Point/Bear Point Loop   Moderate/4.3 km loop: From the day-use picnic area walk 1 km west along the park access road to the Park Headquarters, close to the park gate. Starting across the road from the Heritage Farm, follow trail markers 0.5 km north and keep right at the junction. Hike down the hill and parallel the fence marking the park's active farm. The route runs through fields, forest and patches of old growth to the farm's north end. Turn east at the signposted junction to Bear Point. When you reach the coast, cut right (south) and take either the shoreline trail or a gentler inland path back to the starting point. Many trails in this area interconnect.

Beaver Point to Yeo Point   Moderate/4.4 km, one way: From the picnic area this trail runs north along the serpentine coastline. Expect plenty of up-and-down hiking. Exceptional viewpoints abound, particularly at the many jagged headlands en route. This shoreline trail accesses pocket

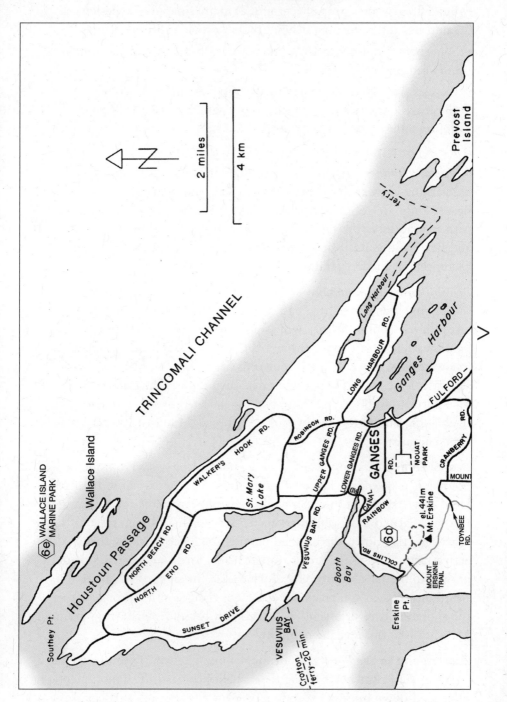

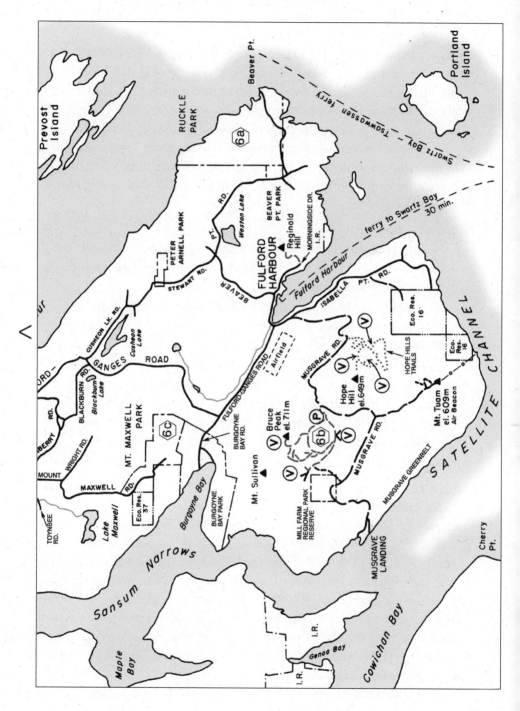

coves, rocky beaches and offers the best opportunities to see marine and other wildlife.

Beaver Point Park to King's Cove   Moderate/3.8 km, one way: This hilly inland trail begins at Beaver Point Park, near Ruckle Park's southwest boundary. From the Beaver Point Road parking area the trail extends almost 4 km to King's Cove and the seascapes at Swanson Channel. En route are several viewpoints where the trail negotiates heights of land. At the second major junction northwest of Merganser Pond, turn north at the signpost for King's Cove, 0.5 km away. Close to this junction, on Merganser Pond's northwest fringe, is a stately stand of Saltspring Island's largest Douglas-fir.

WORTH NOTING

- Near the headlands, scan the waters for killer whales, otters, seals, sea lions and a variety of waterbirds. Deer and grouse are frequently encountered in the forests and fields.
- The Ruckle family donated the parkland to the province in 1974. Present-day members of the family continue to live on and work part of the land that Henry Ruckle began clearing in 1872.
- The park has 3 group camping areas with a total of 78 walk-in field campsites. Eight vehicle sites are available. Other amenities include a day-use picnic area, pit toilets, seasonal fresh water. For current updates on park regulations, seasonal services, interpretive programs and information on camping or daily parking fees contact BC Parks.
- Read about the Gulf Islands on page 110.

NEARBY

Peter Arnell Park (13 ha) is en route to Ruckle Provincial Park. Along Beaver Point Road, turn left onto Stewart Road and continue 2 km and watch for a park sign, near the top of a rise. If you reach a sharp bend, you have missed the marker. On the left side of the road is a picnic area and monument to Peter Arnell, a young surveyor who was accidentally killed on Galiano Island in 1968. He was born in England, but has family connections to Saltspring Island. On the road's right side is a signed trail that runs through a young forest and roughly follows the park's perimeter. Park access from the north is via Cusheon Lake Road. Perched on a ridge, the park has no real viewpoints, but through the trees are tantalizing glimpses of vistas beyond. The 1.5 km trail is suitable for a range of abilities, but is not wheelchair accessible.

Beaver Point Park (16 ha) is along Beaver Point Road, just over 6 km from the Fulford Harbour ferry terminal. The park, adjacent to Ruckle Provincial Park, features 0.5 km of easy walking trails that wind through an old growth coniferous forest. There are large maple trees and trails that link to several Ruckle Park hiking paths. The Beaver Point Community Hall and one-room Beaver Point School, built in 1885, are nearby.

ADDITIONAL INFORMATION
www.bcferries.com (BC Ferries)
www.env.gov.bc.ca/bcparks (BC Parks)
Refer to NTS 92B/14 (1:50,000)

SALTSPRING ISLAND gets its name from the salt springs located on private land at the island's north end. Earlier, in Salish dialect, it was called Tuam, meaning, "facing the sea", or "one on each end" (pertaining to Bruce and Tuam peaks). In 1854, James Douglas referred to the island as Chaun; Captain Grant, in 1856, as Saltspring. Captain Richards named it Admiral Island in 1859 after Rear Admiral Baynes. Local usage prevailed and in 1910 the name Saltspring was officially adopted.

6b. Bruce Peak, Saltspring Island   Maps M6, M6A, M6B

DIFFICULTY/DISTANCE   Moderate to strenuous/up to 4 km, one way

HIGHLIGHTS   Bruce Peak (711 m) is the highest point on the Gulf Islands. In clear weather, the spectacular views at the summit offer a perfect 360 degree panorama. Old roads and well-established trails criss-cross the region. Choose your own route to one of the countless viewpoints or tackle one of the steeper trails or old roads up to the summit area.

ACCESS   From the Fulford Harbour ferry dock take Fulford-Ganges Road for 1.3 km and turn left onto Isabella Point Road. This is the Km 0 starting point. Continue south on Isabella Point Road and at Km 0.5, swing right onto Musgrave Road. Be prepared for some rough, bumpy, rocky sections and switchback corners. Stay on Musgrave Road and climb up to pass a lake, on the right. Directly ahead, the road forks at Km 7. Musgrave Road cuts left. For Bruce Peak turn right onto Mount Bruce Road. The parking area is 0.3 km ahead, close to another fork in the road.

Map M6B Bruce Peak

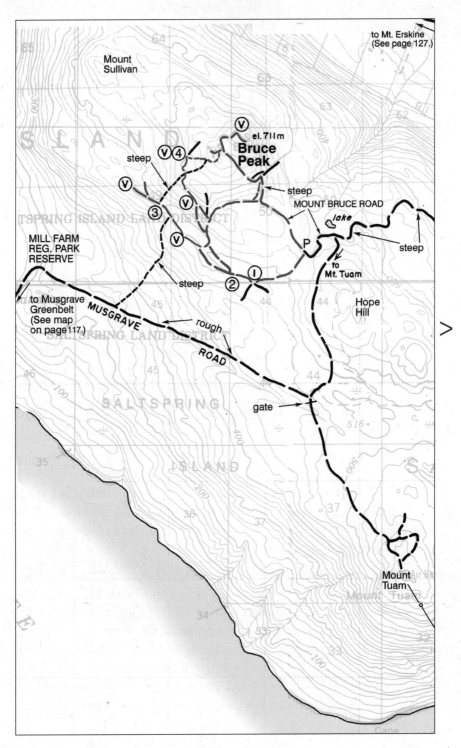

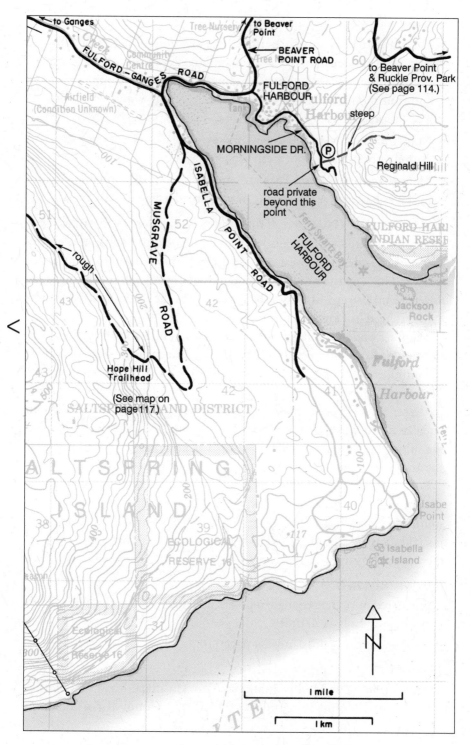

CAUTIONS

- Carry adequate water and wear sturdy footwear.
- Musgrave Road is a rough, twisting, dirt and gravel road that climbs sharply to about 600 m in elevation and then descends just as precipitously to sea level at Musgrave Landing. Choose your season to visit and your mode of transportation carefully. A high-slung vehicle or 4 × 4 is preferable.
- Numerous side trails lead down onto private land. Please obey any posted notices and do not trespass.
- Many roads in the Bruce Peak area are overgrown and unmarked. Motor bikes have gouged deep ruts in other roadways.

HIKE DESCRIPTION   From the limited parking area you can follow a number of old roads and trails to a variety of lookout points. At a nearby road fork, a little to the west, make a right turn to stay on Mount Bruce Road and hike up the rough jeep road to the summit and communication towers. A little over 1 km from the parking area the road splits. Keep right up the rugged hill for the summit.

Another option is to keep left at the fork and hike southwest for about 10 minutes to an intersection of old roads ①. Keep right to a second fork ②, minutes ahead. To the right is a major trail with good viewpoints westward. Whenever there is a choice, take the left fork until you see the lesser peak "Brucey" and its transmission tower, on your right. At an open area at ④, an old road, scoured by motorbikes, veers north. Keep to the minor trail, close by. Hike east, up a steep grade, to the transmitter site and over to the main lookout.

For an even longer hike, from ② take the left branch and contour northwest on old roads to several viewpoints and a steep trail that plummets south and joins Musgrave Road at a point 2 km beyond Mount Tuam Road. Just ahead at ③ cut off the old road onto a steep trail that will set you on the way to the summit.

WORTH NOTING

- Small, red or orange triangle markers designate some trails. Please keep to obvious trails at all times.
- Read about the Gulf Islands on page 110.

NEARBY

Mount Tuam   For Mount Tuam, stay on Musgrave Road for another 2 km beyond Mount Bruce Road to the gated Mount Tuam Road, on the left. Park at roadside and walk just over 2 km to the federally owned Mount Tuam summit (602 m). The hike is along an easy grade of a dirt road, which can be seasonally dusty or muddy. The sweeping vista takes in Satellite Channel, Saanich Peninsula, Cowichan Bay and the outer Gulf Islands. Do not descend the slopes in any direction or you will be trespassing on private land.

Mill Farm Regional Park Reserve   The Capital Regional District's Mill Farm Regional Park Reserve (338 ha) protects one of Saltspring Island's historic farm and mill sites and its fragile habitat. The endangered Phantom Orchid grows here. A 26 ha section of the reserve features the Gulf Island's largest remaining stands of old growth Douglas-fir. As you hike around the old farm site, look for an old millwheel and a pond. Access is along Musgrave Road, just under 2.5 km past Mount Tuam Road, where the road curves abruptly to the left at a hairpin corner.

Musgrave Greenbelt   To reach the Musgrave Greenbelt (35 ha), continue past the Mount Bruce Road cutoff and negotiate Musgrave Road for another 7 km of rough gravel, dirt and steep hills to Musgrave Landing, at sea level. Near the bottom of the last hill, keep left to the shore. Parking is in a grassy field. The greenbelt was once a farm. Easy hiking along old roads leads to a beach. The large rock has been dubbed "Musgrave Island". More meandering trails await along the waterfront.

Hope Hill Trails can be accessed along Musgrave Road, about 4 km from Fulford-Ganges Road. The trailhead is 0.5 km beyond a hairpin corner. Look for an old logging road, on the left. Numerous trails and old roads, some marked with ribbons or red triangle markers, climb above the 500 m level. If you are unfamiliar with this region, hike with someone who knows the terrain. Stay on marked routes as most side trails extend onto private land. Please do not trespass. Note that the Hope Hill summit (649 m) is also private property. See map on page 117.

Reginald Hill   From the Fulford Harbour ferry dock take Fulford-Ganges Road for 0.3 km and then make an immediate right onto Beaver Point Road. Next turn right onto Morningside Drive and drive 1 km to its end. Parking is available here. Beyond this point, the road enters a private residential development. Walk about 100 m past the subdivision gate to the first driveway to the left. Look for and follow the trail markers up the steep, forested path to the summit, where there is a short loop trail. Please do not trespass on adjacent private property. Reginald Hill (241 m) rewards hikers with a fine view of Fulford Harbour. This hike is 1.5 km, one way. Allow about 50 minutes up; 40 minutes down.

ADDITIONAL INFORMATION
www.bcferries.com BC Ferries
www.crd.bc.ca Capital Regional District
Refer to NTS 92B/11, 92B/12, 92B/13,
and 92B/14 (1:50,000)

6c. Mount Maxwell Provincial Park, Saltspring Island   Maps M6, M6A, M6C

DIFFICULTY/DISTANCE   Easy/up to 2 km, one way

HIGHLIGHTS   Mount Maxwell Provincial Park (231 ha) features some of Saltspring Island's best viewpoints. If you are able to negotiate the somewhat rough road up to the top of Mount Maxwell, you will discover short, groomed trails leading to several popular viewing areas. Longer trails stretch through the park's forests and dangle on steep bluffs. The day-use area at the summit has a picnic area.

ACCESS   On the Fulford-Ganges Road, either 12.4 km from the Fulford Harbour ferry terminal or 2 km south of Ganges, turn southwest onto Cranberry Road and proceed to an obvious T-Junction. Toynbee Road is to the right. Swing left (south) onto Mount Maxwell Road. The pavement ends 4 km from Fulford-Ganges Road. The next 5 km of gravel may be seasonally rough. Be alert where Wright Road cuts off to the left. Here Mount Maxwell Road cuts sharply to the right and continues its ascent to the main parking area. Some trails near the summit are wheelchair accessible.

CAUTIONS
- A number of park trails are close to dangerous cliffs and dropoffs. Use caution when hiking in these areas and closely supervise children.
- Carry adequate water.
- Mount Maxwell Road is narrow and has some hills with washboard sections. It is not suitable for trailers or RVs. The road is not plowed in the winter. Visibility can be bad when the road is dusty in the summer.
- No camping, fires or mountain bikes are allowed on park trails. Please keep to designated routes.

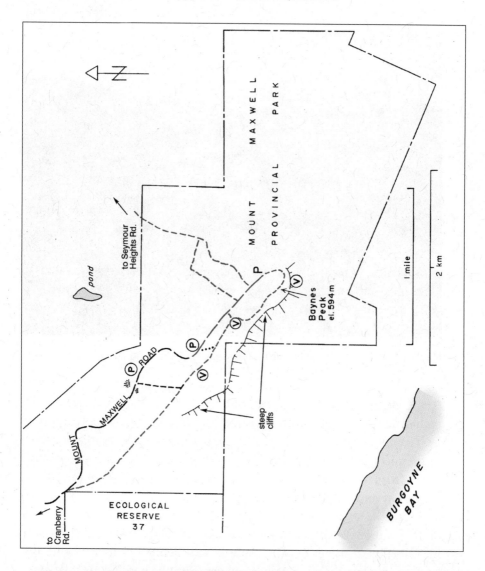

MOUNT MAXWELL PROVINCIAL PARK is named for the mountain that was officially named, in 1858, Mount Baynes. The name commemorated Rear Admiral Robert Lambert Baynes, commander of the Royal Navy's Pacific Station from 1857 to 1860. Through local usage the towering Saltspring Island landmark became known as Maxwell's Mountain or Mount Maxwell, after the farmer who once worked the valley below it from the 1860s on. The Baynes family disputed the name. In 1912 the matter was resolved by retaining the name Mount Maxwell, while remembering the admiral by naming its finest viewpoint Baynes Peak.

Baynes Peak, on Mount Maxwell, offers one of Saltspring Island's best viewpoints. RICHARD K. BLIER

HIKE DESCRIPTION Several of Saltspring Island's best viewpoints, including the popular Baynes Peak (594 m), are easy walks (0.4 km or less) from the main parking area. For public safety, viewing areas adjacent to the sheer bluffs are fenced. The spectacular Gulf Island vistas include the Fulford Valley, Burgoyne Bay, Sansum Narrows, Vancouver Island, Maple Bay and the American San Juan Islands.

From the main parking area a scenic ridge trail parallels the rock bluffs for about 2 km as it snakes through open forest. Heading generally in a northwest direction, the route is well defined at its east end and becomes less distinct the further you get from the parking area. Be extra cautious when travelling near the cliff edges. The ridge trail eventually connects with the park road.

There are numerous unmarked trails on the north side of Mount Maxwell Road. One trail begins 300 m from the parking area. Walk back along the park road and look for a side path on the right. These park trails wind through the salal along the park's northern fringe. There are no boundary markers but you can estimate the park limits by the size of the forest. The larger trees are within the park.

- Park forests consist mainly of Douglas-fir, Garry oaks and arbutus.
- Blacktail deer browse these woodlands but you may also encounter a wandering black bear and even feral goats and sheep.
- Peregrine falcons, turkey vultures, eagles and other birds of prey are frequently spotted in the skies. The park's cliff crevices are important nesting areas for several bat species.
- Facilities include viewing areas, picnic tables and pit toilets.
- Read about the Gulf Islands on page 110.

NEARBY *Burgoyne Bay Provincial Park* Nestled beneath Mount Maxwell's shadow is Burgoyne Bay Provincial Park (524 ha). To reach this beautiful waterfront destination, from the Fulford Harbour ferry terminal, take Fulford-Ganges Road and travel 4.7 km to Burgoyne Bay Road. Turn left and continue to where the Burgoyne Bay Road forks near its end at sea level.

Waterfront trails twist along the rocky shoreline and an extensive tidal flat. Unimproved, but well-worn paths lead inland through the forests. The park is a Saltspring Island Protected Area created to preserve an historic farm and fields, First Nations archaeological sites and crucial parts of the forests, shoreline and waters of Burgoyne Bay. Park changes will come slowly; the area includes Saltspring Island's last undeveloped salmon-bearing estuary.

ADDITIONAL INFORMATION
www.bcferries.com (BC Ferries)
www.env.gov.bc.ca/bcparks (BC Parks)
Refer to NTS 92B/13 and 92B/14 (1:50,000)

6d. Mount Erskine Provincial Park, Saltspring Island
Maps M6, M6A

DIFFICULTY/DISTANCE Strenuous/1.4 km, one way

HIGHLIGHTS Mount Erskine Provincial Park (107 ha) is located about 4 km north of Mount Maxwell Provincial Park. Trails lead to several fine viewpoints close to the Mount Erskine summit (441 m). The vistas take in Vancouver Island and Thetis, Kuper, Galiano and Valdes islands. The Shoal Islands near Crofton are also visible.

ACCESS   Take BC Ferries to Fulford Harbour, then follow Fulford-Ganges Road for 14 km to Rainbow Road, in Ganges. For travellers arriving via the Vesuvius Bay ferry, it is 7 km to Rainbow Road. From Ganges, go west onto Rainbow Road, which becomes Collins Road, and travel 4.9 km. Look for red triangular trailhead markers on the left side roadside trees. Parking is extremely limited. Do not block driveways. Note there are two trailheads fairly close to each other. The southern access is more obvious and less steep.

CAUTIONS
- On the trail, be prepared to skirt fallen trees. Expect slippery sections.
- Carry adequate water for the steep hike.
- The Mount Erskine summit is situated on private land. Please do not trespass.

HIKE DESCRIPTION   From either trailhead, the way is obvious and begins to rise abruptly. Eventually the two steep routes merge and continue to climb. Near the top the trail forks into a short loop from which you can access several viewpoints. The southwest lookout takes in Sansum Narrows and Vancouver Island. Galiano Island and other Gulf Islands are to the north. Parts of Saltspring Island, including St. Mary Lake, are also visible. Allow a little over 1 hour, one way, to reach the summit area.

WORTH NOTING
- The Mount Erskine forest is predominantly old growth Douglas-fir with the occasional arbutus and Garry oak grove. Look for hairy manzanita on the hike up.
- The park is habitat of the provincially red-listed Peregrine falcon and Sharp-tailed snake.
- Please read about the Gulf Islands on page 110.

NEARBY   Mount Maxwell Provincial Park. See page 124.

ADDITIONAL INFORMATION
www.bcferries.com (BC Ferries)
www.env.gov.bc.ca/bcparks (BC Parks)
Refer to NTS 92B/13 and 92B/14 (1:50,000)

6e. Wallace Island Provincial Marine Park
Maps M6, M6A

DIFFICULTY/DISTANCE   Easy/up to 4 km, one way

HIGHLIGHTS   Wallace Island Provincial Marine Park (72 ha) is located in the middle of Trincomali Channel, halfway between Galiano Island and Saltspring Island's northeast tip. For this reason, the park is included in the *Hiking Trails 2* Saltspring Island section. Easy trails go to either end of Wallace Island and offer opportunities for nature appreciation and wildlife viewing as well as access to spectacular seascapes.

ACCESS   **Water access only.** Approach Wallace Island with caution; submerged jagged reefs and rocky shoals abound. Conover Cove has public mooring and a pier. Be alert navigating Conover Cove's shallow entrance, particularly at low tide. Additional anchorage and a small dinghy dock are located at Princess Cove. Small boats, canoes and kayaks can be landed on the beaches.

CAUTIONS

- Stay on designated trails to avoid damaging fragile vegetation and soil structure.
- There is private property halfway down Wallace Island's west side. Respect the privacy of the landowners and do not trespass in this area, northwest of Princess Cove.
- Bring along adequate water. Pumped water is available seasonally. Boil, treat or filter before use.
- No fires are permitted. Campers should equip themselves with small camp stoves. Carry out all your litter.

CAPTAIN RICHARDS originally dubbed Wallace Island Narrow Island in 1859. At the same time he named Houstoun Passage, north of Saltspring Island, after Captain Wallace Houstoun. Unfortunately he made a slip of the pen when entering the captain's surname, recording Houston instead of Houstoun. Although the correct spelling was formally adopted in 1942, the incorrect spelling still crops up from time to time. Captain Parry renamed Narrow Island as Wallace Island when he was surveying the area in 1905. At that time he also named Panther Point after a ship that was wrecked on the point's offshore reefs in 1874. Trincomali Channel is named after Captain Houstoun's ship, HMS *Trincomallee*.

AN EARLY PIONEER, a Scotsman named Jeremiah Chivers, lived on Wallace Island for 38 years. He died there in 1927, at the age of 92. Gnarled fruit trees mark the site of his former orchard and garden. A summer camp existed on the island in the 1930s. David Conover built a resort on Wallace Island in the 1940s. He later wrote two books based on his family's experiences: *One Man's Island* and *Once Upon An Island*, both out of print but worth searching for.

HIKE DESCRIPTION From Conover Cove, well-maintained, flat trails wind through Douglas-fir, Garry oak and arbutus forests. You can hike to Chivers Point, at Wallace Island's north end or head south to Panther Point. This main trail runs about 4 km down the center of Wallace Island. Side paths lead to tiny coves and viewpoints. There are plenty of places to stop and savour your surroundings. Be sure to take note of the many folded-over, twisted rock formations you will encounter along island trails.

WORTH NOTING
- Wildflower viewing is best in March, April and May.
- You might spot a blacktail deer, river otter or mink on your island wanderings. Harbour seals frequent area waters, and over the winter, watch for Steller's or California sea lions.
- Birdwatching is excellent through spring, summer and fall. Eagle sightings are very common.
- Facilities include picnic and information shelters, 18 designated walk-in campsites with pit toilets at Conover Point, Cabin Bay and Chivers Point.
- For current information on seasonal mooring and camping fees, park services and other details contact BC Parks.
- Read about the Gulf Islands on page 110.

NEARBY Saltspring Island and its many trails are just south of Wallace Island. See map on page 116.

ADDITIONAL INFORMATION
www.env.gov.bc.ca/bcparks (BC Parks)
Refer to NTS 92B/13 (1:50,000)

7

Galiano Island and Mayne Island

7a. Dionisio Point Provincial Marine Park, Galiano Island   Maps M6, 7A

DIFFICULTY/DISTANCE   Easy/up to 2km, one way

HIGHLIGHTS   Dionisio Point Provincial Marine Park sits on 147 ha of land at Galiano Island's northern tip. You can only get there by water. The park features rocky headlands, a sandy beach and an exotic-looking tidal lagoon. Other highlights include the fluctuating tidal waters of Porlier Pass, between Galiano and Valdes islands, and the inspiring Strait of Georgia seascapes. The region's diverse marine life is revealed in the tidepools exposed at low tides.

ACCESS   Water access only at this park.

Gulf Islands cruising.   ERIC BURKLE

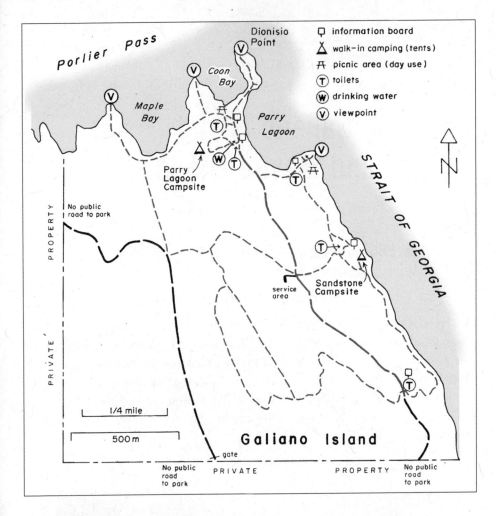

CAUTIONS

- Dangerous tidal currents and rip tides surge through Porlier Pass. Use caution when travelling on shoreline rocks and beaches. Keep children under close supervision.

- Seasonal pumped water is available. Remember to always boil, treat or filter all water prior to use.

- Keep to designated roads and trails at all times to protect the park's delicate vegetation.

- Private property abuts the park. Please do not trespass. Read and follow any posted notices.

- No fires are permitted. Bring along a portable cooking stove.

HIKE DESCRIPTION   A variety of trails wend through upland forest or along the spectacular shoreline. Some paths follow old roads to the park boundaries. Favourite paths include one that leads to tiny pocket beaches fronting Porlier Pass. Another winds out to the rocky isthmus at Dionisio Point, near Coon Bay. Many beaches here are soft sandstone and display the evidence of wind and waves.

WORTH NOTING

- Seasonal spring wildflowers brighten the upland forest meadows. Please do not pick the flowers.
- Watch for seals, sea lions, whales and waterbirds in the offshore waters.
- There are shell midden and five archaeological sites within the park. These areas are fenced for their preservation. Interpretive signposts are located at Maple Bay.
- Divers are attracted to various wreck sites in the surrounding waters.
- The park has two designated walk-in camping areas; both with self-registration. One tenting site is at Parry Lagoon, in the upland area just west of the lagoon. The second campsite, Sandstone, fronts the Strait of Georgia. Both campsites require an uphill hike to reach. Other park facilities include a day-use picnic area, pit toilets and information shelters. Secure your food well at night to deter scavenging raccoons. Contact BC Parks for current information on camping fees and park regulations.

NEARBY   Bodega Ridge Provincial Park. See page 134.

ADDITIONAL INFORMATION
www.bcferries.com (BC Ferries)
www.env.gov.bc.ca/bcparks (BC Parks)
Refer to NTS 92B/13, 92G/4 (1:50,000)

CAPTAIN JOHN F. PARRY named Dionisio Point, during a 1905 coastal survey, to honour Dionisio Alcala Galiano, who explored the region in 1792. Galiano was commander of the Spanish frigate, *Sutil*. Captain Richards had already named Galiano Island after the same person, in 1859. The Spanish explorer Narvaez named Porlier Pass in 1791, after a Spanish official.

7b. Bodega Ridge Provincial Park, Galiano Island
Map M6

DIFFICULTY/DISTANCE   Moderate/6 km, one way

HIGHLIGHTS   Many people consider Galiano Island's Bodega Ridge to be the finest ridge walk in BC. Located within Bodega Ridge Provincial Park (233 ha), the ridge has exceptional viewpoints and is an excellent place for birdwatching and nature appreciation.

ACCESS   Starting at Galiano Island's Sturdies Bay ferry dock, take Sturdies Bay Road for 2.7 km to the junction with Georgeson Bay Road, near the Hummingbird Inn. This intersection is known locally as "the corner". Turn right (north) onto Porlier Pass Road and continue another 14 km to Cottage Way. Turn right and wind up the switchbacks on the paved road for 1.7 km to the marked south end trailhead. Parking is limited here. Please do not block driveways.

A second access point is beyond Cottage Way, another 5.2 km north along Porlier Pass Road. At Cook Road, swing right and watch for the driveway at the Bodega Resort. The northern Bodega Ridge trailhead starts nearby. Look for signposts.

CAUTIONS
- To access the ridge from either trailhead, hikers must cross 1 km of private property. Area landowners are co-operating in allowing hikers to cross their land. Please respect any posted notices. Carry out your litter and do not cut trees.
- The trail is narrow in places and you may encounter large, fallen trees. Use caution near the cliff edges. Supervise small children carefully.
- Wear sturdy footwear and carry adequate water.
- Stay on designated park trails to avoid trampling delicate soil structure and vegetation.
- This day-use park has no amenities. No camping or fires are permitted.

HIKE DESCRIPTION   From the Cottage Way trailhead the trail climbs to follow an old road. About 0.5 km along, the wide track swings right and down into a valley. Take the left trail for the ridge and the first of many viewpoints. The inspiring vistas include Saltspring, Wallace and other Gulf Islands, Vancouver Island and the distant Olympic Mountains, and the seascapes over Trincomali Channel and the Strait of Georgia. At its north end, the trail passes a small, steep-sided valley. Allow about

30 minutes to reach the ridge from the Cottage Way trailhead. Bodega Ridge is 4 km in length and rises to an elevation of 328 m. The distance between the north and south trailheads is about 6 km.

WORTH NOTING

- Seasonal wildflowers carpet the forest floor in the early spring. Equally brilliant flowers cover the sandstone shelf below the cliffs and are easily visible to passing boaters and paddlers.
- Bodega Ridge is habitat to the endangered Peregrine falcon and the rare, non-poisonous, sharp-tailed snake.
- The lower forest consists mainly of Douglas-fir and western red cedar. Higher up, Garry oak and arbutus thrive. Hairy manzanita dominates the ridge.
- Listen and look for woodpeckers in the forests; turkey vultures, eagles and other birds of prey overhead.
- Read about the Gulf Islands on page 110.

NEARBY *Montague Harbour Provincial Marine Park* (97 ha) features several trails. Maintained paths lead to a Montague Harbour beach, a lagoon and saltwater marsh. Other trails loop around a small peninsula. Parker Island, Mount Sutil and Trincomali Channel form the seaside backdrop. The waterfront offers ample opportunity to explore the intertidal marine life and watch for wildlife. This larger, serviced campground is popular with boaters. The campground has 25 vehicle and 15 walk-in campsites, one of which is a group camping area. Other facilities include a dock and boat ramp, picnic tables, fire rings, seasonal tap water and pit toilets. Contact BC Parks for current information on seasonal services, reservations and fees.

Access as above for Bodega Ridge. At the Km 2.7 Sturdies Bay/ Georgeson Bay Road junction, near the Hummingbird Inn, keep left and

GALIANO ISLAND'S BODEGA HILL and Quadra Hill were both named by Captain Parry in 1905, after a Spanish naval officer, Captain Juan Francisco de la Bodega y Quadra, who had taken part in exploration along the BC coast in the 1770s. Although their countries were rivals, when Captain George Vancouver met Quadra at Nootka in 1792 to accept restoration of British lands seized earlier by the Spanish, the two men developed a personal friendship. This resulted in Vancouver's naming of what is now Vancouver Island as "the Island of Quadra and Vancouver".

follow Georgeson Bay Road, then Montague Road for 4 km to Clanton Road. Keep straight ahead onto Montague Park Road for 1 km to the park.

ADDITIONAL INFORMATION
www.bcferries.com (BC Ferries)
www.env.gov.bc.ca/bcparks (BC Parks)
www.galianoisland.com (Galiano Island Chamber of Commerce)
Refer to NTS 92B/13 and 92B/14 (1:50,000)

7c. Mount Galiano, Galiano Island   Map M6

DIFFICULTY/DISTANCE   Moderate to strenuous/3 km, one way

HIGHLIGHTS   Mount Galiano (311 m) is Galiano Island's most visible landmarks and towers above Active Pass's western entrance. A slightly arduous, but rewarding hike up the steep trail to the summit ends at one of the best viewpoints anywhere on the Gulf Islands.

ACCESS
Active Pass Drive via Burrill Road   From Galiano Island's Sturdies Bay ferry terminal follow Sturdies Bay Road for 0.7 km and turn left (south) onto Burrill Road. This road swings left to become Bluff Road. Continue up through Bluffs Park to the stop sign at Georgeson Bay Road. Turn left (south) to Active Pass Drive.

Active Pass Drive via Georgeson Bay Road   From the ferry dock stay on Sturdies Bay Road for 3 km to the junction with Porlier Pass Drive and Georgeson Bay Road. Locals call this intersection "the corner". Turn left here at the Hummingbird Inn and stay on Georgeson Bay Road for 1.5 km. The route winds through meadow and forestlands. Where the road curves sharply to the right, turn left onto Active Pass Drive. From here it is 0.5 km to the parking area.

Active Pass Drive narrows as it passes through the tiny Georgeson Bay neighbourhood. The road then drops down a hill to a limited parking area. Do not block driveways and respect the privacy of area residents. Near the roadside pulloff look for the Mount Galiano signpost and walk down Phillimore Point Road for about 50 m to the marked trailhead, on the right.

Secondary access to Mount Galiano is possible via trails from the north. One is found along Georgeson Bay Road, just south of Bluff Road. The other trail begins at the end of Lord Road, which is reached via

Ferry entering Active Pass. RICHARD K. BLIER

Morgan Road, also off Georgeson Bay Road. These alternate routes meet the main trail part way up to the summit. Consult a detailed Galiano Island road map for further directions.

CAUTIONS

- Bring along ample water.
- Stay on designated trails and obey any posted notices.
- The Mount Galiano trail skirts a sheer cliff on the way to the summit. There are sheer, rocky outcrops and bluffs in the summit meadows. Exercise caution when hiking in these areas.
- Build no fires and leave no litter. No camping is allowed.

HIKE DESCRIPTION   From the Phillimore Road trailhead the trail begins a steady climb to the summit. The 3 km trail is steep in spots as it snakes up the forested slope. Metal markers indicate the route. After about 40 minutes hiking, turn left (south) where an overgrown logging road joins in on the right. This junction is clearly marked. Note: If you accidentally turn north (right) you will start heading back down the mountain on the old road, which serves as an alternate route to Mount Galiano. See Access on page 136.

Beyond the logging road junction, the trail steepens even more. The climb up the last pitch to the summit ends at a panoramic vista of Active Pass and the Gulf Islands. The stunning view includes Mayne, Saturna, Saltspring and the Pender islands. On a clear day you can see as far as the Olympic Mountains. The summit area features several large Garry oak meadows and is known for its colourful spring wildflowers. Allow at least 1 hour to reach the top.

WORTH NOTING

- In April of 1991, 81 ha of second and third growth forests on Mount Galiano were preserved as a nature conservancy area. The Galiano Club spearheaded the campaign to save this area and now manages the land.
- Read about the Gulf Islands on page 110.

NEARBY   Bluffs Park. See page 139.

ADDITIONAL INFORMATION
www.bcferries.com (BC Ferries)
www.galianoclub.org (Galiano Club)
Refer to NTS 92B/14 (1:50,000)

ACTIVE PASS, between Galiano and Mayne islands, was named in 1855 when the US steamer *Active* first transited the passage. In 1857, the *Active* and the Royal Navy's *Plumper,* under Captain G. H. Richards, were both in Semiahoo Bay to assist in boundary negotiations along the 49th parallel. Semiahoo Bay is close to White Rock, BC. While there, the officers of the *Plumper* arrested a man for illegal trade in alcohol. The *Active* transported him to Esquimalt and justice.

On the trip, the crew learned that the man had obtained vast quantities of gold dust in trade with Fraser Valley First Nations people. The following winter, when the men returned to San Francisco, the news broke. The 1858 Fraser River gold rush was on. That year, Captain Richards named the passage after the *Plumper,* but he dropped the designation after correspondence with the American boundary commissioner. The loyal Mayne Island inhabitants retained the name of Plumper Pass for their post office until 1900.

7d. Bluffs Park, Galiano Island   Map 6

DIFFICULTY/DISTANCE   Easy/0.5 km, one way

HIGHLIGHTS   Galiano Island's Bluffs Park (128 ha) features several viewpoints that overlook Active Pass and Mayne Island. You can drive to the best lookouts and follow short ridge trails to many more. These are perfect places from which to watch the frequent ferry and boat traffic in the constricted waters of Active Pass. Numerous well-travelled paths wind through the shady, neighbouring forest and provide more hiking options.

ACCESS   From the Galiano Island ferry terminal at Sturdies Bay take Sturdies Bay Road for 0.7 km and turn left (south) on Burrill Road. After negotiating a sharp right corner the road turns to gravel and becomes Bluff Road. Climb this narrow, winding road to the Bluffs Park viewpoint, about 4 km from the ferry dock. Turn left for the parking area. The walk to the park from the ferry dock is about 1 to 1.5 hours, one way.

CAUTIONS
- Carry adequate water.
- Some trails within Bluffs Park lead onto private property. Please stay on marked park trails. Follow any posted notices and do not trespass.
- A speed limit of 10 km/hr applies within the park.
- Camping or fires are not permitted. Bicycles are restricted to the road. The RCMP and area residents patrol the area.

HIKE DESCRIPTION   The main Bluffs Park viewpoint is 122 m above Active Pass and offers great views south over Georgeson Bay, Active Pass, Prevost, Mayne and the Pender islands. Hike in either direction along the bluffs to discover your own perfect viewpoint. One path offers a fine view of Mount Galiano. Many trails cut through the adjacent forest and access more hiking areas. Some intersecting side paths descend from the bluffs to other park access points.

WORTH NOTING
- Galiano Islanders purchased Bluffs Park in 1948. The area is held as a nature conservancy area administered by the Galiano Club. In 2006, the CRD and the Land Conservancy procured adjacent property that links Bluffs Park with Matthews Point Regional Reserve.
- Read about the Gulf Islands on page 110.

Matthews Point Regional Park Reserve (32.8 ha), located right next to Galiano Island's Bluffs Park, protects an arbutus, Garry oak and Douglas-fir forest near the Active Pass bluffs and a small beach area. The point, which overlooks Active Pass, is known for its colourful spring wildflowers. Unimproved, unsanctioned trails exist. Possible future improvements are under study. Access is via Bluffs Road. Contact the Capital Regional District at www.crd.bc.ca for more information.

Bellhouse Provincial Park (2 ha) is a tiny day-use destination for hikers, picnickers and anyone who enjoys scenic seascapes. Short trails meander through a small Douglas-fir, maple, arbutus, western red cedar and hemlock forest to the shores of Active Pass. These paths access Burrill Point, named after two brothers, Frederick and Joseph, who once ranched nearby. The point consists mainly of exposed rock with a thin cover of mosses and grasses. Remember to tread lightly near these sensitive areas and stay on park trails. A submerged shelf is revealed at low tide; an ideal time to spend looking at the park's unique sandstone formations.

Fishboat, ferry and freighter traffic is usually heavy in Active Pass. Directly across the narrows stands the historic Georgina Point lighthouse, on Mayne Island. On a clear day the Coast Mountains are visible. Park facilities include picnic tables, benches and pit toilets. No fires, camping or bicycles are allowed. Access to the park is via Sturdies Bay and Burrill roads and Jack Drive, 1.3 km from the ferry dock. The walk from the ferry terminal to the park takes approximately 30 to 45 minutes. BC Parks has more information at www.env.gov.bc.ca/bcparks.

ADDITIONAL INFORMATION
www.bcferries.com (BC Ferries)
www.galianoclub.org (Galiano Club)
Refer to NTS 92B/14 (1:50,000)

7e. Mount Parke Regional Park, Mayne Island   Map M6

DIFFICULTY/DISTANCE   Moderate/1.8 km, one way

HIGHLIGHTS   Mount Parke (260 m) is Mayne Island's highest point. Steep, challenging trails at Mount Parke Regional Park (49 ha) climb almost to the summit and offer the island's best viewpoints, mostly along the mountain ridge. This Capital Regional District nature appreciation park is a great destination for hikers, birdwatchers and naturalists.

ACCESS   From Mayne Island's Village Bay ferry terminal take Village Bay Road to Fernhill Road. Swing right (east) and follow Fernhill Road to Montrose Road. Turn right (south) to the end of the road and the parking area.

CAUTIONS
- The Mount Parke trail is steep. Wear suitable footwear.
- Carry ample water.
- Stay on existing trails to minimize damage to soil and vegetation. Carry out all litter.
- Exercise caution near the sheer cliffs. There is no safety barrier or fence. Supervise small children closely.
- The Mount Parke summit is on private land. Obey any posted notices and please do not trespass.
- Fires, camping, bicycles or motorized vehicles are not permitted. This day-use park is open sunrise to sunset.

HIKE DESCRIPTION   From the parking area the trail follows a road right-of-way to the park boundary. About 0.3 km from the parking area is a major trail junction, near a pit toilet. Keep straight ahead or take the right hand path to hike an easy 1.3 km loop through Mount Parke's lower forest. This 30 minute circle hike passes an unusually large arbutus tree.

To access the ridge, follow the trail on the left. Things start out relatively flat, then the steep sections begin. From the junction it is 1.5 km to the main viewpoint. The signposted Halliday Lookout, at 185 m, is the highest public viewpoint on Mayne Island. The panoramic vista includes Vancouver and the Mainland mountains, Navy Channel, and Saturna, Prevost, Saltspring and Vancouver islands. Extend your hike further along the ridge to more viewing areas. One rough trail runs north to link with the lower forest trails. Allow 30 to 45 minutes hiking time to reach the ridge.

- A variety of spring wildflowers adorn Mount Parke's slopes and ridges.
- Mount Parke forests are mainly western red cedar, alder, arbutus and Douglas-fir. Oregon grape and large ferns are common at trailside.
- Mayne Island and Mount Parke were named by Captain Richards. The Royal Navy's Richard Charles Mayne was Lieutenant on the surveying vessels *Plumper*, 1857-1860, and *Hecate*, 1861. Lieutenant John J. Parke, a US topographical engineer, was a surveyor and chief astronomer for the boundary commission of 1857.
- Read about the Gulf Islands on page 110.

NEARBY

Plumper Pass Community Park features a moderately rough loop trail that meanders 2 km through second growth forest on Mount Parke's north side. The route follows old roads and trails and there are steep sections. The park abuts Mount Parke Regional Park and has linking trails. Access is via Village Bay, Fernhill, Felix Jack and Kim roads. Consult a detailed Mayne Island road map. Contact www.mayneisland.com for more park details.

Bennett Bay and Campbell Point (17 ha) are part of Parks Canada's Gulf Islands National Park Reserve (GINPR). See page 110. Bennett Bay is situated on Mayne Island's east side, near Campbell Point. There are 3 km of easy walking trails and a stunning sandy beach. The Campbell Point peninsula has the remains of an old growth forest. Offshore is Georgeson Island, also part of the GINPR. Please avoid the unsanctioned paths near the Campbell Point peninsula cliffs. These are succumbing to incessant erosion and pose a public safety hazard. Access is via Village Bay, Fernhill, Bennett Bay and Wilkes roads, with parking available at the end of Wilkes or Bennett Bay roads. Refer to a Mayne Island road map. For more information visit www.pc.gc.ca/gulf.

ADDITIONAL INFORMATION

www.bcferries.com (BC Ferries)
www.crd.bc.ca (Capital Regional District)
Refer to NTS 92B/14 (1:50,000)

8

Pender Islands

8a. North Pender Island   Map M6

DIFFICULTY/DISTANCE   Easy to strenuous/180 m to 2 km, one way; 5 km loop

HIGHLIGHTS   North Pender Island has a surprising number of places to hike. Some trails run through community parks, other paths are within the Parks Canada Gulf Islands National Park Reserve (GINPR). Many trails access environmentally sensitive areas, so tread lightly.

ACCESS   For concise directions to area trailheads consult a detailed North Pender Island road map.

CAUTIONS

- Carry adequate water.
- Stay on designated trails and do not trample fragile soil structure and vegetation.
- Many trails abut private property. Respect the privacy of area land-owners and do not trespass.

HIKE DESCRIPTIONS

George Hill   Moderate to strenuous/2 km, one way: George Hill is located on North Pender Island's north end. The well-groomed forested trail is steep as it climbs to some of North Pender Island's best lookouts. There are two viewpoints on the way up; both feature resting benches. A third bench is situated near an upper viewpoint. Trail improvements at this community park include steps, handrails and ramps. Allow 30 minutes hiking time, one way.

Access from the Otter Bay ferry terminal is via MacKinnon, Otter Bay and Port Washington roads. From the latter, zig and zag along Bridges

Road, then take Stanley Point Drive to the corner of Ogden and Walden roads. The marked trailhead is on the corner's south side.

Mount Elizabeth Park   Easy/180 m, one way: The highlight at Mount Elizabeth Park is the profusion of swordferns that blanket the shady forest floor. The community park is named after a family member of early Pender Island settlers. Allow about 10 minutes hiking time, one way.

Access from the Otter Bay ferry terminal is via MacKinnon Road to Otter Bay Road. Turn right and follow Otter Bay Road to Amies Road. Swing left onto Amies Road and head east to Hope Bay and the junction of Hooson and Clam Bay roads. Turn left (north) onto Clam Bay Road and watch for the trail signpost and map on the left about 2 km from Hooson Road.

Mount Menzies Park   Moderate/2 km loop: The loop trail at Mount Menzies Park meanders through a mature forest and climbs gently to a ridge. The trail traverses rough terrain so wear sturdy footwear and watch your footing as you hike. The resting bench marks the boundary of the community park. From here, simply loop back to the start. Allow about 25 minutes to complete the park loop. Extend your hike and explore along the bluffs by following the old road east from the end of Hooson Road. A network of trails leads to impressive Plumper Sound seascapes.

Access as above for Mount Elizabeth Park to the junction of Clam Bay and Hooson roads. Turn right onto Hooson Road and continue south to the end of the road.

Roesland   Easy/0.5 km, one way: Roesland (formerly a cottage resort) is now part of Parks Canada's GINPR. This area features a short trail that crosses a footbridge and leads to an impressive Roe Islet viewpoint near Otter Bay. Allow 15 minutes hiking time, one way. Roesland's previous owners still live on a section of the property. Please respect their privacy and obey any posted notices. The Pender Island Heritage Museum is housed in Roesland's restored 1908 farmhouse. Plan a visit to learn about Pender Island history. Contact www.penderislandmuseum.org for hours of operation and more information.

To reach Roesland from the Otter Bay ferry terminal, drive up the hill to MacKinnon Road and turn right to Otter Bay Road. Swing right onto Otter Bay Road and then turn right onto South Otter Bay Road. Continue another 1.5 km and watch for Parks Canada signpost on the right (west) side of the road.

Roe Lake Trail Moderate/5 km loop: The Roe Lake Trail, part of the GINPR, leads to and around a freshwater lake, a Gulf Island rarity. To protect delicate ecosystems, please stay on designated trails at all times. From the trailhead the trail winds southeast through a second growth Douglas-fir upland forest above Shingle Bay. At Roe Lake, turn left or right to loop around the lake perimeter. There are countless confusing side paths in this region so watch for official signage to stay on the main routes. One access trail, very popular with locals, starts at Roe Lake's southwest corner and descends to the end of Galleon Way, in the Magic Lake Estates. Allow up to 1.5 hours to complete the lake loop. Roe Lake is closed to fishing.

Access to Roe Lake is as for Roesland above. From Roesland, follow South Otter Bay Road to Shingle Bay Road. Turn left and drive 0.3 km to the official Parks Canada trailhead, marked by a signpost and map on the road's left (east) side.

Heart Trail/Prior Centennial Campground Easy to moderate/1 km, one way: The Heart Trail starts at the GINPR's Prior Centennial Campground (16 ha) and winds about 1 km through a second growth forest of western red cedar, alder, maple and fir. The trail ends at Ketch Road, in the Magic Lake Estates. There are a few steep sections. Allow about 20 minutes, one way.

To reach the Heart Trail and Prior Centennial Campground, from the Pender Island Otter Bay ferry terminal go up the hill to MacKinnon Road and turn right to Otter Bay Road. Turn right and follow Otter Bay Road to Bedwell Harbour Road, about 3 km from the ferry dock. Turn right (south) onto Bedwell Harbour Road, which becomes Canal Road just north of the Driftwood Shopping Centre. Continue 3.5 km to the Prior Centennial Campground entrance, on the right.

Oak Bluffs Trail Strenuous/0.4 km, one way: This short but surprisingly steep trail off North Pender Island's Pirates Road leads to excellent bluff

PRIOR CENTENNIAL CAMPGROUND (16 ha) was once a provincial park. Parks Canada now administers the campsite as part of the GINPR. Overnight facilities include 17 tent/vehicle campsites, picnic tables, pit toilets and fire pits. Seasonal fire restrictions may apply. This popular park is usually busy from June through the fall, particularly on summer weekends. For current information on reservations, camping fees, seasonal closures and park policies contact Parks Canada.

views of Swanson Channel, Vancouver Island and Washington State's Mount Baker. There are wooden steps at the trail's start and a wooden stairway halfway up. Exercise extreme caution when travelling anywhere along the sheer bluffs. Allow 15 to 20 minutes, one way, to reach the viewpoints.

Access as for the Heart Trail and Prior Centennial Campground. Continue on Canal Road another 0.5 km beyond the park entrance to Aldridge Road. Here Canal Road turns left toward the bridge over the narrow channel that separates North and South Pender islands. Turn right (south) onto Aldridge Road to Schooner Way. Turn right again and follow Schooner Way west to the Magic Lake Estates and Pirates Road. Turn southeast (left) onto Pirates Road and drive another 2.5 km to the small roadside parking area, on the right.

WORTH NOTING   Read about the Gulf Islands on page 110.

NEARBY   South Pender Island hiking trails (See below.)

ADDITIONAL INFORMATION
www.bcferries.com (BC Ferries)
www.crd.bc.ca/penderparks (Capital Regional District)
www.pc.gc.ca/gulf (Gulf Islands National Park Reserve)
Refer to NTS 92B/14 (1:50,000)

8b. South Pender Island   Map M6

DIFFICULTY/DISTANCE   Strenuous/2 km to 3 km, one way

HIGHLIGHTS   *Mount Norman* (244 m) and its magnificent viewpoint is South Pender Island's highest spot. Formerly a CRD Park, Mount Norman is now part of Parks Canada's Gulf Islands National Park Reserve (GINPR). See page 110. A rigorous hike up old roads and trails to the summit leads to one of the Gulf Island's best viewpoints.

ACCESS   From the North Pender Island ferry terminal in Otter Bay climb the hill to MacKinnon Road and turn right. Next, swing right onto Otter Bay Road and drive to Bedwell Harbour Road, about 3 km from the ferry dock. Turn right (south) onto Bedwell Harbour Road—which becomes Canal Road just north of the Driftwood Shopping Centre—and drive 5 km to pass Prior Centennial Park and Aldridge Road to reach the narrow bridge over the constricted channel that separates the Pender Islands. Cross the bridge over to South Pender Island. From here you have a choice of Mount Norman trailheads.

MOUNT NORMAN AND PENDER ISLAND were named by Captain Richards. The Royal Navy's William Henry Norman was paymaster on HMS *Ganges,* flagship of Rear Admiral R. L. Baynes. See page 125. Daniel Pender, also from the Royal Navy, was second and later third master of the surveying ship *Plumper,* then the *Hecate.* From 1863 to 1870 he commanded the *Beaver* as surveys of the West Coast were completed.

To the Ainslie Point Road Trailhead   From Canal Road cut right onto Ainslie Point Road and continue 0.4 km to the signposted trailhead and parking area, on the left.

To the Canal Road Trailhead   At the narrows bridge, keep left to stay on Canal Road. Drive 2.4 km and watch on the right for the gated access road for the Mount Norman parking lot and trailhead. This is the main access point.

CAUTIONS

- Wear sturdy footwear and carry extra water. The Mount Norman hike is steep, tiring and thirst-inducing.
- No fires, camping or motorized vehicles are allowed at this day-use park.
- From the Ainslie Point Road trailhead the trail crosses private land. Please keep to the trail and do not trespass.

HIKE DESCRIPTION   The Mount Norman trails traverse moderate to steep terrain. Both follow old roads that become trails farther up the slopes. Part way up the two well marked trails merge and continue the seemingly endless climb to the viewpoint and a short loop trail, at the top. Vistas from the Mount Norman summit include Vancouver Island, Bedwell Harbour, the northern San Juan Islands and the Gulf Islands; to the east, the Lower Mainland and Mount Baker, in Washington State.

The 3 km Canal Road access trail takes about 45 minutes to an hour to hike, one way. The Ainslie Point Road access trail is shorter by about a third; is less scenic and a little steeper. It should take about 35 minutes to hike, one way. Adjust your travel times accordingly if you add a visit to Beaumont Marine Park to your hiking agenda. See Worth Noting below.

WORTH NOTING

- Chocolate lilies blanket Mount Norman meadows in the springtime.
- Near the Ainslie Point Road trailhead, a steep side path branches off the main trail and plunges 2.5 km to sea level at Bedwell Harbour and

Beaumont Marine Park (58 ha). Now part of the GINPR, Beaumont Park is one of the most-visited marine parks in the Gulf Islands. Facilities include 11 walk-in campsites, picnic tables, pit toilets and mooring buoys. Allow 30 to 40 minutes to hike down from the Mount Norman Trail; considerably longer on the way back up.

- Facilities at Mount Norman include pit toilets, information signposts, a summit boardwalk and viewing platform with benches.
- Mount Norman was the first Capital Regional District nature appreciation park on the Outer Gulf Islands. Created in 1993, it was subsequently transferred to the GINPR.
- Read about the Gulf Islands on page 110.

NEARBY

The William Walker Trail begins near the Mount Norman Canal Road trailhead. This moderately steep community trail winds 2.5 km through shady forest and through a woodlot to parallel Canal Road and emerge near Spalding Road. A further 1 km extension runs along the beach on Canal Road's north side. The trail passes an impressive, ancient Douglas-fir and there are gaps in the forest that reveal the ocean.

Brooks Point (4.9 ha) on South Pender Island's southeast tip is now a regional park, administered by the Capital Regional District. The land was partially donated as parkland by Alan Brooks and his family. Easy trails at this spectacular waterfront destination lead through grassy meadows and shady forests to rocky headlands, beaches and a navigation beacon at Gowlland Point. Boardwalks traverse wetter trail sections. Brooks Point features a jagged point of land at Drummond Bay and the area's mixed forest includes Douglas-fir and thick salmonberry. The shoreline has a variety of intertidal life and is a good spot for bird or whale watching. The seaside views include the Strait of Georgia, Boundary Pass and the San Juan Islands. This day-use park has no amenities and is open from sunrise to sunset. Access is via Otter Bay, Bedwell Harbour, Canal, Spalding, Gowlland Point and Kloshe roads. Consult a detailed Pender Island road map. Further information is available through the CRD.

ADDITIONAL INFORMATION

www.bcferries.com (BC Ferries)
www.crd.bc.ca/penderparks (Capital Regional District)
www.pc.gc.ca/gulf (Gulf Islands National Park Reserve)
Refer to NTS 92B/14 (1:50,000)

Brooks Point on South Pender Island. JOYCE FOLBIGG

9

Saturna Island

9a. Winter Cove   Maps M6, M9

DIFFICULTY/DISTANCE   Easy/1.5 km loop

HIGHLIGHTS   Winter Cove day-use area (91 ha), on Saturna Island's northwest end, is known for spectacular Strait of Georgia seascapes. The often rushing, reversing tidal flows in Boat Passage between private Samuel Island and Saturna Island are captivating. Visitors will enjoy the short, delightful loop trail that runs along shorelines and through salt marsh, open meadows and forest to Boat Passage. Winter Cove is part of the Gulf Islands National Park Reserve (GINPR).

ACCESS   Take BC Ferries to Saturna Island. From the ferry terminal go straight up the hill on Ralph Road which turns into East Point Road. Around 1.7 km from the ferry dock, East Point swings left (north) and Narvaez Bay Road is straight ahead. Turn left to stay on East Point Road and travel just over 3 km to the Winter Cove Road junction. Turn left for 0.5 km to the park entrance and parking area.

CAUTIONS
- Strong, fluctuating tidal currents are prevalent in Boat Passage. Use extreme caution when anywhere near this constricted channel. Closely supervise your children.
- No camping is allowed.
- The park gate is locked at night.

HIKE DESCRIPTION   From the parking area, walk through the forest to a fork. Keep on the path to the right for the expansive views of the Strait of Georgia. When you reach a small shoreline bluff that overlooks the water, turn left and follow the trail northwest to Boat Passage. Return to the parking area via the coastal trail that skirts protected Winter Cove.

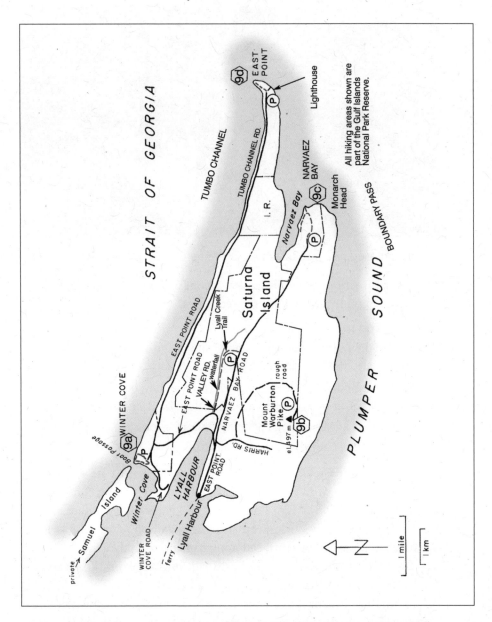

IN THE EARLY MORNING HOURS of July 1st, 2007, the famous *Robertson II* grounded in the waters off Winter Cove Park. Built in Nova Scotia in 1940, the wooden, ex-fishing schooner struck treacherous Minx Reef and became inexorably wedged on the rocks. A salvage effort was attempted and subsequently abandoned. The sea eventually reclaimed the heritage vessel.

A delightful loop hike awaits visitors at Winter Cove. Richard K. Blier

Whatever direction you follow, allow about 30 minutes to complete the loop. Allot extra time to savour the seascapes.

WORTH NOTING

- Since 1990, Winter Cove has been the site of the annual Saturna Island Canada Day (July 1st) lamb barbeque.
- Facilities include day-use picnic areas, pit toilets, a boat launch and a sports field. Pumped water is available. Boil, treat or filter it.
- The park has kayaking and canoeing opportunities.
- Read about the Gulf Islands on page 110.

NEARBY *Lyall Creek Trail* (2 km, one way) begins its sharp descent to the mouth of Lyall Creek from the trailhead along Narvaez Bay Road. At the junction of East Point Road and Narvaez Bay Road, around 1.7 km from the ferry dock, keep straight ahead on Narvaez Bay Road for another 1.5 km. The trailhead and roadside parking area are on the left. Access is also possible on Valley Road, off East Point Road. Expect moderately steep sections in the upper Lyall Creek Valley. The waterfall is one highlight. Verdant mosses and ferns thrive in the shady forest. Local conservation efforts have restored the stream's chum salmon run. Allow 40 minutes hiking time, one way.

ADDITIONAL INFORMATION
www.bcferries.com (BC Ferries)
www.pc.gc.ca/gulf (Gulf Islands National Park Reserve)
Refer to NTS 92B/14 (1:50,000)

9b. Mount Warburton Pike, Saturna Island   Maps M6, M9

DIFFICULTY/DISTANCE   Easy/up to 1 km, one way

HIGHLIGHTS   Mount Warburton Pike (497 m) is Saturna Island's highest point, and the second highest, below Bruce Peak, on all of the Gulf Islands. The view from the summit is superb. You can drive to the top and wander along Warburton Ridge to viewpoints. The area is within Park Canada's Gulf Island National Park Reserve (GINPR).

ACCESS   Starting at the Saturna Island ferry terminal, go straight up the hill on Ralph Road which becomes East Point Road. Near the general store, about 1.7 km from the ferry dock, East Point Road swings sharply to the left with Narvaez Bay Road straight ahead. Stay on Narvaez Bay Road and then make an immediate right onto Harris Road. Continue just under 1 km and turn left (east) onto Staples Road. This steep, narrow, gravel road follows a serpentine course to the Mount Warburton Pike summit, near the federal tower installations. From the bottom of Staples Road to the top of Warburton Pike is 4 km.

CAUTIONS
- Carry adequate water.
- If you extend your hike any distance over 1 km along the ridge it is easy to become disoriented among the lookalike bluffs and meadows. Anyone unfamiliar with the region should travel with someone who knows the area.
- The farm below Warburton Ridge and some adjacent land is private property. Obey any posted notices and please do not trespass.
- Sheep graze in this area. Keep all dogs leashed.
- Staples Road passes through an ecological reserve. Please do not stop in this area. Signs alert visitors to the regulations prohibiting fires, motorized vehicles, camping, hunting, vegetation removal or tree cutting in a reserve.
- All vehicles, including bicycles must stay within the parking area atop Mount Warburton Pike. Attempts are underway to rejuvenate the vegetation and soil at the summit area. Do your part to help. Tread lightly on the ridge trails.

HIKE DESCRIPTION   Park near the towers and hike in either direction along well worn trails and old roads on the Mount Warburton Pike ridge. One rutted old road descends the mountain on one side of the towers. There are excellent viewing spots near the tower, east along the ridge and further down the slopes, in the Garry oak meadows. The vistas include Plumper Sound, the Pender Islands, Moresby, Portland, Saltspring and the American San Juan Islands.

WORTH NOTING

- Mount Warburton Pike is named after a wealthy Englishman who once owned 565 ha of land on Saturna Island. Spanish explorers named Saturna Island in 1791 after their naval schooner *Saturnina*, commanded by Jose Maria Narvaez.
- Read about the Gulf Islands on page 110.

NEARBY Narvaez Bay. See below.

ADDITIONAL INFORMATION
www.bcferries.com (BC Ferries)
www.pc.gc.ca/gulf (Gulf Islands National Park Reserve)
Refer to NTS 92B/14 (1:50,000)

MANY OF THE ROUGH TRAILS that cover the Warburton Ridge and meadows were made by feral goats, which inhabit the region. If you hear a strange bleating sound as you wander the ridge, it probably emanated from the hill below, and came from an alert male goat warning you off. The animals contour along the mountain slopes and weave a purposeful course through the grassy Garry oak meadows and behind camouflaging rocky outcrops and trees. Scan the meadows closely and watch for slight movement. The goats blend in perfectly with their surroundings making them hard to spot. Many visitors feel a visit to Mount Warburton Pike is not complete without a sighting of the elusive goats.

9c. Narvaez Bay, Saturna Island   Maps M6, M9

DIFFICULTY/DISTANCE Moderate/2.5 km, one way

HIGHLIGHTS Saturna Island's Narvaez Bay (250 ha) is now part of Parks Canada's Gulf Islands National Park Reserve (GINPR). An old road serves as the access trail through a Douglas-fir and Garry oak forest and steadily drops to sea level at Narvaez Bay. For inspiring seascapes, nature appreciation, wildlife viewing or simply pleasant hiking, consider a visit to beautiful Narvaez Bay.

ACCESS From the Saturna Island ferry terminal, go straight up the hill on Ralph Road which becomes East Point Road. Near the general store around 1.7 km from the ferry dock, East Point Road swings sharply to the left with Narvaez Bay Road straight ahead. Stay on Narvaez Bay Road and head east another 4.8 km to the end of the road. There is a stretch of gravel en route. The trail starts at the turnaround, next to a locked gate.

CAUTIONS

- Bring along ample water.
- Use care when hiking on the rugged points and headlands. The rocks may be slippery. Keep away from the steep cliff edges.
- Stay on the obvious trails to avoid damaging the area's regenerating vegetation and soil structure.
- Monarch Head is not within the boundaries of the GINPR. Please follow any posted notices and do not trespass on the adjacent private land.
- Building fires is prohibited.

HIKE DESCRIPTION From the trailhead near the locked gate at the end of Narvaez Road, go through the gate and hike along the old road. The trail descends steadily and steepens a bit on the approach to the flatter land at sea level. Note: Getting back to the parking area will take longer on the return hike; the route is mostly uphill. The trail passes several overgrown old roads and curves past a fenced field to the shores of Narvaez Bay. Allow about 40 minutes hiking time, one way.

Hike along the shoreline beach or head over to several points of land on the large, rocky promontory that juts out into Narvaez Bay. Little Bay, on the left (west) side of the headland, is easily reached. Echo Bay, the spectacular cove on the promontory's right (east) side, is equally accessible. Use utmost care when hiking or scrambling on the rocks anywhere near the unpredictable ocean waves. Many visitors spend several hours exploring the Narvaez Bay waterfront, forest trails and roads.

WORTH NOTING

- Facilities include a handful of walk-in campsites, picnic tables, information signposts and pit toilets. Please carry out all your litter.
- Read about the Gulf Islands on page 110.

NEARBY The Lyall Creek Trail. See page 152.

ADDITIONAL INFORMATION

www.bcferries.com (BC Ferries)
www.pc.gc.ca/gulf (Gulf Islands National Park Reserve)
Refer to NTS 92B/14 (1:50,000)

9d. East Point, Saturna Island Maps M6, M9

DIFFICULTY/DISTANCE   Easy/5 to 15 minutes

HIGHLIGHTS   East Point day-use area (2.5 ha) has stunning seascapes of the San Juan Islands and the Strait of Georgia. A choice of short hiking trails offers easy opportunities for nature appreciation and wildlife viewing. As well as a variety of seabirds, you might even spot killer whales. East Point is part of the Gulf Islands National Park Reserve.

ACCESS   Take BC Ferries to Saturna Island. Start at the Saturna Island ferry terminal and go straight up the hill on Ralph Road, which becomes East Point Road. At the 1.7-km mark, cut left (north) to stay on East Point Road. (Narvaez Bay Road continues straight ahead.) East Point Road parallels the Strait of Georgia and turns into Tumbo Channel Road. Just under 15.5 km from the ferry terminal park at the limited parking area and turnaround near the East Point lighthouse.

CAUTIONS
- East Point Road is hilly. Watch for narrow corners and sections of bumpy pavement. Be wary of roadside deer.
- Please do not trespass on federal land at the lighthouse.

HIKE DESCRIPTION   The *Viewpoint Trail* leads to a sandstone bluff overlooking Boundary Pass. Large freighters ply these waters.

The *East Point Trail* descends a hill and meanders out to East Point. This is where most killer whale sightings occur. The roiling currents off Tumbo Channel and Boiling Reef are a highlight.

WORTH NOTING
- Late spring and fall are the best times to spot killer whales.
- The day-use park has pit toilets.
- Construction of the original East Point lighthouse was completed in 1888. In 1948, a steel tower replaced the earlier structure.
- Read about the Gulf Islands on page 110.

NEARBY   Winter Cove. See page 150.

ADDITIONAL INFORMATION
www.bcferries.com (BC Ferries)
www.pc.gc.ca/gulf (Gulf Islands National Park Reserve)
Refer to NTS 92B/14 (1:50,000)

10

Oceanside
to Cameron Lake

10a. Rosewall Creek Provincial Park   Map M10

DIFFICULTY/DISTANCE   Easy/0.3 km, one way

HIGHLIGHTS   Rosewall Creek Provincial Park (54.3 ha), along Highway 19A just south of Fanny Bay, features an easy loop trail along the forested banks of Rosewall Creek. The park is located on Vancouver Island's east coast, in the Oceanside region that includes Parksville and Qualicum Beach. Other small coastal communities to the north—Qualicum Bay, Bowser, Deep Bay and Fanny Bay—are known as "Lighthouse Country" and are also part of Oceanside.

ACCESS

Via Highway 19 (Inland Island Highway)   From Highway 19 turn east at the Exit 87 traffic lights and take Cook Creek Road to Highway 19A. This junction is just north of Deep Bay and Bowser. Turn left (north) and follow Highway 19A about 2 km. Turn right (east) onto Berray Road to the parking area. It is on the road's left (north) side, just before the E & N railway crossing.

Via Highway 19A   From Qualicum Beach drive north through Qualicum Bay, Bowser and Deep Bay to Cook Creek Road. Continue another 2 km north to Berray Road, turn right (east) to the park.

CAUTIONS
- Trails extend along Rosewall Creek beyond the park boundaries. These rougher paths are not maintained.
- Periods of heavy rain or melting snows cause creek waters to rise. Low-lying areas may flood.

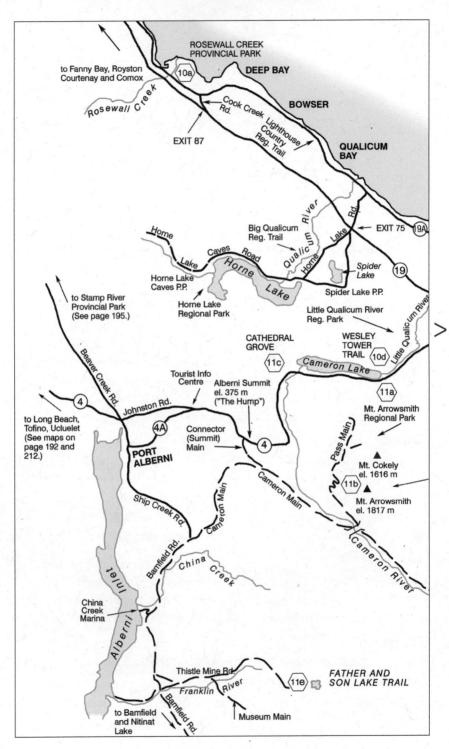

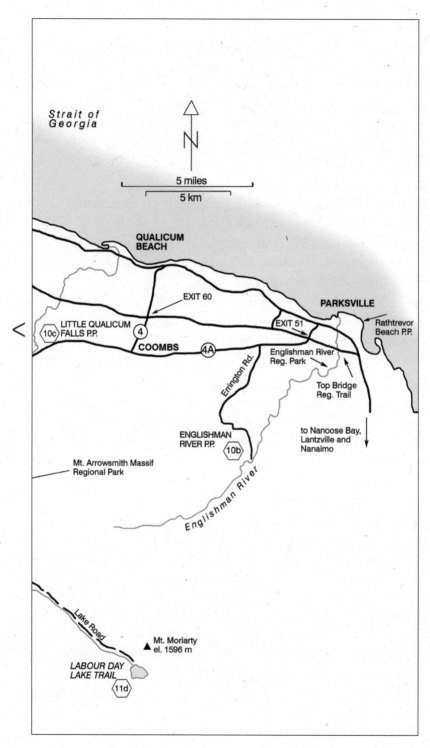

Strait of Georgia

N

5 miles
5 km

QUALICUM BEACH

EXIT 60

PARKSVILLE

LITTLE QUALICUM FALLS P.P.

10c

4

COOMBS

4A

Rathtrevor Beach P.P.

EXIT 51

Englishman River Reg. Park

Top Bridge Reg. Trail

Errington Rd.

ENGLISHMAN RIVER P.P.

10b

to Nanoose Bay, Lantzville and Nanaimo

Mt. Arrowsmith Massif Regional Park

Englishman River

Lake Road

Mt. Moriarty
el. 1596 m

LABOUR DAY LAKE TRAIL

11d

- Stay on designated trails to minimize plant and soil damage. Heed any posted notices.

HIKE DESCRIPTION   From the parking area, short trails lead to the picnic areas and loop through a predominantly big leaf maple and western hemlock forest on both banks of Rosewall Creek. The maple trees are strikingly colourful in the fall. The upstream trail goes under the highway bridge to several beautiful views along the creek. Expect some uneven sections. The trail continues upstream, beyond the park boundaries, to a picturesque waterfall.

WORTH NOTING

- Rosewall Creek is important habitat for spawning coho salmon. This region is a favourite haunt of wintering waterfowl.
- Facilities at this day-use park include picnic tables on both sides of the creek. Pit toilets are close to the parking area. The loop trail to the picnic areas is wheelchair accessible.
- Rosewall Creek Provincial Park was created in 1956 to honour Lieutenant Ian MacDonald, a member of the Canadian Scottish Regiment and once a resident of Fanny Bay. He was killed in action during the WW II Allied invasion of Normandy.

NEARBY

Below are several Regional District of Nanaimo (RDN) parks and trails and two provincial parks close to Rosewall Creek Provincial Park. Consult a detailed road map for directions. Updates on the RDN trails are available at www.rdn.bc.ca.

Lighthouse Country Regional Trail   Currently a RDN work-in-progress, this trail near Bowser and Qualicum Bay features two loops on either side of Nile Creek. The north side loop is 2 km in length; the south side features a 5 km loop. Trails are currently rough and undeveloped and the bridging of Nile Creek remains incomplete. A planned hiker/biker bridge will link the two sections. Access to the Lighthouse Country Trail's north end is at Bowser's Wildwood Community Park. The south end is reached off Highway 19 via Charlton Drive and Linx Road. Park near the cul-de-sac at the end of Linx Road. Vehicles are prohibited beyond the parking area. Hike across the railway tracks and down the woodlot road and watch for signs on the left that pinpoint the trailhead.

Big Qualicum River Department of Fisheries and Oceans (DFO) Trail   This relatively level trail starts at Qualicum Bay's Big Qualicum

River Hatchery and follows a gravel service road along the Big Qualicum River's northwest side. The RDN warns that the trail, which runs approximately 10 km upriver, ends before it reaches Horne Lake Caves Road. The terminus is a large, yellow gate. The trail is an excellent route from which to view spawning fall salmon. The trailhead is at the hatchery on Fisheries Road, accessed via Horne Lake Road, off Highway 19A. Allot some time to visit the Big Qualicum River Salmon Hatchery. Contact Fisheries and Oceans Canada at www.pac.dfo-mpo.gc.ca for more information.

Spider Lake Provincial Park (65 ha) is accessed from Highway 19 (Exit 75) or Highway 19A and Horne Lake Road. Follow the park signposts. From the parking area, short, easy trails lead to several picnic sites on the shores of Spider Lake. This day-use park is popular with swimmers and paddlers.

Horne Lake Regional Park Nestled at Horne Lake's west end, the RDN's Horne Lake Regional Park (109 ha) has over 5 km of easy lakeshore and river hiking and walking. The campground features over 80 campsites in two separate lakeside locations, picnic tables, a boat launch and pit toilets. There are no electrical hookups or showers. Summer adventure camps and family retreats are offered. Contact the RDN at www.rdn.bc.ca for more information on campground fees and seasonal rates.

The Horne Lake Outdoor Centre is located at the park and offers a wide variety of outdoor programs for schools and groups. Beginners can learn basic skills for rappelling, caving, paddling or camping. Among the seasonal programs are a limited number of Cave Rescue Workshops that allow participants the chance to train with members of the British Columbia Cave Rescue Society. For current listings of available visitor programs and reservation policies please contact www.hornelake.com.

Access to Horne Lake Regional Park from Highways 19 (Exit 75) and 19A is via Horne Lake Road, then Horne Lake Caves Road. The latter is a narrow, bumpy, gravel artery that is often used by logging trucks. Watch for and follow the blue park signposts to the lake's west end.

Horne Lake Caves Provincial Park (158 ha), near Horne Lake's west end about 12 km west of Highway 19, is a prime destination for spelunkers (cavers) all year long. Two small caves are open to the public for self-guided explorations. Seasonal guided tours of the larger cave systems range from easy family outings to more lengthy, advanced forays to underground waterfalls. Some tours involve rappelling. Helmet and map rentals are available.

Children under five years of age are not permitted on cave tours. Due to uneven terrain, persons with limited mobility or the very old may find the trails difficult to traverse. All visitors should wear sturdy footwear and warm clothing. Temperature in the caves stays around eight degrees Celsius, even when summer swimmers are cooling off in Horne Lake, a short distance away. Except for the Summer Family Cavern Tours, which run on a first-come, first-served basis, reservations are required for all other cave tours. Contact BC Parks or www.hornelake.com for more details on seasonal guided cave tours, fees and reservations, safety precautions and park regulations.

Access to the park as for Horne Lake Regional Park, then continue another 1 km to the main parking area. The caves are reached by crossing the Big Qualicum River footbridge to the Caving Centre and kiosk. From here a 1.3 km riverside trail winds to several of the park's caves.

ADDITIONAL INFORMATION
www.env.gov.bc.ca/bcparks BC Parks
Refer to NTS 92F/7 (1:50,000)

10b. Englishman River Falls Provincial Park
Maps M10, M10B

DIFFICULTY/DISTANCE   Easy/2 km loop

HIGHLIGHTS   Englishman River Falls Provincial Park (97 ha) has over 3 km of hiking trails, including a spectacular loop trail that wanders along the Englishman River and beside a river canyon to viewpoints near two boisterous waterfalls.

ACCESS   Along Highway 19 (Inland Island Highway) take the Port Alberni turnoff (Exit 51) to Highway 4A. Head 3 km west on Highway 4A toward Port Alberni and watch for the signposted Englishman River Falls Park turn at Errington Road. Swing left (south) and follow Errington Road for 8 km to the parking area where there is room for over 100 vehicles. Daily parking fees apply.

CAUTIONS
- Avoid the dangerously steep and slippery river banks. Stay on designated trails at all times to protect fragile vegetation and soil structure.
- Swimming is allowed only in the pool below the Lower Falls. Closures may be imposed during high river flows. Obey all public safety notices.
- No fishing is permitted within park boundaries.

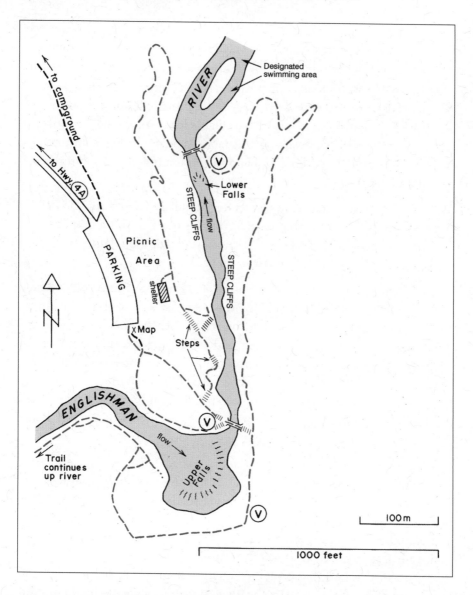

HIKE DESCRIPTION From the parking area near the campground hike in either direction to loop along both sides of the Englishman River to the Upper Falls and the Lower Falls. The trail crosses the river twice. Stop on either of the bridges for breathtaking sights of the Englishman River. When the river runs high, roiling waters plunge through deep, rocky gorges. Allow 45 minutes to one hour to complete the loop hike. Another hiking option is to explore the trail that winds upriver from the Upper Falls to more viewpoints.

WORTH NOTING

- Park trees include Douglas-fir, arbutus, hemlock, maple and western red cedar. The forest floor is carpeted with delicate ferns, moss and many seasonal wildflowers.

- Detailed park trail maps are posted near the information shelters. A large day-use area with a river viewing platform sits adjacent to the camping area. Fresh tap water is available seasonally. Other facilities include over 100 campsites, picnic tables, a picnic shelter, a flush toilet building near the parking area and various pit toilets situated through-out the park.

NEARBY Listed below are several Regional District of Nanaimo (RDN) parks and trails and a popular provincial park. Consult a detailed area road map for concise directions to these areas. Additional information on the RDN trails is available at www.rdn.bc.ca.

Rathtrevor Beach Provincial Park Parksville's Rathtrevor Beach Provincial Park (347 ha), off Highway 19A just east of the Englishman River bridge, features an expansive sandy beach. At lowest tide it is possible to walk this beautiful strand for almost 2 km. Over 5 km of shady trails twist through the park's upland forest. Most of the trails are wheelchair accessible. This area is great for birdwatching and a prime destination for observing the annual spring brant migration. The park's full-service campground fills up over the summer. Contact BC Parks for current camping and day-use parking fees, policies and reservation information.

Top Bridge Trail and Park From Rathtrevor Beach Provincial Park the easy *Top Bridge Trail* extends 5 km via roads and trails to *Top Bridge Park* (6 ha), west of Highway 19's Exit 46 just south of Parksville. There are numerous access points en route. Sections of the trail pass through private property. Please respect the privacy of area residents.

   Top Bridge Park has a picturesque river canyon, a swimming hole, petroglyphs and a network of trails designed specifically for mountain bikers. A park highlight is the Englishman River suspension bridge that links to Englishman River Regional Park. Road access is at the end of Allsbrook Road, reached via Bellevue Road off Highway 4A. Park near the red gate and hike down into the river valley. Top Bridge Park is also accessed from the end of Chattell Road, via Kaye Road off Highway 4A. Further details are available at www.city.parksville.bc.ca.

Englishman River lower falls. JOYCE FOLBIGG

Englishman River Regional Park   Acquired by the RDN, the Nature Trust of BC and their partners, Englishman River Regional Park (207 ha) and Conservation Area protects important wildlife and salmon habitat in and around the Englishman River. A community salmon hatchery is located within the park, near Middlegate Road. Unofficial trails exist. Future plans include careful trail improvements and the eventual creation of linear routes to connect to other municipal and regional parks. Access is via the Top Bridge Trail or at the end of Allsbrook Road, reached via Bellevue Road off Highway 4A. The park's west side is accessed at the end of Middlegate Road, reached via Leffler, Ruffles and Bellevue roads off Highway 4A.

ADDITIONAL INFORMATION
www.env.gov.bc.ca/bcparks (BC Parks)
Refer to NTS 92F/1 and 92F/8 (1:50,000)

10c. Little Qualicum Falls Provincial Park
Maps M10, M10C

DIFFICULTY/DISTANCE   Easy to moderate/4 km loop

HIGHLIGHTS   Little Qualicum Falls Provincial Park (440 ha) is a popular hiking and camping destination. Several trails lead to rocky gorges and a boisterous set of waterfalls on the Little Qualicum River. The park has 6 km of interesting trails and features a seasonal, serviced campsite with an adventure playground for children. Park boundaries incorporate Cameron Lake's south side and include two delightful lakeside picnic sites along Highway 4.

ACCESS   South of Parksville, at the Highway 19A junction, stay on Highway 19 (Inland Island Highway) for 14 km and take the Qualicum Beach/Port Alberni exit to Highway 4. Turn west onto Highway 4 and continue just over 9 km to the park entrance. Watch for park signposts 2 km and 400 m before the highway cutoff. Turn right and take the park access road 1.3 km to the large parking lot. Just west of the park's service road, but before the bigger main parking lot, watch for two small parking areas on the left side of the park entrance road. Trails from here lead almost directly to the upper falls. Some park trails and other facilities are wheelchair accessible.

CAUTIONS
- Read and follow all posted warnings and notices. Stay behind fences and guardrails. Little Qualicum River has two waterfalls. In other spots, the river churns through rocky chutes and creates treacherous currents. Keep back from potentially slippery river banks and cliff edges. Closely supervise all children.
- For public safety, swimming is prohibited downstream from the upper falls, north to the park boundary. BC Parks does not recommend river swimming elsewhere in the park. The park's Cameron Lake picnic site is the safest location for swimmers.
- While some park trails are relatively flat, others cross uneven terrain. Wear proper footwear.
- Stay on designated trails to avoid trampling delicate soil structure and vegetation.
- Carry water. Treat, filter or boil all river water.

Map M10C   Little Qualicum Falls

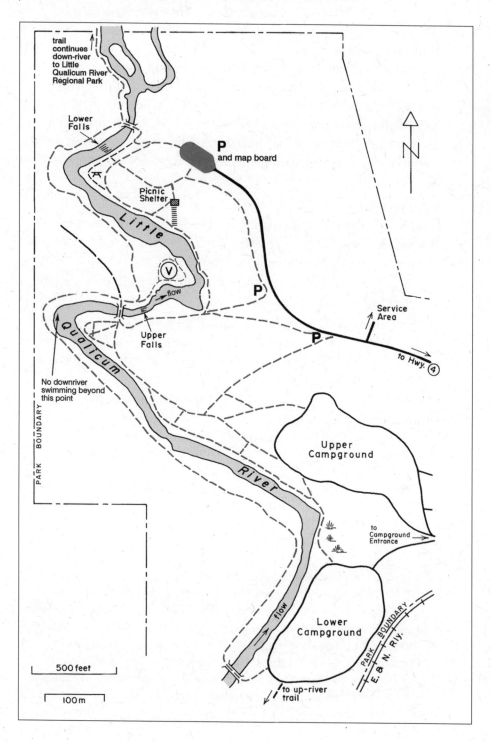

trail continues down-river to Little Qualicum River Regional Park

Lower Falls

P and map board

Picnic Shelter

Little

V

flow

Upper Falls

P

Qualicum

Service Area

to Hwy. ④

No downriver swimming beyond this point

PARK BOUNDARY

River

Upper Campground

to Campground Entrance

500 feet

100 m

flow

Lower Campground

PARK BOUNDARY

E. & N. Rly.

to up-river trail

HIKE DESCRIPTION Starting from either the main parking area or the campgrounds to the south, it is possible to follow well marked trails along one bank of the Little Qualicum River and return on the other. This enjoyable loop hike accesses two lovely waterfalls and several river viewpoints. A popular viewing area is perched on the river's west bank, a little downstream from the upper falls. Allow about 40 minutes to complete a loop hike. Remember to spend some time exploring the numerous side trails that intersect the shadowy forest closer to the campsites. Incorporate these paths into a riverside trail to create your own circle hike.

WORTH NOTING

- Area trails run through a mature Douglas-fir forest interspersed with stands of second growth trees. Trail improvements include stone steps, wooden stairs and bridges at river crossings.
- A developed trail links Little Qualicum Falls Provincial Park with the nearby Little Qualicum River Regional Park. See below.
- The Cameron Lake picnic site is along Highway 4, 4.3 km west from the park's main entrance road. The Beaufort picnic site is approximately 2.5 km west. Both day-use locations are on Cameron Lake's south side. Facilities include picnic tables and pit toilets.
- Cameron Lake (477 ha) is bordered by steep mountains. Area topography and frequent, steady winds create ideal conditions for wind surfers. This deep, narrow lake is one of only a few on Vancouver Island to contain brown trout.

NEARBY

Little Qualicum River Regional Park (44 ha) protects a unique river corridor just downstream from Little Qualicum Falls Provincial Park. Informal, rough trails and routes exist along both sides of the river.

LITTLE QUALICUM FALLS PROVINCIAL PARK has a serviced campground with 94 campsites. There are two separate camping areas. Pumped water is available during peak operating times. Other facilities include a covered picnic area, picnic tables, a playground for kids, pit and flush toilets, and information signposts. Fires are permitted at designated campsites only. Seasonal fire closures may apply. The campsite fills up early over the summer. Contact BC Parks for information on available park services and fees, opening hours, reservations, interpretive programs and current park policies.

A maintained trail connects the park with Little Qualicum Falls Provincial Park. Exercise caution when exploring the unofficial trails in this region. This undeveloped Regional District of Nanaimo (RDN) park can be reached from Highway 19A. Take Bayliss and Corscan roads to the Meadowood Way trailhead. Access is also possible from a maze of secondary and logging roads branching off Highway 4. For more details contact the RDN at www.rdn.bc.ca.

Wesley Tower Trail This steep trail begins along Highway 4, just east of Cameron Lake. The viewpoints from the Wesley Ridge are highlights. See below.

Historic Arrowsmith (CPR Regional) Trail This challenging RDN trail begins directly opposite the Cameron Lake picnic site and climbs to the site of an old ski hill, in behind Mount Cokely. See page 172.

ADDITIONAL INFORMATION
www.env.gov.bc.ca/bcparks (BC Parks)
Refer to NTS 92F/7 (1:50,000)

10d. Wesley Tower Trail   Maps M10, M10D, M11A

DIFFICULTY/DISTANCE   Strenuous/2 km, one way

HIGHLIGHTS   The steep, challenging Wesley Tower Trail begins near Cameron Lake's eastern fringe and climbs up to the bluffs atop a high ridge. Hikers are rewarded with exceptional viewpoints of Cameron Lake and the surrounding mountains.

ACCESS   From Highway 19 (Inland Island Highway) or Highway 19A in Qualicum Beach, take Highway 4 towards Port Alberni. About 3 km past the entrance to Little Qualicum Falls Provincial Park, watch closely for a small roadside pulloff on the highway's north (right) side. This parking spot is between the highway bridges over Lockwood and McBey creeks. If you reach Chalet Road or the Cameron Lake picnic site just to the west, you have travelled too far.

CAUTIONS
- Anyone unfamiliar with semi-wilderness or wilderness hiking should travel with someone who knows the area well. Consider going on a scheduled hike with a local outdoors group.
- Use extreme caution when parking along Highway 4.
- Carry adequate water.

- In some places the Wesley Tower Trail is indistinct. Look for ribbons in the trees to assist in finding your way. There are numerous, unmarked old roads and trails near the communications tower.
- Tread carefully as you descend some sections of the trail. It is often trickier hiking down a steep grade than it is going up.

HIKE DESCRIPTION   From the roadside parking area along Highway 4, cross the Little Qualicum River on the railway trestle and continue about 200 m. Watch for the trailhead on the right (north). The trail climbs sharply through a second growth forest and eventually reaches an area of bluffs. The seemingly endless ascent finally ends at the top of the bluffs where an excellent viewpoint overlooks Cameron Lake. From here, the trail is less steep and follows the ridge northwest along the bluffs to run through old growth Douglas-fir.

An old road near the top leads to the telecommunications tower. From this vantage spot you can see Qualicum Beach, Parksville and other parts of Vancouver Island's east coast. A little exploring near the summit will reveal additional viewpoints offering glimpses of Mount Arrowsmith and Horne and Spider lakes. Allow about 2 hours hiking time, one way.

WORTH NOTING
- A welcoming resting bench is situated at the bluff's west-facing viewpoint, halfway up the Wesley Tower Trail. Named the Forever Tuesday bench, it honours deceased members of the Tuesday Walkers Club. This Port Alberni hiking group has existed for over 40 years.
- Stands of arbutus and hairy manzanita are common near the bluffs.
- Experienced hikers can extend their hike by following a 2 km route west along the Wesley Ridge to a high point of land that offers a spectacular 360 degree panorama. Route finding skills may be required.

NEARBY   Little Qualicum Falls Provincial Park, Historic Arrowsmith (CPR Regional) Trail and Cathedral Grove (See pages 166, 172 and 183 respectively.)

ADDITIONAL INFORMATION
www.justabunchahikers.ca (Port Alberni Hiking Group)
www.avcoc.com (Alberni Valley Chamber of Commerce)
Refer to NTS 92F/7 (1:50,000)

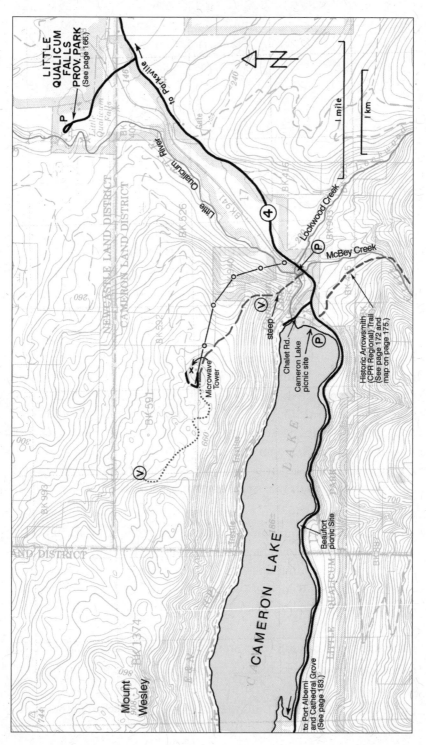

LITTLE
QUALICUM
FALLS
PROV. PARK
(See page 166.)

P

Little Qualicum Falls

Little Qualicum River

to Parksville

BK 900

gate

BK 941

17

BK 526

4

Lockwood Creek

BK 416

BK 903

P

McBey Creek

260

BK 592

V

steep

V

Chalet Rd.

Cameron Lake
picnic site

P

Historic Arrowsmith
(CPR Regional) Trail
(See page 172 and
map on page 175.)

BK 591

x

Microwave
Tower

660

300

700

CAMERON LAKE

86

Beaufort
picnic Site

NEWCASTLE LAND DISTRICT

CAMERON LAND DISTRICT

AND DISTRICT

Mount
Wesley

BK 1374

098

744

to Port Alberni
and Cathedral Grove
(See page 183.)

1 mile

1 km

11

Cameron Lake to Port Alberni

11a. Historic Arrowsmith (CPR Regional) Trail
Maps M10, M10D, M11A

DIFFICULTY/DISTANCE Moderate to strenuous/7 km and 10 km loops

HIGHLIGHTS Historic Arrowsmith Trail, known also as the CPR Regional Trail, dates back to 1912 and is likely the oldest intact trail on Vancouver Island. The steep, well-defined Regional District of Nanaimo (RDN) route passes many memorable viewpoints as it gains elevation to the site of a former ski facility on Mount Cokely (1616 m), north of Mount Arrowsmith (1817 m). The trail features an upper loop and is the hiking gateway to Mount Arrowsmith Regional Park, adjacent to Mount Arrowsmith Massif Regional Park. The trailhead is along Highway 4, near Cameron Lake's east end. You can also reach the upper loop trails via rugged logging roads that snake up the Cameron River Valley.

CAUTIONS
- **These challenging mountain trails are best suited for fit, experienced hikers.** Fog, rain and low cloud may swirl in unexpectedly. In these conditions route finding skills are an asset. If you are unfamiliar with semi-wilderness or wilderness hiking, travel with someone who knows the area well. Consider joining a guided hike offered by the RDN or a local club.
- Exercise extreme caution when crossing Highway 4, near Cameron Lake.
- Expect numerous creek crossings, uneven terrain and muddy, slippery sections. Wear sturdy footwear.
- Please stay on designated trails to minimize erosion, which happens

quickly in steep terrain. Do not cut corners on switchbacks.

- Carry adequate water. Boil, treat or filter all creek water.
- Be ready for sudden adverse weather. Bring extra food, warm clothing and raingear.
- The region is habitat to bear and cougar. Be alert when hiking.
- Secure your vehicle and remove all valuables.

MAIN ACCESS

Via Highway 4 and Cameron Lake   From Highway 19 (Inland Island Highway) take the Qualicum Beach/Port Alberni cutoff (Exit 60) to Highway 4. Turn west onto Highway 4 and continue approximately 13.5 km to Cameron Lake's east end. Just past Chalet Road swing right to the parking area at the Cameron Lake picnic site. The Historic Arrowsmith Trail begins as an old road on the south side of Highway 4, opposite the picnic area.

HIKE DESCRIPTION

Historic Arrowsmith (CPR Regional) Trail   Moderate to strenuous/10 km loop: From the Highway 4 trailhead follow the old road, marked with temporary signage, about 1 km to a trail sign and map. A hike highlight is ahead—the McBey Creek bridge and nearby waterfall. The bridge was reconstructed in 2004. McBey Creek is also known as Pipeline Creek. There is a second waterfall and viewpoint farther ahead.

It is a steady, moderately steep climb from the Cameron Lake to where the trail divides, about 1.5 hours from the trailhead. The left fork is called the East (Arrowsmith) Loop. In the 1950s, MacMillan Bloedel, the local logging company at the time, relocated a portion of the Historic Arrowsmith Trail in anticipation of McBey Creek logging, which never

THE CANADIAN PACIFIC RAILWAY opened what they called the CPR Trail in 1912 so that their guests could stay at the Cameron Lake Chalet and travel on horseback up to "The Hut" at the 1400 m level. The switchbacking grade was for pack horses. The old chalet and hut have gone, but horses were still going up decades later. In 1998, lower portions of the Historic Arrowsmith Trail were heli-logged. The following summer the logging company cleared debris and repaired damaged trailbeds. Later, major erosion resulted due to lack of forest cover. The FMCBC repaired this damage through a great expenditure of volunteer labour. The RDN now maintains the trail and has a lease for it from private forest companies, on whose land the trail passes.

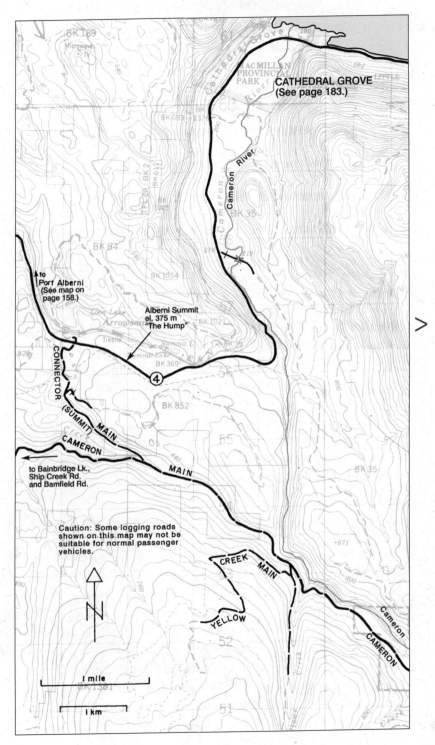

CATHEDRAL GROVE
(See page 183.)

to
Port Alberni
(See map on
page 158.)

Alberni Summit
el. 375 m
"The Hump"

④

CONNECTOR

(SUMMIT) MAIN

CAMERON MAIN

to Bainbridge Lk.,
Ship Creek Rd.
and Bamfield Rd.

Caution: Some logging roads
shown on this map may not be
suitable for normal passenger
vehicles.

N

CREEK MAIN

YELLOW

Cameron
CAMERON

1 mile

1 km

Map M11A   Mount Arrowsmith

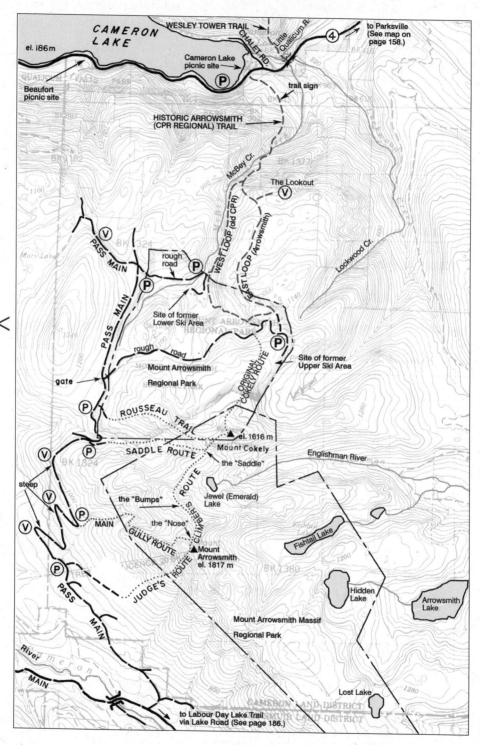

CAMERON LAKE

el. 186m

WESLEY TOWER TRAIL

CHALET RD.

Little Qualicum R.

to Parksville
(See map on
page 158.)

Beaufort
picnic site

Cameron Lake
picnic site

trail sign

HISTORIC ARROWSMITH
(CPR REGIONAL) TRAIL

McBey Cr.

The Lookout

Lockwood Cr.

PASS MAIN

WEST LOOP (old CPR)

EAST LOOP (Arrowsmith)

rough
road

Site of former
Lower Ski Area

rough   road

ORIGINAL COKELY ROUTE

Site of former
Upper Ski Area

gate

Mount Arrowsmith

Regional Park

ROUSSEAU TRAIL

el. 1616 m

Mount Cokely

the "Saddle"

Englishman River

SADDLE ROUTE

ROUTE

Jewel (Emerald)
Lake

steep

the "Bumps"

CLIMBER'S

the "Nose"

Fishtail Lake

MAIN

GULLY ROUTE

JUDGE'S ROUTE

Mount
Arrowsmith
el. 1817 m

Hidden
Lake

Arrowsmith
Lake

PASS MAIN

Mount Arrowsmith Massif

Regional Park

River   meron

MAIN

Lost Lake

CAMERON LAND DISTRICT
MUIR LAND DISTRICT

to Labour Day Lake Trail
via Lake Road (See page 186.)

happened. The original trail along McBey Creek, now known as the West (Old CPR) Loop, remained intact. Today, both trails form a popular loop hike on Mount Cokely's northern flank.

The *West (Old CPR) Loop* follows the old route up McBey Creek. There are glimpses of rushing rapids and clamorous waterfalls en route. The trail hugs the creek all the way to a disused lower ski hill, within the boundaries of Mount Arrowsmith Regional Park. See Worth Noting on page 178. An old spur road (formerly P60) off Pass Main in the Cameron River Valley provides a second access point to the Historic Arrowsmith Trail. See McBey Creek Upper Access below. From the former lower ski area, the trail climbs south and then east up the slope to join the East Loop at its highest point, just below the road to the defunct upper ski hill.

If you turn left (east) at the trail junction onto the *East (Arrowsmith) Loop*, watch for a marked side path that leads to the Lookout, a magnificent Cameron Lake, Strait of Georgia and Gulf Islands viewpoint. Here, in season, clumps of penstemon and other sub-alpine flowers flourish. Hiking time from Cameron Lake to the Lookout is about 2 hours, one way. Past the Lookout the trail is less steep and passes several tarns and ponds as it climbs south. The high point is below the access road to the old upper ski hill, also within Mount Arrowsmith Regional Park. Both the East and West loops are easy to follow and merge via a connector trail at their upper terminus near the upper ski hill road. A return loop hike takes 6 to 7 hours and makes for a long day. From the ski road it is possible to hike and scramble along what was the *Original Cokely Route* and climb farther up Mount Cokely's north side toward the summit. The RDN strongly emphasizes that this route to Mount Cokely is best suited for fit, well equipped, experienced hikers only.

ACCESS

To Upper McBey Creek via Highway 4 At the Alberni Summit (The Hump) along Highway 4, just east of Port Alberni, turn south onto Connector (Summit) Main and drive 2.7 km to the Cameron Main T-junction. It is a steep descent into the Cameron River Valley. Note that Connector (Summit) Main is occasionally closed due to active logging. An alternative route, via Ship Creek Road is described on page 177. Both logging mainlines are subject to access restrictions due to logging activities or fire hazard.

Turn left (east) onto Cameron Main, travel 7.2 km and cross the Cameron River bridge to the river's north side. Just 0.5 km ahead is the Pass Main junction. Reset your vehicle's trip meter to zero and swing left

Mount Arrowsmith saddle. Port Alberni in the background. Peter Rothermel

(north) onto Pass Main. The mainline begins a long, steady climb and negotiates sharp switchbacks to eventually level out just north of Mount Cokely. Avoid any branch roads on the way up, including the old upper ski hill road, until you reach the side road at Km 10.2 (formerly P60), which accesses to the Historic Arrowsmith Trail. Park near the mainline or drive as far as you can to road's end near McBey Creek and former location of the lower ski area. To hike the mostly downhill grade along the access road takes 20 minutes.

ALTERNATE ACCESS

To McBey Creek from Port Alberni via Ship Creek Road: In Port Alberni, from Highway 4 or Highway 4A, follow the signs for Bamfield and China Creek Marina. This will lead to the southern outskirts of town and the corner of Anderson and Ship Creek roads. Continue another 3.5 km on Ship Creek Road to where Cameron Main enters on the left. Bamfield Road is to the right. Turn left and head 8.5 km east to where Connector Main joins Cameron Main. From here, continue east as per McBey Creek Upper Access above. See map on page 158.

WARNING   Both McBey Creek access routes involve travel along gravel logging roads. Loaded logging trucks and industrial traffic may be frequent. Read Forest Road Travel on page 19 carefully. Sections of Pass Main and roads closer to the trailhead may be rough and not suitable for all vehicles.

HIKE DESCRIPTION

Upper McBey Creek Loop Strenuous/7 km loop: Cross McBey Creek to its east side and the West (Old CPR) Loop of the Historic Arrowsmith Trail. There is no bridge here and fording the creek can be boot-soaking if its waters are running high. Turn right (south) and hike upstream to where the well-used West Loop turns east. Follow markers up to the site of the former upper ski area. A connector trail below the old ski hill road links to the East (Arrowsmith) Loop. Look for trail markers and hike north along the East Loop to the Lookout. The trail then turns west and drops into the McBey Creek Valley and the junction with the West Loop. Head left (south) at the junction and follow McBey Creek upstream to the starting point. Hike the Upper McBey Loop in a clockwise or counter clockwise direction. Whichever route you choose, it avoids the climb up the McBey Creek Valley from Cameron Lake. Allow 4.5 to 5 hours to complete the loop.

WORTH NOTING

- Hiking times will vary according to weather, trail conditions and a person's fitness level.
- From Cameron Lake to the old upper ski area expect an elevation gain of 1000 m. The trail's lower reaches cross (with permission) private forestland.
- Interim signage along the Historic Arrowsmith Trail pinpoints key road junctions and trailheads. Look for diamond-shaped markers. The RDN plans more permanent signage.
- Mount Arrowsmith Regional Park (516 ha) includes alpine habitat on Mount Cokely's north side and sits adjacent to Mount Arrowsmith Massif Regional Park. (See page 182.) Administered by the Alberni-Clayoquot Regional District (ACRD), the park once featured a ski operation. Note that within the park, off road vehicles (including 4 x 4 trucks, ATVs, dirt bikes and snowmobiles) are not allowed beyond existing park roads or parking areas. For more information contact the ACRD at www.acrd.bc.ca.
- Some mainlines and branch roads in this region are now reactivated (improved and upgraded) to access logging cutblocks. Many routes are being renamed. This book provides area logging road names that have been in regular use for years.
- The *Alberni Valley Trail Guide*, available at the Port Alberni Visitor Info-Centre, contains information on some Mount Arrowmith area trails.

11b. Mount Arrowsmith and Mount Cokely Hiking Routes   Maps M10, M11A

Several long-established Mount Arrowsmith and Mount Cokely trails and routes are reached along Pass Main. These challenging strenuous hikes include the Judge's, Main Gully, Saddle and Rousseau routes. Access as for Upper McBey Creek to the Pass Main/Cameron Main junction. From Cameron Main, turn left (north) onto Pass Main and reset your vehicle's trip meter to zero. See page 176. See also Cautions on page 172.

Mount Arrowsmith

Judge's Route   strenuous/2.5 km, one way: From the Pass Main/ Cameron Main junction climb Pass Main for just under 3 km. Heading up the hill there are four major spur roads on the right (north) side of the mainline. The fourth and last side road, about 0.5 km from the first of a series of four Pass Main switchbacks, is the signposted start of the Judge's Route. A parking area is just ahead, on the left side of Pass Main.

The Judge's Route is the easiest non-technical summer route to Mount Arrowsmith. It is still a strenuous, steep climb through forest and open alpine to the summit. Elevation gain is just over 1,000 m and there is no water en route. The ascent is rewarded by sweeping vistas of the Coast Mountains, the Gulf of Georgia and Strathcona Park's rugged peaks. Members of the Island Mountain Ramblers (a hiking group) discovered this route in the early 1970s. One member was Ralph Hutchinson, who shortly after became a provincial court judge, hence the "Judge's" Route. On the way up look for beautiful yet delicate trailside saprophytes such as Indian pipe and striped coral root. Tread lightly. Allow at least 5 to 6 hours for a return hike.

MOUNT ARROWSMITH was named in honour of Aaron Arrowsmith and his nephew John Arrowsmith, brilliant cartographers of the early 19th century. First Nations people were first into Vancouver Island Mountains. They called Mount Arrowsmith "Sharp Faces" from the Port Alberni side and "The Sleeping Maiden" from the east. Over the years, the character of Mount Arrowsmith has changed considerably. Through logging and development of now-defunct ski areas, much of the old magic is gone. Still, the access roads and trails do lead hikers up to the sub-alpine for hikes on several interconnecting trails and routes.

Mount Arrowsmith, Judge's Route. PETER ROTHERMEL

Main Gully Route (strenuous/2.3 km, one way): The Main Gully Route was the only way to the Arrowsmith summit until the Judge's Route was discovered in the early 1970s. (See page 179.) This popular, though somewhat technical, snow gully route starts along Pass Main, at the fourth and last switchback past the Judge's Route parking area. The route heads southeast and drops down to cross a year round running creek. It then turns east, along the creek's south side, to ascend through a valley of old growth sub-alpine forest. These woodlands are valuable winter habitat for ungulates such as elk and deer.

The route climbs above the tree line to pass three cirques (small, amphitheatre-like valleys) in successive elevation. From the upper cirque, experienced climbers can continue east to access the Climber's Route at a point below the "Nose", a major feature on Mount Arrowsmith. See the Climber's Route on page 181.

Mount Cokely
Saddle Route Strenuous/2 km, one way: From the Pass Main/Cameron Main junction take Pass Main for 7.3 km. After numerous switchbacks and viewpoints the road veers inland to a hairpin corner. The Saddle Route starts here along a marked old spur road on the right.

The Saddle Route ascends a steep valley and parallels a small creek. Expect rocky sections and protruding roots on the way up. The trail threads through sections of bluffs and breaks out from the tree line into open alpine, just below at the Cokely/Arrowsmith col. This area is also known as the "Saddle". Snow patches may linger into late spring. August is when area meadows are ablaze with dazzling wildflowers.

At the saddle, turn north and head up Mount Cokely's west ridge and turn east (with some exposure) to the summit. Retrace your steps or loop back another way by following Mount Cokely's west ridge and the Rousseau Trail. North of the saddle, look for a big cairn with a stick pointing the direction off the ridge. Expect a return hike on the Saddle Route to take 3 to 3.5 hours. A loop hike that incorporates the Rousseau Route will take slightly longer.

From the "Saddle" hikers can travel south along the *Climber's Route* to cross a plateau and then scramble over Mount Arrowsmith's four sub-peaks, known as the "Bumps". A descent from the last bump leads to a small col near the junction with the Main Gully Route, just below the "Nose", an exposed Mount Arrowsmith arete. (See page 175.) The final 60 m pitch up the "Nose" is technical and requires well-honed climbing skills for a roped belay up and a rappel down. There are two bolted belay stations on the "Nose". From the top it is a short scramble to Mount Arrowsmith's summit.

Rousseau Route   Strenuous/2.2 km, one way: From the Pass Main/ Cameron junction, climb Pass Main for just under 8 km and watch for a signposted old road on the right, at the top of a hill, just past a switchback. Park well off to the side of the mainline. The Rousseau Route was constructed sometime prior to WWII. The route was named after Ralph Rousseau, a Port Alberni mountaineer who was killed in 1954 by a fall into a crevasse on Mount Septimus.

The Rousseau Route weaves east through the forest and then steepens as it climbs to Mount Cokely's west ridge. Continue east up the ridge to the junction with the Saddle Route, indicated by a large cairn just north of the Cokely/Arrowsmith col or saddle. Bear left (northeast) and scramble (with some exposure) to the Mount Cokely summit. Allow 4 to 4.5 hours for a return hike. A longer loop hike via the Saddle Route above and the Rousseau Route is possible and involves a 10 minute walk along Pass Main to return to your vehicle. See page 180.

WARNING   Though considered moderately easy summer trails, the Judge's, Saddle and Rousseau routes are deemed technical in the off-season. Over the winter and spring, people must have ice axes and crampons and be experienced with using these tools. As well, they should have avalanche rescue skills training and the tools for self-rescue. Area routes are intended for seasoned hikers and climbers able to safely find their way in sometimes-indistinct alpine terrain. See below for information on guided tours, ideal for inexperience hikers.

NEARBY

Mount Arrowsmith Massif Regional Park (1300 ha) under the jurisdiction of the RDN, was created in 2008 with assistance from the Federation of Mountain Clubs of BC (FMCBC) and the Alpine Club of Canada (ACC). The park protects Mount Cokely and Mount Arrowsmith and nearby alpine lakes and meadows. The pristine lakes include Lost, Hidden, Fishtail and Jewel (Emerald). Lost and Emerald are unofficial names.

The FMCBC from Vancouver Island have maintained trails on the Arrowsmith Massif for decades. Member clubs include the Alberni Valley Outdoors Club, ACC (Vancouver Island Section) and Island Mountain Ramblers. The FMCBC and the ACC have assumed the role of park stewards and are committed to continue trail upgrades and erosion control. Volunteers regularly repair trail damage inflicted by careless or ignorant hikers. Immediate improvements are trailhead and roadside signage and fluorescent diamond-shaped markers along trails and routes. Large "Mount Arrowsmith" signs are now up along Highway 4 and at key logging road junctions. Smaller signs pinpoint popular trailheads. All the roadside markers have a white background with blue stencilled letters.

The RDN, in co-operation with local hikers and mountaineers, offers guided hikes in the Mount Arrowsmith area. Geared towards an introduction to alpine hiking, these are particularly popular with and beneficial to novice hikers. Contact the RDN for seasonal schedules. Updates on the Arrowsmith Massif are available at www.mountainclubs. org or www.mountarrowsmith.org. Additional information on Mount Arrowsmith area trails and technical climbing routes is available from Peter Rothermel at 250-752-2529; e-mail: prother@telus.net.

ADDITIONAL INFORMATION
www.avcoc.com (Alberni Valley Chamber of Commerce)
www.for.gov.bc.ca/dsi (BC Forest Service South Island District)
www.rdn.bc.ca (Regional District of Nanaimo)
www.westernforest.com/wiwag (West Islands Woodlands Community
    Advisory Group)
Refer to NTS 92F/2 and 92F/7 (1:50,000)

11c. Cathedral Grove (MacMillan Provincial Park)
Maps M10, M11A, M11C

DIFFICULTY/DISTANCE   Easy/up to 2 km loop

HIGHLIGHTS   Cathedral Grove (15 ha), part of MacMillan Provincial Park (301 ha), is situated along Cameron Lake's southwest shore. About 10 km west of Little Qualicum Falls Provincial Park, Cathedral Grove features easy loop trails through a majestic old growth forest along the banks of the Cameron River. On both sides of Highway 4, fern-bordered paths guide visitors into the cathedral atmosphere of the Cameron River floodplain. Park trails are open year round.

ACCESS   Just south of Parksville, at the Highway 19A junction, stay on Highway 19 (Inland Island Highway) for 14 km and take the Qualicum Beach/Port Alberni turnoff (Exit 60) to Highway 4. Turn west onto Highway 4 and continue just over 19 km to Cathedral Grove. Parking is available on either side of the highway. Some park trails and facilities are wheelchair accessible.

CAUTIONS
- **The Riverside Trail, a loop path along the river on the park's southeast corner, is currently closed.** High water and flooding have washed away two bridges and obliterated other sections of the trail. Until repairs are made, please avoid this area and comply with all posted notices. Contact BC Parks for updates.
- Be extra cautious and double check for traffic when crossing Highway 4 to access park trails on the other side. This main highway from Parksville to Port Alberni is extremely busy and dangerous, despite a speed limit reduction near the parking areas. Be alert at all times and carefully monitor all children.
- Do not hike the trails in windy, stormy weather. The potential for falling branches poses a public safety hazard.
- Hundreds of thousands of visitors hike the Cathedral Grove trails each year. Stay on marked routes at all times to minimize damage to fragile vegetation and soil structure.
- This is a day-use park. No fires or camping allowed. Smoking is banned anywhere within park boundaries. Cyclists must stay on the roads.

Map M11C Cathedral Grove

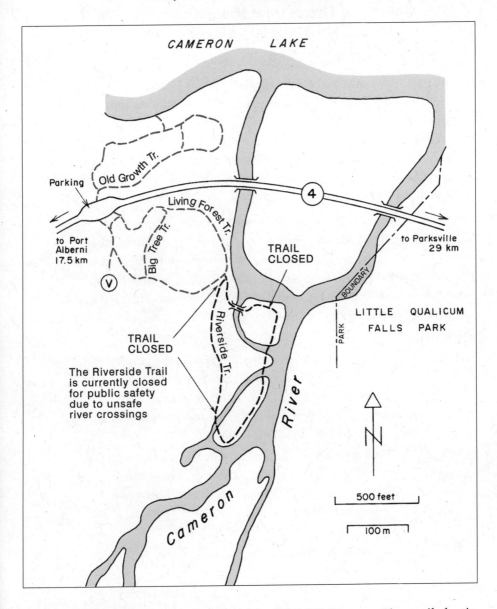

HIKE DESCRIPTIONS   The park's self-guided interpretive trails begin at the parking areas on either side of Highway 4. These are well groomed, obvious paths, with wooden boardwalks over some muddier sections. Allow 15 to 20 minutes to complete any of the loop hikes.

The Old Growth Trail winds through massive western red cedar on the highway's north side. A side path accesses the often windswept shores of

Cameron Lake. On the south side of Highway 4, the *Living Forest Trail* is a popular walk. This loop trail features numerous interpretive signposts that describe the diverse stages of a forest's life. Visitors can see various examples right at trailside. Along the Living Forest Trail, a side path leads to a viewing platform that overlooks a 1997 forest blowdown. The *Big Tree Trail* cuts off the Living Forest Trail and passes some of the park's biggest trees. One mammoth Douglas-fir is over 9 m in circumference. The *Riverside Trail* is currently closed. See Cautions on page 183.

WORTH NOTING

- Cathedral Grove's ancient forest consists primarily of old growth Douglas-fir, western red cedar, grand fir and western hemlock. Some trees are between 500 and 850 years old.

- In the mid-1940s, MacMillan Bloedel's forest magnate H. R. MacMillan donated 136 ha of land to the province, so the area could be preserved in its natural state. Today threats come from river flooding and wash-outs, severe wind storms and patch logging on the park's fringes. Even the advanced age of some trees conspires against them. Weakened and near the end of their natural life cycle, the trees are more susceptible to falling over or to disease.

- In January 1997 a powerful windstorm ripped a swath through the narrow Cameron River Valley creating extensive blowdowns, some as wide as 45 m. Ten per cent of Cathedral Grove trees were damaged and a number of park trails were destroyed. The windthrow left massive trees piled up to resemble a giant's game of pick-up-sticks. An observation platform has been constructed for visitors to view this stark blowdown area.

- Park facilities include interpretive signage, a viewing platform and pit toilets. The latter are located on either side of Highway 4, near the parking areas. A seasonal concession stand operates near the parking lot over the summer.

NEARBY   Historic Arrowsmith (CPR Regional) Trail. See page 172.

ADDITIONAL INFORMATION
www.env.gov.bc.ca/bcparks (BC Parks)
Refer to NTS 92F/7 (1:50,000)

11d. Labour Day Lake Trail   Map M10

DIFFICULTY/DISTANCE   Moderate/0.7 km, one way to lake, 2.6 km lake loop

HIGHLIGHTS   The Labour Day Lake Trail offers hikers the chance to loop around a secluded wilderness lake nestled in the Cameron River Valley. Fringed by old growth trees, the lake is a BC Forest Service (BCFS) Recreation Reserve. For campers there are 3 BCFS user-maintained campsites situated around the lake's perimeter. To get to the trailhead be prepared to travel just under 24 km on area logging roads. But then that is part of the adventure.

ACCESS

Via Highway 4 and Connector (Summit) Main   At the Alberni Summit (The Hump) along Highway 4, just east of Port Alberni, turn south onto Connector (Summit) Main and drive 2.7 km to a T-junction. Turn left (east) onto Cameron Main, travel 7.2 km and cross the Cameron River bridge to the river's north side. Just 0.5 km ahead, Pass Main cuts off to the left. For Labour Day Lake stay east on Cameron Main for another 4.7 km to where the road forks. Avoid the route that cuts off to the right; head straight ahead on Lake Road another 8.5 km to the trailhead.

Indian Pipe.   JOYCE FOLBIGG

Expect many confusing intersections and side roads en route. When in doubt, keep left and stay on the Cameron River's north side. Park in an obvious roadside clearing on the right. The trail, also on the right, begins 50 m up the road. Note that Connector Main may be occasionally closed due to active logging. At these times, use the alternate access via Ship Creek Road. Both routes are subject to access restrictions due to active logging or fire hazard.

ALTERNATE ACCESS

From Port Alberni via Ship Creek Road   In Port Alberni, from Highway 4 or Highway 4A, follow the signs for Bamfield and China Creek Marina. This will lead to the southern outskirts of town and the corner of Anderson and Ship Creek roads. Continue another 3.5 km on Ship Creek Road to where Cameron Main enters on the left. Bamfield Road is to the right. Turn left onto Cameron Main and head 8.5 km east to where Connector (Summit) Main joins the mainline. From here, continue as for Connector Main Access on page 186.

CAUTIONS

- Getting to the Labour Day Lake Trail involves travel along gravel logging roads. Loaded logging trucks and industrial traffic may be frequent. Read Forest Road Travel on page 19 carefully. Sections of the backroads closer to the trailhead may be rough and not suitable for all vehicles. If you are unfamiliar with wilderness hiking or gravel backroading, go with someone who knows the area well.
- The trail crosses numerous creeks; some with wooden bridges in various states of repair. Use caution at all times.
- Expect some uneven terrain, muddy sections and slippery, deteriorating bridges. Wear sturdy footwear.
- Carry adequate water. Boil, treat or filter all lake water.
- No motorized vehicles are permitted near Labour Day Lake to avoid potential damage to sensitive vegetation, trails and bridges.

HIKE DESCRIPTION   From the trailhead on Lake Road, the trail heads downhill through a logged off area towards Labour Day Lake (70.8 ha). At the lake you can go in either direction and hike the lake perimeter to several user-maintained wilderness campsites. There are plenty of creek crossings and bridges along the way. Allow 20 minutes hiking time to the lake and an additional 2 to 2.5 hours to loop around the lake. Hiking times will vary according to weather, trail conditions and a person's fitness level.

- There is a wetland and pebble beach at Labour Day Lake's south end.
- This area is habitat for Roosevelt Elk.
- Labour Day Lake is a favourite destination for hike-in anglers. The relatively short trail to the lake makes it feasible to portage a canoe or carry a float tube in.
- Pass Main is a steep artery that switchbacks up the flanks of Mount Arrowsmith and Mount Cokely to Mount Arrowsmith Regional Park. Pass Main provides hikers with an alternate access to the Historic Arrowsmith (CPR Regional) Trail. See page 172.
- Some mainlines and branch roads in this region are now reactivated (improved and upgraded) to access logging cutblocks. Many routes are being renamed. This book provides area logging road names that have been in regular use for years.

NEARBY

Mount Moriarty (1596 m) is reached via a rugged, steep route that begins at the BCFS campsite on Labour Day Lake's east side. The trail climbs to a lofty bluff that provides striking vistas of the surrounding area. Experienced hikers travel further along the ridge to the summit. Hiking distance from Labour Day Lake: 2 km, one way. Route finding skills may be required.

ADDITIONAL INFORMATION

www.for.gov.bc.ca/dsi (BC Forest Service South Island District)
www.westernforest.com/wiwag (West Islands Woodlands Community Advisory Group)
Refer to NTS 92F/2 and 92F/7 (1:50,000)

11e. Father and Son Lake Trail Map M10

DIFFICULTY/DISTANCE Moderate/1.5 km, one way

HIGHLIGHTS Hikers, anglers and wilderness campers alike make the effort to hike up to Father and Son Lake (13 ha), southeast of Port Alberni. Their reward is a magical setting that includes a secluded high-elevation lake, a BC Forest Service (BCFS) wilderness campsite, pristine old growth forest and lofty mountain ridges that abound with spring wildflowers.

ACCESS In Port Alberni, from Highway 4 or Highway 4A, follow the signs for Bamfield and China Creek Marina. This will lead to the southern outskirts of town and the corner of Anderson and Ship Creek roads. Continue another 3.5 km on Ship Creek Road to the junction with Cameron Main, a logging mainline, that comes in on the left. From this point, Cameron Main provides alternate access to the Mount Arrowsmith area and the Labour Day Lake Trail. See pages 176 and 186 respectively. Turn right (west) at the signposted junction onto Bamfield Road, reset your vehicle's trip meter to zero and head towards Bamfield.

The road to the right at Km 6 is the marked entrance to China Creek Marina. Stay on the Bamfield Road and at Km 9.7 cut left onto Museum Main. (If you miss this turn it is possible to take Museum Hookup at Km 11.2 and link back up to Museum Main.) Drive a little under 4 km on Museum Main and swing left onto Thistle Mine Road. Road upgrades make it easier to continue to the end of the road, approximately 8 km from Museum Main cutoff. Look for flagging marking the trailhead on the road's east (right) side.

CAUTIONS
- Getting to Father and Son Lake involves travel along gravel logging roads. Loaded logging trucks and industrial traffic may be frequent. Read Forest Road Travel on page 19 carefully. Some area mainlines have been improved to facilitate logging. Sections of these backroads may be seasonally rough and not suitable for all vehicles. If you are unfamiliar with wilderness hiking or gravel backroading, go with someone who knows the area well.
- Use exteme caution when travelling the narrow road near the cliffs beyond the China Creek Marina turn.
- Be ready for capricious weather. Bring extra food, warm clothing and raingear.

- Expect uneven terrain, protruding roots and branches, muddy sections and slippery creek crossings. Wear sturdy footwear.
- Carry your own water. Boil, treat or filter all lake water.

HIKE DESCRIPTION From its start on Thistle Mine Road, the Father and Son Lake Trail begins a steady climb, mainly through a shady, old growth forest. The route is well marked, so getting lost is not a worry. The trail levels off a bit but remains steep as it snakes another 1 km to serene Father and Son Lake, nestled in a mountain bowl. Allot some time to savour the vistas on the way up to the lake. A trail of sorts curves around the lake but many parts are rough and deteriorating. Take advantage of the opportunity to explore and scramble around the surrounding ridges where the views are magnificent. Allow 45 minutes hiking time to reach the lake, one way.

WORTH NOTING
- Father and Son Lake is a popular destination for hike-in anglers. Rainbow trout inhabit the lake.
- The BCFS wilderness campsite at Father and Son Lake features 3 rustic sites, fringed by old growth amabalis fir, hemlock and western red cedar. There are no facilities. Practise low-impact camping.
- This region is home to cougar and black bears. Be alert while hiking.
- China Creek Marina, operated by the Port Alberni Port Authority, features a large campground that caters to Alberni Inlet saltwater anglers. There are 250 campsites (many fully serviced) and moorage for 250 vessels. Contact 250-723-9812 for current information.
- Some mainlines and branch roads in this region are now reactivated (improved and upgraded) to access logging cutblocks. Many routes are being renamed. This book provides area logging road names that have been in regular use for years.

NEARBY Labour Day Lake Trail (See page 186.)

ADDITIONAL INFORMATION
www.for.gov.bc.ca/dsi (BC Forest Service South Island District)
www.westernforest.com/wiwag (West Islands Woodlands
   Community Advisory Group)
Refer to NTS 92F/2 (1:50,000)

12

Port Alberni to the West Coast

12a. Log Train Trail Regional Park   Map M12

DIFFICULTY/DISTANCE   Easy to moderate/3 km to 21 km, one way

HIGHLIGHTS   Port Alberni's Log Train Trail Regional Park is a multi-use trail system popular with hikers, joggers, walkers, cyclists and horse riders. This linear trail is comprised of two sections. The north end follows an old railway grade and runs 21 km northwest from Port Alberni, in the shadow of the Beaufort Range of mountains. The southern part, though much shorter, is more challenging since the trail leads through a deep ravine at Rogers Creek.

CAUTIONS
- Carry adequate water.
- There are many confusing, unmarked side roads, trails, mountain bike routes and game trails along the Log Train Trail. Stay on the designated main trail at all times.
- Trails often run close to private property. Respect the privacy of area residents. Please do not trespass.

THE LOG TRAIN TRAIL follows an old logging railway grade that extends northwest from Port Alberni. The first part of the rail line was built to accommodate the Bainbridge Mill, which operated from 1917 to 1927. Ten years later the tracks were extended into the Ash River Valley and to tidewater at Alberni Inlet. From 1937 to 1953 steam locomotives hauled timber along this railway. With the advent of truck logging, the line was abandoned.

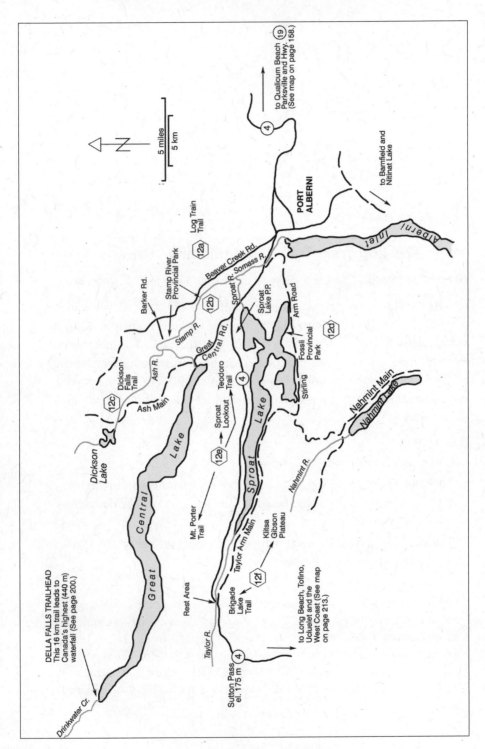

ACCESS *To the North End of the Log Train Trail* As you approach Port Alberni, heading west on Highway 4, keep right at the Visitor InfoCentre and stay on Highway 4 (Johnston Road) for 0.5 km to Maebelle Road. Turn right (north) onto Maebelle Road and continue to the end. At Mozart Road, park on the gravel near the marked trailhead. Secondary access points are via Cherry Creek, Smith or Bainbridge roads and, at the trail's north end, Woolsey Road.

HIKE DESCRIPTION

North Section of the Log Train Trail Easy/21 km, one way: The north section of the Log Train Trail initially passes through a second growth forest of Douglas-fir, western red cedar and hemlock, in the area just east of Cherry Creek. The route offers occasional valley views through the trees. The Cold Creek waterfall is another highlight. Around 4 km from the Mozart Road trailhead a major trail cuts off to the right (east) and leads into the Horne Lake area.

The Log Train Trail winds another 3.5 km along farmlands and fields to the junction with an old road leading to the R.B. McLean Mill National Historic Site. (See Sidebar page 194.) Just north of this site, close to where the E & N Railway crosses the trail, is the old Bainbridge Mill site. From here the Log Train Trail continues another 14 km north through a young forest to a couple of viewpoints near the trail's end at Woolsey Road, close to Somers Road.

ACCESS *To the South End of the Log Train Trail* As you approach Port Alberni, heading west on Highway 4, keep left at the Visitor Info-Centre onto Highway 4A (Port Alberni Highway) which becomes Redford Street. After 0.5 km turn right (north) onto Maebelle Road and park on the gravel. The trail begins on the south side of Highway 4A. Use caution when crossing the highway.

HIKE DESCRIPTION

South Section of the Log Train Trail Moderate/3 km, one way: The south section of the Log Train Trail offers tougher hiking than the generally flatter north end. From the trailhead on Highway 4A's south side the trail runs south to the ravine at Rogers Creek. The logging railway trestle that once spanned Rogers Creek was 286 m long. The trail descends steep switchbacks down to the footbridge over the creek and the junction with Rogers Creek Nature Trail. (See page 195.) The Log Train Trail continues up the ravine's south side and across another gully to Burde Street.

R.B. McLean steam sawmill. JOYCE FOLBIGG

THE R.B. MCLEAN MILL NATIONAL HISTORIC SITE (13 ha) features a restored, steam-operated sawmill that began operation in 1926 and continued until 1965. Most of the machinery was left on site. In 1989, the McLean family graciously donated the site and the abandoned equipment to the City of Port Alberni. The federal and provincial governments, along with the Alberni Valley Museum, the City of Port Alberni, the Alberni-Clayoquot Regional District and the Western Vancouver Island Industrial Heritage Society are partnered in restoring the sawmill.

Do not pass up a chance to visit western Canada's last working steam sawmill. The site is accessed along the Log Train Trail or by vehicle from Port Alberni via Beaver Creek and Smith roads. Visitors can also ride a seasonal steam train (a refurbished 1929 Baldwin logging locomotive) from the restored 1912 station in downtown Port Alberni to the mill. The 10 km journey via the Alberni Pacific "Steam" Railway takes about 35 minutes.

For information on the R.B. McLean Mill National Historic Site and the Alberni Pacific "Steam" Railway, including general fees and group rates, seasonal hours of operation, reservations, interpretive programs and tour schedules, contact the Alberni Valley Heritage Network at www.alberniheritage.com.

A 5.2 km connector trail links the Log Train Trail with Ship Creek Road, in Port Alberni's south end. A future trail will run all the way to China Creek Marina, near the start of the CNPR Trail. Planning continues on the CNPR Trail, which will follow the historic Canadian Northern Pacific Railway grade almost 4 km along the Alberni Inlet. Contact the Alberni-Clayoquot Regional District for updates.

WORTH NOTING

- Members of the Port Alberni Equine Society were instrumental in the Log Train Trail's development. The trail's official opening was in 1990.
- Gates are located at trail access points on Woolsey, Bainbridge and Smith roads, and at the Horne Lake cutoff, near Cherry Creek Road.
- The Ministry of Transportation and Highways leases the right-of-way along the Log Train Trail to the Alberni-Clayoquot Regional District.

NEARBY *Rogers Creek Nature Trail* offers relatively easy hiking as it meanders 3 km, one way, along the south bank of Rogers Creek. Expect some uneven terrain. Sections of the upriver trail are sometimes difficult to locate. The Log Train Trail and numerous unmarked trails and side paths intersect the route. Access is along Highway 4A, 1.4 km south of the Travel InfoCentre, on the south side of the Rogers Creek bridge. The parking area is on the highway's left (east) side.

ADDITIONAL INFORMATION
www.acrd.bc.ca (Alberni-Clayoquot Regional District)
www.avcoc.com (Alberni Valley Chamber of Commerce)
www.westernforest.com/wiwag (West Islands Woodlands Community
    Advisory Group)
Refer to NTS 92F/2 and 92F/7 (1:50,000)

12b. Stamp River Trails   Map M12

DIFFICULTY/DISTANCE Easy to moderate/0.5 km to 7.5 km, one way

HIGHLIGHTS Just west of Port Alberni several scenic trails snake along both sides of the Stamp River. The *Stamp Long River (Sayachlas ta' saa'nim) Trail* extends along the Stamp River's east bank and is accessed at Stamp River Provincial Park and a secondary road to the north. The *Greenmax Anglers' Trail*, closer to Sproat Lake, runs along the Stamp River's west side. Short paths at *Stamp River Provincial Park* are ideal for viewing fall salmon runs. Area trails offer picturesque hiking along one of Vancouver Island's most scenic rivers, with plenty of great opportunities for nature appreciation and wildlife viewing along the way.

CAUTIONS

- If you are unfamiliar with semi-wilderness hiking, travel with someone who knows the area well.
- Watch for rising river levels. Keep away from riverside cliffs and slippery banks.
- Be prepared for adverse weather. Bring extra warm clothing, food and raingear.
- Carry water. Boil, treat or filter all river and creek water.
- Expect uneven terrain, protruding roots and branches, slippery sections, up and down hiking and some steep switchbacks. Wear sturdy footwear.
- Keep to designated trails. Avoid trampling delicate soil structure and vegetation.
- These trails pass through bear and cougar territory. Although your chances of an encounter are slim, be alert when hiking.
- Secure your vehicle and remove all valuables.

ACCESS

To Stamp Long River Trail (south end) and Stamp River Provincial Park
In Port Alberni, from the foot of Johnston Road near the Somass River, turn right (west) on Highway 4 (Pacific Rim Highway), cross the bridge and then make an immediate right onto Beaver Creek Road. Continue another 11.7 km north following the Stamp River Falls Provincial Park signposts. At the park entrance, swing left and drive 1.7 km to the parking area. The Stamp Long River Trail begins near the information signpost.

To Stamp Long River Trail via Barker Road (north end) To access the Stamp Long River Trail's north end, continue north approximately 5 km past the main park entrance on Beaver Creek Road and turn left onto Barker Road. En route, be sure to keep left, about 4 km north of the Stamp River Park main entrance, to stay on Beaver Creek Road. The paved road to the right that descends a steep hill is Somers Road. From Beaver Creek Road head west on Barker Road for 1 km to a short, rough access road that leads to the trailhead. Most visitors park here, but with a 4 × 4 or high-clearance vehicle it is possible to drive right to the riverside trail.

HIKE DESCRIPTIONS

Stamp Long River Trail Moderate/7.5 km, one way: From Stamp River Provincial Park the trail runs along the Stamp River's east side. Note the only entry points are at the north and south trailheads; there is no mid-trail access. Near its south end start, the route swings inland to avoid a slide area. There are countless rapids to see and riverside viewpoints, both near the water and higher up on the riverbank. An impressive stand of old growth Douglas-fir and western red cedar is located at the trail's north end. Allow approximately 3 hours hiking time, one way.

Stamp River Provincial Park Easy/0.5 km, one way: There are 2 km of interconnecting trails at Stamp River Provincial Park (327 ha). A popular 0.5 km path leads south from the parking area to the fish ladders and riverside viewpoint from which visitors may observe the fall salmon runs from August through December. The trail leads to Stamp Falls and several river rapids. Extend your hike a few kilometres downriver on an improved trail, where new bridges make the creek crossings a lot easier.

ACCESS *To Greenmax Anglers' Trail* In Port Alberni, from the foot of Johnston Road near the Somass River, turn right at the T-junction and head west on Highway 4 (Pacific Rim Highway) for 8.3 km to Coleman Road, just north of the lofty Sproat River bridge. Swing right (east) on Coleman Road past Airport Road to the Greenmax Woodlot access road, marked by a yellow gate. Park nearby, but do not block the road.

HIKE DESCRIPTION *Greenmax Anglers' Trail* Moderate/4 km, one way: From the gate the trail follows the woodlot road through a logged area and climbs a small hill. At the top, take the road to the right and head east to the Stamp River. Once at the river, the trail drops steeply to the water's edge, near a waterfall. Turn left and hike another 2.4 km northwest through an old growth forest. There are numerous summer swimming holes en route and plenty of casting spots. The trail ends at the Eagle Rock fishing pool. Allow 1.5 hours hiking time, one way.

WORTH NOTING

- These trails are popular with anglers. Always check current fishing regulations.
- Watch for eagles, hawks and a variety of waterbirds.
- Stamp River Provincial Park was created when Stamp Falls and Money's Pool provincial parks merged into one. Facilities include 23 campsites surrounded by a stand of old growth trees, a day-use

picnic area, seasonal tap water, interpretive signposts and pit toilets. Contact BC Parks for current information on seasonal camping fees and park services.

NEARBY The Log Train Trail (See page 191.)

ADDITIONAL INFORMATION
www.acrd.bc.ca (Alberni-Clayoquot Regional District)
www.avcoc.com (Alberni Valley Chamber of Commerce)
www.env.gov.bc.ca/bcparks (BC Parks)
www.westernforest.com/wiwag (West Islands Woodlands Community Advisory Group)
Refer to NTS 92F/7 (1:50,000)

12c. Dickson Falls Map M12

DIFFICULTY/DISTANCE Moderate/0.3 km, one way

HIGHLIGHTS One of Port Alberni's scenic secrets is boisterous Dickson Falls, on the Ash River, north of Great Central Lake. Getting to the trailhead involves travelling just under 12 km on a logging road mainline. The reward is seeing one of the Alberni Valley's lesser known waterfalls.

ACCESS In Port Alberni, at the T-junction at the foot of Johnston Road, near the Somass River, turn right and follow Highway 4 (Pacific Rim Highway) west for 9.6 km. Near Sproat Lake Provincial Park, turn right (north) onto Great Central Road and continue 7.5 km to the foot of Great Central Lake.

At the Ark Resort, bear right onto Ash Main and cross the Sproat River bridge. On the span's north side, reset your vehicle's trip meter to zero and follow Ash Main for 11.7 km. Park safely well off to the right side of the road, next to a deteriorating side road. If you reach the Ash River bridge at Dickson Lake, just over 1 km down the road, you have gone too far and will have to backtrack.

CAUTIONS
• Reaching Dickson Falls involves travel along gravel industrial roads, which may be seasonally rough. Public access restrictions could apply. Read Forest Road Travel on page 19 carefully. Anyone unfamiliar with semi-wilderness hiking should travel with someone who knows the area well.

Dickson Falls, on the Ash River, are reached via logging roads, northwest of Port Alberni.   RICHARD K. BLIER

- The Dickson Falls trailhead is not marked and so is easy to miss.
- Watch for sharp, slippery rocks along the Ash River and closer to Dickson Falls where fine, wind-drifted spray often soaks the riverbanks.
- Bring some water. Boil, treat or filter any river water.
- Carry out any litter.

HIKE DESCRIPTION   From the roadside pulloff along Ash Main, the trail begins as a disused spur road that leads uphill and soon narrows into a well-worn trail. It is not a far distance to the Ash River but watch your steps carefully as you traverse the uneven, rocky terrain. The trail emerges on a slightly elevated bank of the Ash River that overlooks Dickson Falls. It is possible to work your way closer to the falls by hiking along the riverbank.

- Dickson Falls takes on the look of a grand staircase when the waters of the Ash River run high.
- Anglers note that the Ash River is closed to fishing all year from Dickson Falls to boundary markers, 30 m downstream.
- The relatively short Sproat River drains Sproat Lake and runs east to the confluence of the Stamp and Somass rivers.

NEARBY *Della Falls* The amphibious adventure to Della Falls (440 m), Canada's highest cascade, starts at the foot of Great Central Lake, near the Ark Resort. This rugged wilderness hike into Strathcona Park's southeast corner is recommended for intermediate to experienced hikers. First challenge is the 35-km journey up Great Central Lake to the Della Falls trailhead. Great Central Lake is surrounded by steep mountains that often funnel winds and create high waves and hazardous conditions for small craft. Be wary on the water. Next is the steady climb from lakehead up the Drinkwater Creek Valley to the base of the falls, 7 hours and 16 km away. The Della Falls Trail is featured in *Hiking Trails 3: Northern Vancouver Island* published by the Vancouver Island Trails Information Society.

The Ark Resort offers boat and canoe rentals and a water taxi service or you can use your own boat, canoe or kayak to reach the remote trailhead. Backpacking gear is also available for rent. Visitors can arrange to park their vehicles at the resort for a small fee. For more information and current trail reports contact www.arkresort.com.

ADDITIONAL INFORMATION
www.for.gov.bc.ca/dsi (BC Forest Service South Island District)
www.westernforest.com/wiwag (West Islands Woodlands Community
  Advisory Group)
Refer to NTS 92F/6 and 92F/7 (1:50,000)

12d. Fossli Provincial Park   Maps M12, M12D

DIFFICULTY/DISTANCE   Moderate/2.5 km to 4.5 km, one way

HIGHLIGHTS   Fossli Provincial Park (53 ha) is located on Sproat Lake's Stirling Arm, just west of Port Alberni. Trails lead along St. Andrew's Creek to a small beach on Sproat Lake. The suspension bridge over the creek is a highlight. Fossli is a Norwegian word for waterfalls and there are several within park boundaries.

Map M12D Fossli Provincial Park

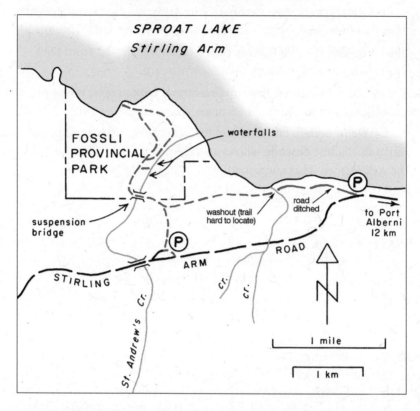

ACCESS In Port Alberni, at the foot of Johnston Road near the Somass River, turn right at the T-junction and follow Highway 4 (Pacific Rim Highway) 3 km west and cross the Somass River bridge. On the bridge's south side, turn left onto Mission Road to pass through a logging yard and continue up a hill to a major junction, 3 km from the highway turn-off. Cous Main is the logging road to the left. Keep straight ahead onto Stirling Arm Road for Sproat Lake and Fossli Park.

Continue west to an intersection near a pipeline. The logging road on the right is an alternate route to and from Stirling Arm Road and Highway 4 via Stirling Arm Drive and McCoy Lake Road. Stay on Stirling Arm Road for another 4 km to where an unmarked side road swings off on the right. This branch road, 9.3 km from Highway 4, is the longer *East Access* trailhead to Fossli Provincial Park. Be sure to park safely off to the side of the mainline. Space here is extremely limited. With a four-wheel-drive vehicle you can negotiate the ditched branch road a short distance to a wider parking spot.

For the *West Access*, proceed another 1.6 km west down Stirling Arm Road. Immediately before you cross the St. Andrew's Creek bridge, turn right onto an old road, which is sometimes marked with ribbons. A roadside parking area is just ahead.

CAUTIONS
- Reaching Fossli Provincial Park involves travel along gravel industrial roads. Read Forest Road Travel on page 19 carefully.
- Trail signage is incomplete. If you are unfamiliar with semi-wilderness hiking, travel with someone who knows the area well.
- Bring ample water. Boil, treat or filter any creek or lake water.
- Carry out all your litter.

HIKE DESCRIPTIONS
East Access Trail   Moderate/4.5 km, one way: This is the lengthier and rougher of two trails to Fossli Provincial Park. From the mainline, hike along the branch road to parallel Sproat Lake's Stirling Arm. Proceed with caution at the bad washout where the trail zigs and zags a bit before turning away from the lake to begin a steady climb. Locating the trail at the washout can be difficult. At a road junction, where the West Access Trail joins in from the south, keep west on the right hand trail to the St. Andrew's Creek suspension bridge. On the creek's far side, the trail turns north and negotiates a steep hill. At the bottom of the grade a side trail goes to St. Andrew's Creek. The main trail loops through a mainly deciduous forest to an old homestead on Sproat Lake. All that remains is a small grassy area at lakeside. From the mainline to Sproat Lake, the East Access hike takes 1.5 to 2 hours, one way.

West Access Trail   Moderate/2.5 km, one way: This is the shorter, easier and preferred access to Fossli Park. From the branch road parking area the trail heads north and follows an old logging road downhill. Parts of the grade are rocky and slippery, so watch your steps. At an obvious road junction the East Access Trail meets the West Access Trail near the park's southern boundary. Bear left (west) to St. Andrew's Creek and the suspension bridge. For a description of the trail from the footbridge to Sproat Lake see East Access Trail. above. To hike the West Access Trail allow 1 hour, one way.

WORTH NOTING
- Helen and Armor Ford donated the land to the province in 1974.

- Hike west of the old homestead to a point of land near a beaver pond. This area is popular with birdwatchers.
- The park has a lakeside picnic table and tiny beach area, which is also accessible by boat.

NEARBY   The rugged trails and routes to the *Klitsa/Gibson Plateau* and the *Brigade Lake Trail* can be reached via Stirling Arm Road and Taylor Arm Main logging roads. This is an alternate, longer way in to these trailheads. See page 207.

ADDITIONAL INFORMATION
www.for.gov.bc.ca/dsi (BC Forest Service South Island District)
www.env.gov.bc.ca/bcparks (BC Parks)
www.westernforest.com/wiwag (West Islands Woodlands Community Advisory Group)
Refer to NTS 92F/2 and 92F/7 (1:50,000)

12e. Trails and Hiking Routes along Highway 4 (North Side)   Map M12

DIFFICULTY/DISTANCE   Moderate to strenuous/2.6 km to 5.5 km, one way; 7.8 km loop

HIGHLIGHTS   The *Teodoro Trail, Sproat Lake Lookout* and *Mount Porter Trail* are three remote hiking destinations accessed along the north side of Highway 4 (Pacific Rim Highway), west of Port Alberni. The hard part is getting to some of the trailheads, a challenge that involves travelling (or hiking up) steep, gravel logging roads. The effort is always worth it; the trails lead to some of the most breathtaking panoramas on Vancouver Island.

CAUTIONS
- Reaching these trails and routes requires travel along gravel logging roads. Public access may be periodically restricted due to active logging. Many of these access roads are not suitable for all vehicles and will require a four-wheel-drive truck with good clearance. Read Forest Road Travel on page 19 carefully.
- If you are unfamiliar with semi-wilderness or wilderness hiking, travel with someone who knows the area well. Arrange to join a scheduled hike with a local hiking group.
- Carry adequate water.

An eagle's-eye view over Sproat Lake to the mountains on the lake's south side. RICHARD K. BLIER

ACCESS

To the Teodoro Trail   As you approach Port Alberni from Parksville, driving west on Highway 4, keep right at the Visitor InfoCentre to the foot of Johnston Road, near the Somass River. Turn right at the T-junction and follow Highway 4 (Pacific Rim Highway) west for another 10.2 km. Turn right (north) onto the logging mainline just past Great Central Road and Sproat Lake Provincial Park. Continue about 1.5 km to a branch road. Turn left and drive another 3.5 km west to the Weiner Creek bridge and the roadside parking area. Hike across the bridge and follow the road about 200 m to the trailhead marker, on the right.

HIKE DESCRIPTION

Teodoro Trail   Moderate to strenuous/7.8 km loop: The Teodoro Trail winds up through a second growth forest to an area of open bluffs. Here, near stately stands of old growth Douglas-fir, are fine vistas of Sproat Lake and surrounding mountains. The route continues several kilometres along the bluffs and then cuts south to drop back down to the logging road. Head 250 m east along the road and watch for trail markers, on the right. Here the trail leaves the road and runs east to eventually descend a hill to an old road that parallels the power lines near Weiner Creek. Turn left (north) and hike uphill to the Weiner Creek bridge parking area. Allow at least 4 hours for the loop hike.

ACCESS

To the Sproat Lake Lookout   See Teodoro Trail access above. In Port Alberni, at the T-junction at foot of Johnston Road, turn right and drive west on Highway 4 just under 13.5 km to a deactivated logging road on the highway's right (north) side. This road is west of Great Central Lake Road and the West Bay Hotel. Turn right off the highway and park at the bottom of the logging road.

HIKE DESCRIPTION

Sproat Lake Lookout   Moderate/5.5 km, one way: To reach the Sproat Lake Lookout from the parking area close to Highway 4, hike up the logging road 1.6 km to a spur road on the right near a gate post. Take the spur road to a T-junction. Turn left (west) and follow the road about 200 m, then take a 150 m all-terrain vehicle (quad) route (on the right) to an older, overgrown road. Swing left (northwest) for the lookout. Most of this hike is along old roads and trails with strenuous, steep sections en route. There are many confusing, unmarked side trails and old roads, so know your territory or travel with a friend who does. Signage and flagging in this area is incomplete but some exists along the upper route. The views from the rocky viewpoint take in Sproat Lake, Mount Klitsa, the Beaufort Range and Mount Arrowsmith. It is possible to loop around the lookout area on old roads. Allow 2.5 hours hiking time, one way.

ACCESS

To the Mount Porter Trail   See Teodoro Trail access on page 205. In Port Alberni, from the foot of Johnston Road, turn right and take Highway 4 west for approximately 34 km to Doran Lake Road, on the highway's north side. This logging road, frequented by anglers, is just west of the head of Sproat Lake. Turn right onto Doran Lake Road and climb about 8 km to Doran Lake. The access road, subject to constant washouts, has countless waterbars (small ditches) across the roadway and could stymie some drivers. Park at a lower elevation and hike along the road as conditions warrant. From Doran Lake a confusing maze of rough branch roads leads another 2.5 km to the trailhead. It is best to travel these backroads with a knowledgeable partner. The Mount Porter Trail begins at the end of a branch road.

HIKE DESCRIPTION

Mount Porter (1328 m)   Moderate/2.6 km, one way: From the trailhead, the trail cuts through a logged area and begins a steady climb to some bluffs. The viewpoint nearby is perfect for a rest stop and offers vistas south over Sproat Lake to Mount Klitsa. The trail continues up to a lofty ridge. You will know you have reached this high point when a majestic view of Great Central Lake unfolds. The trail continues east along the ridge to the Mount Porter summit and its spectacular Sproat Lake panorama. Allow around 2 hours to reach the summit.

WORTH NOTING

- The Teodoro Trail is named after Mexican Teodoro Cabrera, an environmental activist who was jailed in 1999 for protesting old growth forest logging.
- The bluffs near the Sproat Lake lookout are awash with pockets of bright, spring wildflowers.
- The *Alberni Valley Trail Guide*, available at the Port Alberni Visitor InfoCentre, contains detailed information on area access roads and trails.

NEARBY   Dickson Falls. See page 198.

www.avcoc.com (Alberni Valley Chamber of Commerce)
www.for.gov.bc.ca/dsi (BC Forest Service South Island District)
www.islandhikes.com (hiking updates)
www.justabunchahikers.ca (Port Alberni hiking group)
www.westernforest.com/wiwag (West Islands Woodlands Community
   Advisory Group)
Refer to NTS 92F/2 and 92F/7 (1:50,000)

12f. Trails and Hiking Routes along Highway 4 (South Side) Map M12

DIFFICULTY/DISTANCE   Strenuous/1.8 km to 5.5 km, one way

HIGHLIGHTS   West of Port Alberni, on Sproat Lake's south side, are two excellent wilderness hiking destinations reached by gravel logging roads. The *Klitsa/Gibson Plateau Trail* accesses Mount Klitsa (1642 m) and various lakes high up on the Klitsa/Gibson Plateau (6000 ha), a beautiful sub-alpine region of lakes, tarns and ridges. The *Brigade Lake Trail* climbs up a valley to Brigade Lake, west of Mount Gibson (1332 m). There are opportunities for hiking, mountain viewing, nature appreciation and wilderness camping.

CAUTIONS
- Reaching these trails and routes requires travel along gravel logging roads. Public access may be periodically restricted due to active logging. Many of these access roads are not suitable for all vehicles and will require a four-wheel-drive truck with good clearance. Read Forest Road Travel on page 19 carefully.
- No trail signage exists at the Highway 4 cutoff or along the logging mainlines and branch roads leading to the trailheads. If you are unfamiliar with semi-wilderness or wilderness hiking, travel with someone who knows the area well. Consider joining a guided hike offered by a local club. These rugged trails are best suited for fit, experienced hikers.
- Be prepared for wilderness conditions and rapidly changing weather. Low cloud and fog can swirl in without warning. In these adverse conditions route finding skills are a prerequisite. Bring rain gear, extra warm clothing and backup food.
- Carry ample water. Boil, treat or filter all creek and lake water.
- This region is habitat for black bear and cougar. Be alert when hiking.

ACCESS

To Klitsa/Gibson Plateau Trail   In Port Alberni, at the foot of Johnston Road near the Somass River, turn right at the T-junction and follow Highway 4 (Pacific Rim Highway) 36.5 km to the Taylor River Rest Area, west of Sproat Lake. Stay on the highway and cross the Taylor River bridge. On the river's south side make an immediate left turn onto South Taylor Main and travel east 4.6 km to Branch 552E, close to where a bridge (now removed) once spanned the Taylor River.

Turn right (south) and drive approximately 1.5 km to the end of the branch road or park and walk the distance. Expect the road hike to take an hour. This once overgrown artery has been improved to facilitate construction of a Micro Hydro Dam project but the route may still be impractical to attempt in a regular passenger vehicle. The road is cleared to within 200 m of the trailhead. From the end of the upgrades, watch for new flagging and hike the remaining 200 m to the Klitsa/Gibson trailhead, marked by ribbons.

A much longer alternate access from the east is possible. From Fossli Provincial Park's West Access Trail (See page 202.) head west on Sproat Lake's logging road mainlines for 26.5 km to the Branch 552E turn.

HIKE DESCRIPTION

The Klitsa/Gibson Plateau Trail   Strenuous/1.8 km, one way: From the trailhead the route cuts through a logged area to the old growth timber. Signage on the steep, challenging trail is virtually non-existent save for some sun-bleached flagging here and there. The slightly worn route seems to disappear in places, so hikers must remain observant to stay on course. Keep to the right (west) side of the creek all the way to the first lake. Blowdowns, which require scrambling, may block parts of the route and increase hiking times.

The trail's toughest grade is on the final pitch to the plateau. Snow on the upper slopes may linger until June. If the weather co-operates, the 360 degree panorama on top of the plateau is well worth the effort. Extend your hike and explore other rough trails on the plateau. One arduous route involves a tricky creek crossing near the first lake and then climbs a gully and ridge east of the lake to access Mount Klitsa.

ACCESS

To the Brigade Lake Trail   As per Klitsa/Gibson access above to South Taylor Main. From Highway 4, swing left (east) onto South Taylor Main and travel 0.6 km. The side road that climbs a small hill on the mainline's south side is the turn for Brigade Lake. Unless you have a 4 x 4 or high-slung vehicle, it is best to park somewhere near South Taylor Main and hike up the road to the trailhead. Problem hills strewn with sharp rocks and small boulders preclude most regular passenger vehicles. Travel 2 km on the access spur to a road widening near Sutton Creek, the Brigade Lake outflow stream. The trailhead is close by. Park well off to the side of the road.

Alternative access from the east is possible but this involves lengthy travel down logging mainlines on Sproat Lake's south side. From Fossli Provincial Park's West Access Trail (See page 202.) head west for 31.5 km to the Brigade Lake cutoff.

HIKE DESCRIPTION

The Brigade Lake Trail . Strenuous/5.5 km, one way: The first 3.5 km of the Brigade Lake Trail has some boardwalks, bridges and short, wooden steps. Many of these trail upgrades are deteriorating so use caution when hiking in these areas. Expect uneven terrain, protruding roots and branches, wet sections and places where the trail seems to vanish. The last 2 km up to the outflow creek at Brigade Lake can be quite bushy. Some of the original trail has been rerouted due to logging. The trail ends at Brigade Lake. Seasoned hikers accustomed to rough conditions sometimes traverse an unimproved route southeast to Weismuller, Richards, Middle and Vincent lakes.

WORTH NOTING

- These areas are used in the winter by cross-country skiers.
- Some logging mainlines and branch roads in this region are now reactivated (improved and upgraded). Many routes are being renamed. This book provides area logging road names that have been in regular use for years.

NEARBY Fossli Provincial Park (See page 200.)

ADDITIONAL INFORMATION

www.for.gov.bc.ca/dsi (BC Forest Service South Island District)
www.islandhikes.com (hiking updates)
www.westernforest.com/wiwag (West Islands Woodlands Community
     Advisory Group)
Refer to NTS 92F/2, 92F/3, 92F/6 and 92F/7 (1:50,000)

13

West Coast

13a. Clayoquot Sound Provincial Parks Map M13

HIGHLIGHTS This section deviates slightly from the book format to list various provincial parks and ecological reserves within Clayoquot Sound. A boat is required to access the majority of these parks. Though few established trails exist at many Clayoquot Sound parks, it is possible to visit countless pocket beaches, coves, rocky headlands and accessible shorelines. There are opportunities to explore the intertidal zones for waterbirds and other marine life.

ACCESS Boat access only.

CAUTIONS Clayoquot Sound has been the ancestral home of the Nuu-chah-nulth for thousands of years. Included are the Ahousaht, the Hesquiaht and Tla-o-qui-aht First Nations. When exploring this spectacular region, respect their traditional territories. There are numerous First Nations Reserves in Clayoquot Sound. Please do not visit these sites without permission.

PARK DESCRIPTIONS

(a) Clayoquot Arm Provincial Park (3491 ha) protects habitat for spawning salmon and an old growth Sitka spruce forest near Kennedy Lake's Clayoquot Arm.

(b) Clayoquot Plateau Provincial Park (3155 ha) features sinkholes and limestone caves and an old growth forest on a high elevation plateau.

(c) Cleland Island Ecological Reserve (no public access) lies west of Vargas Island (within Vargas Island Park) and protects important marine habitat for water birds. The reserve includes Cleland Island and a marine area with a 10 km radius around the island.

Enjoying the vast Long Beach surf. Eric Burkle

(d) Dawley Passage Provincial Park (154 ha), south of Meares Island, has a varied marine ecosystem and nearby channels are subject to strong tideflows, particularly Fortune Channel.

(e) Epper Passage Provincial Park (306 ha) encompasses two small islands (Morfee and Dunlap) in the marine-rich waters just east of Vargas Island.

(f) Flores Island Provincial Park (7113 ha) preserves three pristine watersheds and their adjacent old growth Sitka spruce forests. The park has spectacular rocky shorelines and sandy beaches. Island wolves may frequent campsites in the early morning, late evening and at night. Ensure your food is secure. Do not feed the island's wolves. This is a violation of the Parks Act.

(g) Gibson Provincial Marine Park (140 ha) at the south end of Flores Island, in Matilda Inlet, is known for the Ahousat Warm Springs and the beautiful beaches of Whitesand Cove.

(h) Hesquiat Lake Provincial Park (62 ha) protects a stand of shoreline forest near Hesquiat Lake.

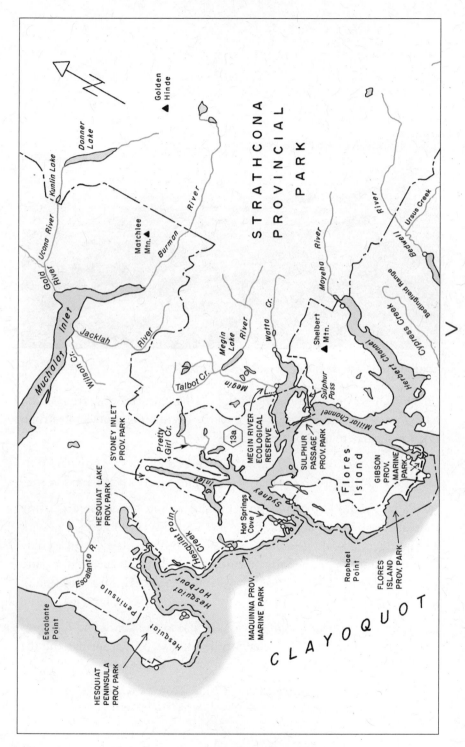

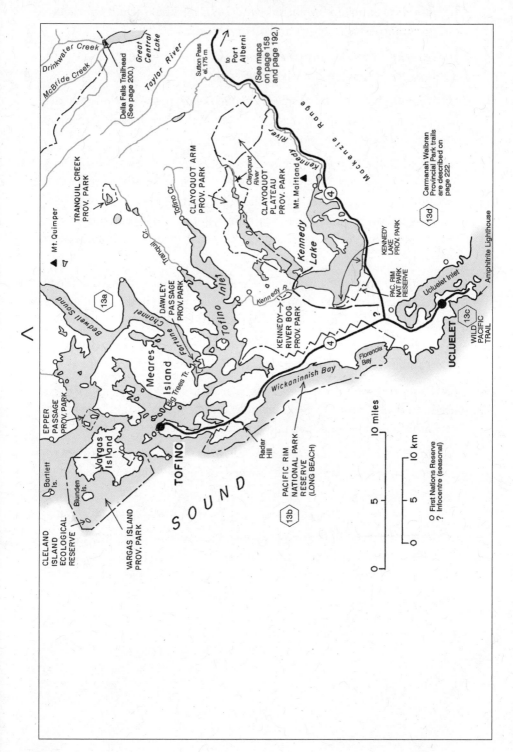

Drinkwater Creek

Great Central Lake

McBride Creek

Taylor River

Della Falls Trailhead (See page 200.)

Sutton Pass el.175 m

to Port Alberni

(See maps on page 158 and page 192.)

Mackenzie Range

Kennedy River

Mt. Maitland

TRANQUIL CREEK PROV. PARK

CLAYOQUOT ARM PROV. PARK

Clayoquot River

CLAYOQUOT PLATEAU PROV. PARK

Tofino Cr.

Mt. Quimper

4

13d

Carmanah Walbran Provincial Park trails are described on page 222.

Amphitrite Lighthouse

Tranquil Cr.

Kennedy Lake

KENNEDY LAKE PROV. PARK

Ucluelet Inlet

Bedwell Sound

13a

DAWLEY PASSAGE PROV. PARK

Tofino Inlet

Fortune Channel

Kennedy R.

PAC. RIM NAT PARK RESERVE

?

13c

WILD PACIFIC TRAIL

Meares Island

Big Trees Tr.

KENNEDY RIVER BOG PROV. PARK

4

UCLUELET

EPPER PASSAGE PROV. PARK

Florencia Bay

Bartlett Is.

Vargas Island

Blunden Is.

TOFINO

Radar Hill

Wickaninnish Bay

PACIFIC RIM NATIONAL PARK RESERVE (LONG BEACH)

13b

CLELAND ISLAND ECOLOGICAL RESERVE

VARGAS ISLAND PROV. PARK

SOUND

10 miles

10 km

5

5

0

0

○ First Nations Reserve
? Infocentre (seasonal)

(i) Hesquiat Peninsula Provincial Park (7891/7888 ha) includes pockets of old-growth forest, shorelines and offshore reefs.

(j) Kennedy River Bog Provincial Park (11 ha) preserves a bog near the Kennedy River that has unusually low acidity.

(k) Maquinna Provincial Marine Park (2667 ha), near Hot Springs Cove, has natural hot springs. Change houses and toilets are provided. No soap, shampoo, alcohol, glass, pets, or camping at the hot springs.

(l) Megin River Ecological Reserve (no public access) and the Megin/ Talbot addition (27,391 ha) in western Strathcona Provincial Park include a pristine watershed. The area features karst topography, old-growth forest and valuable salmon habitat. Karst refers to an area with underground drainage and cavities caused by the dissolution of rock.

(m) Sulphur Passage Provincial Park (2299 ha) includes the scenic channel between Obstruction and Flores islands, the nearby estuary and old-growth forests. This is an important salmon habitat.

(n) Sydney Inlet Provincial Park (2774 ha) protects the fjord (Sydney Inlet) and its old growth forest. The area is a valuable salmon habitat.

(o) Tranquil Creek Provincial Park (Paradise Lake) (299 ha), near the headwaters of Tranquil Creek, includes untouched Paradise Lake and its surrounding alpine meadows and forests.

(p) Vargas Island Provincial Park (5970 ha) features beautiful sandy beaches, a protected lagoon and a rugged, open coastline.

WORTH NOTING
- Be cognizant of fluctuating tides. Contact the Canadian Hydrographic Service at www.waterlevels.gc.ca for current tidal information.

NEARBY Pacific Rim National Park Reserve (Long Beach) and Ucluelet's Wild Pacific Trail (See pages 215 and 219, respectively.)

ADDITIONAL INFORMATION
www.env.gov.bc.ca/bcparks (BC Parks)
Refer to NTS 92C/13, 92E/1, 92E/8, 92F/4, 92F/5 (1:50,000)

13b. Pacific Rim National Park Reserve (Long Beach)
Map M13

DIFFICULTY/DISTANCE   Easy to moderate/500 m to 2.5 km, one way; 800 m to 1 km loops

HIGHLIGHTS   Parks Canada's Pacific Rim National Park Reserve (PRNPR) features numerous hiking trails of varying lengths and degrees of difficulty. They wind through coastal boglands, rainforests and along rugged shorelines to rocky headlands and wild Pacific Ocean beaches. Most trails feature interpretive signs that explain the region's natural and cultural heritage. The majority of the paths have been improved with boardwalks, inclined ramps, wooden staircases or steps.

ACCESS   Take Highway 4 (Pacific Rim Highway) west from Port Alberni, past Sproat and Kennedy lakes to the T-junction with the Tofino/Ucluelet Highway. Allow 1.5 to 2 hours driving time from Port Alberni. The Pacific Rim Visitor Centre is near this intersection. From mid-October to mid-March the infocentre is open weekends only. Turn right (north) and head toward Tofino. Most trails are signposted along the highway. To reach the Half Moon Bay and Willowbrae trails, turn left (south) at the Tofino/Ucluelet T-junction and travel 2 km toward Ucluelet. Swing right (west) onto Willowbrae Road to the trailheads. There is no park signpost at this easy-to-miss cutoff.

IMPORTANT NOTE   Park regulations require visitors to clearly display a valid Park Use Permit on their vehicle when parked anywhere in the park. These passes are available at several locations and select trailheads. Contact Parks Canada for details.

CAUTIONS
- It is impossible to overemphasize the danger posed by the force of ocean waves, especially where they dash against rocks. They can easily hurl full-sized logs about. Periodically and unpredictably an unusually large wave (a rogue wave) or a series of bigger waves will strike the beach. These are capable of plucking people off the rocks and washing them out to sea. When beach hiking or headland scrambling, use extreme caution and closely supervise children at all times. Stay well clear of surge channels. Read and obey all posted warnings concerning undertow. Be aware of the dangers posed by undersea earthquakes that may spawn devastating tsunami (tidal waves).
- Stay on designated trails to protect delicate vegetation and soil.

- Wooden boardwalks and steps are very slippery in damp or frosty conditions.
- Bears, cougars and raccoons are sometimes encountered on these coastal trails. Be alert when hiking. Never approach or feed wildlife.

HIKE DESCRIPTIONS

Most Long Beach area trails are reached along Highway 4, beginning just north of the Tofino/Ucluelet T-junction. Watch for Parks Canada signposts. Many trails are self guided and feature interpretive signposts.

Shoreline Bog Trail   Easy/800 m loop: This boardwalk trail loops through an old growth rainforest where stunted, gnarled lodgepole pine barely survive in the poorly drained, acidic soil. Soaked by annual torrential rains, the ground is covered with sphagnum moss, a plant that thrives in the harsh environment. Alongside the boardwalk watch for sundews, a delicate, insect eating plant. Access off Highway 4 is along Wickaninnish Road, 300 m west of the road to Florencia Bay. The Shoreline Bog Trail is wheelchair accessible.

Nuu-chah-nulth Trail   Moderate/2.5 km, one way: The Nuu-chah-nulth Trail follows a historic route once travelled by the Nuu-chah-nulth First Nations. Starting behind the Wickaninnish Interpretive Centre the trail crosses Quisitis Point and links Wickaninnish Bay (Long Beach's south end) with Florencia Bay. Trailheads are situated at Florencia Bay and near the Wickaninnish Interpretive Centre, both accessed off Wickaninnish Road and Highway 4.

South Beach Trail   Moderate/800 m, one way: From its start along the Nuu-chah-nulth Trail, the South Beach Trail runs through thick salal and descends to South Beach, known for its spectacular wave watching. Dangerous surf and powerful currents are prevalent at this pebble beach. For obvious safety reasons, swimming and other water activities are not recommended. See Cautions on page 215.

Rainforest Trails   Easy/1 km loops: Located on both sides of Highway 4, two trails loop 1 km through a mossy rainforest where giant cedar and hemlock compete for light. This is a popular birdwatching area. Markers along the east side loop describe the life cycle of a rainforest's trees. The loop starting at the parking lot gives more information about what a rainforest consists of and details on area wildlife. Trail improvements include small steps and boardwalk. The parking lot is on Highway 4's west side. Be alert for signs.

Beach hiking on the West Coast. ERIC BURKLE

Comber's Beach   Easy/500 m, one way: Along Highway 4, just south of the Greenpoint Campground, a short gravel path goes from the parking lot to the inspiring sands, dunes and surging waves at Comber's Beach. Just offshore are Sea Lion Rocks, a favourite haulout site for sea lions and a nesting spot for birds. Enjoy the seascapes or walk along the expansive beach. Be wary of incoming tides. This is a great destination for observing migratory shorebirds and active shoreline erosion.

Schooner Cove Trail   Moderate/1 km, one way: From the salal-fringed parking lot the trail drops through a cedar hemlock forest, across two streams to Schooner Cove. This scenic strand is at Long Beach's north end. High tides may temporarily restrict access. There are some wooden ramps and steps en route. The signposted trailhead is along Highway 4.

Willowbrae Trail   Moderate/1.4 km, one way: Walk the historic trail that was once part of the only route between Tofino and Ucluelet, prior to the construction of a road in the 1940s. There are long flights of stairs at the Florencia Bay beach access. The trailhead is on Willowbrae Road, off the highway to Ucluelet. See Access on page 215.

Half Moon Bay Trail   Moderate/500 m, one way: This short, steep trail cuts off the Willowbrae Trail and winds through an old growth hemlock and cedar forest to tiny Half Moon Bay, near Wya Point. This picturesque and relatively sheltered sandy beach is fringed by tall Sitka spruce. The beach approach is very steep. The total distance, one way, from the Willowbrae Trail parking area is 1.7 km. See Willowbrae Trail on page 217.

WORTH NOTING

- No bikes, horses or motorized vehicles are permitted on park trails.
- The Greenpoint Campground is a popular base camp. The site has 94 vehicle sites, a group camping area and 18 walk-in campsites. The latter have bear caches. Other amenities include fresh water, picnic tables, firepits, flush toilets and a sani-dump. From late June through early September interpretive programs are offered at a small indoor theatre. For current updates on park regulations, seasonal services, off season closures, interpretive programs and information on camping, daily parking fees or Park Use Permits contact Parks Canada.
- Visit the Wickaninnish Interpretive Centre at the end of Wickaninnish Road, about 3.5 km west of Highway 4. View displays and exhibits about the region's natural and cultural history or attend a visitor program. There is also a restaurant and gift shop. The centre is closed from mid-October to mid-March.

NEARBY

Radar Hill Radar Hill is said to be one of Vancouver Island's best viewpoints. It is certainly one of the most popular destinations within the PRNPR. Close to the park's northwest boundary just south of Tofino, a narrow, winding paved road leads to the top. From the parking area follow the 100 m path up a slope to the viewpoints. With some assistance these are wheelchair accessible.

The unforgettable panoramas provide an eagle's-eye view of everything the PRNPR has to offer: the Pacific Ocean and the wild west coast beaches, inlets, islands, mountains and coastal temperate forests that make up Clayoquot Sound. At the summit a commemorative plaque honours the Canadian war effort at Kap'yong Hill, Korea. Access is off Highway 4, 21.4 km north of the Tofino/Ucluelet T-junction. A locked gate may preclude vehicle entry in the off-season.

Big Trees Trail, Meares Island Just a 10 minute boat or a water taxi ride away from Tofino, Meares Island features the Big Trees Trail, a spectacular 3 km loop through one of BC's oldest rainforests. The trail snakes through an old growth forest of Sitka spruce, hemlock and western red cedar. The Tla'o'qui'aht First Nations declared Meares Island a Tribal Park in the mid-1980s.

Once on Meares Island, look for ribbons on shoreline trees that mark the trailhead. The first part of the loop traverses mainly level ground. Tread carefully; the weathered boardwalk is narrow and uneven and may be slippery. Use caution on the many wooden steps. The Hanging Garden Tree, a giant, ancient cedar at the end of the boardwalk, is over 2000 years old and more than 18 m in circumference. Past the boardwalk expect muddy, wet sections as the trail swings back to the start. Wear sturdy footwear and carry adequate supplies that include raingear. Allow 2 to 2.5 hours to complete the loop hike.

ADDITIONAL INFORMATION
www.pacificrimvisitor.ca Pacific Rim Visitor Centre
www.pc.gc.ca/pn-np/bc/pacificrim Pacific Rim National Park Reserve
Refer to NTS 92C/13 and 92F/4 (1:50,000)

13c. Wild Pacific Trail, Ucluelet   Map M13

DIFFICULTY/DISTANCE   Easy to moderate/0.3 km to 8.4 km, one way

HIGHLIGHTS   Ucluelet's Wild Pacific Trail winds 8.4 km along jagged headlands and through old growth forest to wild beaches and the magnificent seascapes of Barkley Sound, the Broken Group Islands and the Pacific Ocean. This area provides spectacular hiking and excellent opportunities for whale and storm watching, wildlife viewing. The trail is divided into 3 sections, each with a designated trailhead and parking area.

CAUTIONS
- Sections of the coastal trails pass close to dangerous cliffs, rocks and surge channels. Beware of rogue waves. Stay on designated routes at all times. Closely monitor all children.
- Carry extra clothing and water. Be prepared for sudden, adverse weather.
- Black bears, cougars and wolves may be encountered on the trails. Be alert.
- Expect uneven terrain and muddy sections. Parts of the wooden stairs and boardwalks may be slippery. Wear sturdy footgear.

To the Lighthouse Loop Trailhead   Head west on Highway 4 (Pacific Rim Highway) from Port Alberni to the Long Beach area. At the signposted T-junction, west of Kennedy Lake, turn left (south) to Ucluelet and continue almost to the end of Peninsula Road. Turn right onto Coast Guard Road to the signposted parking area. Secondary access is possible from the marked He-Tin-Kis Park/Terrace Beach parking area off Peninsula Road, just before Coast Guard Road. For a detailed area road map visit the Wild Pacific Trail website at www.wildpacifictrail.com.

HIKE DESCRIPTION

Lighthouse Loop   Easy/2.5 km loop: From the parking area head west to the coast and turn south to the lighthouse at Amphitrite Point, just under 1 km away. Several side paths along the way access cliffside viewpoints and this part of the trail features benches on which to rest and soak in the sights. From the lighthouse the trail swings north along the coast. Expect some uneven terrain. Avoid the boardwalk trail 0.5 km ahead that comes in on the right (east). Instead, keep to the wooden walkway that parallels the shoreline. There is 1.1 km of boardwalk in this area, part of a rainforest loop near He-Tin-Kis Park and Terrace Beach. The trail

Sunset over Wild Pacific Trail, Ucluelet.   BILL PERRY

negotiates several wooden stairs and cuts inland to a marked junction. A left at the fork accesses the He-Tin-Kis Park/Terrace Beach parking lot. Turn right (south) and hike the boardwalk to an obvious gravel path that cuts off the boardwalk and runs back to the Coast Guard Road trailhead. Allow approximately 30 to 45 minutes to complete a loop hike.

ACCESS

To Big Beach Trailhead   In Ucluelet, turn west off Peninsula Road onto Matterson Drive to Marine Drive and the signposted parking area on the corner.

HIKE DESCRIPTION

Big Beach   Moderate/1 km, one way: From the trailhead hike west a short distance to a junction. The trail to the right (north) climbs some stairs to a viewpoint and footbridge, close to Marine Drive. The trail south leads to the large picnic area at Big Beach. Explore the Big Beach shoreline or simply enjoy a seaside picnic.

ACCESS

To Brown's Beach Trailhead   Access as above for Big Beach Trailhead. At the corner of Matterson Drive and Marine Drive turn right and continue another 0.7 km to the marked trailhead on the left (west) side of Marine Drive.

HIKE DESCRIPTION

Brown's Beach   Moderate to strenuous/0.3 km to 3 km, one way: From the new Marine Drive parking area and trailhead take the short trail 0.3 km east toward Big Beach and back to Marine Drive. More adventurous hikers head 0.5 km west past some new development to the coast trail. From here the Wild Pacific Trail snakes another 3 km through west coast wilderness to the paved road to Ucluelet. En route, be sure to explore the numerous short side trails to the viewpoints. Many seaside lookouts feature wooden viewing platforms. At the highway, turn around and retrace your steps to see the region's great scenery from a reverse perspective; or follow the roadside bike trail back to Ucluelet.

WORTH NOTING

- Seals, sea lions, otter and mink are often seen in the surf. Gray whale migrations occur between February and May.
- The forests consist primarily of western red cedar and Sitka spruce
- Most of the Wild Pacific Trail follows rugged coastline trails. These are linked by access trails and area roads; the latter marked with red

lettering. The Lighthouse Loop is well maintained and wide enough in most places for side-by-side hiking.

- The trail is open during daylight hours only. For public safety trail closures may be imposed due to storm surges, high winds or blowdowns.
- Over the summer the Raincoast Education Society offers guided interpretive walks. Attendance is by donation. For more information contact www.raincoasteducation.org.
- Future trails will link the Wild Pacific Trail with the Pacific Rim National Park Reserve (Long Beach), about 14 km to the north.
- Toilets are located at all main trailheads except Brown's Beach. There is also a toilet close to the Amphitrite Point lighthouse.

NEARBY   Pacific Rim National Park Reserve (Long Beach) and Clayoquot Sound Provincial parks. See pages 215 and 210, respectively.

ADDITIONAL INFORMATION
www.wildpacifictrail.com (Wild Pacific Trail)
Refer to NTS 92C/13 (1:50,000)

13d. Carmanah Walbran Provincial Park   Map M13

DIFFICULTY/DISTANCE   Moderate to strenuous/1.3 km to 8.8 km, one way

HIGHLIGHTS   Carmanah Walbran Provincial Park (16,450 ha) was created in 1995 and protects a spectacular old growth rainforest on Vancouver Island's west coast. The area is habitat for a variety of wildlife. The park's cathedral-like atmosphere is spellbinding. Semi-improved, but still rough, valley trails guide hikers to magnificent spruce groves and giant Douglas-fir, many centuries old.

ACCESS   Along Highway 1 (Trans-Canada) just north of Duncan take Highway 18 west for 30 km to the town of Lake Cowichan. From here follow either the North Shore Road via Youbou or the South Shore Road via Mesachie Lake to Cowichan Lake's west end. Near the Heather Campsite, watch for Carmanah Walbran Provincial Park/Port Alberni/Nitinat Lake road signs and head west about 18.5 km to the Nitinat Junction. Here, at the signposted T-junction near Nitinat Lake's east end, reset your vehicle's trip meter to zero and turn left onto South Main. The road on the right is a longer alternative access route that comes in from Port Alberni.

Carmanah Walbran Provincial Park is a world-class wilderness hiking destination. RICHARD K. BLIER

Just over 5 km west of the Nitinat Junction is the turn for the Ditidaht First Nations Centre where there is a tiny grocery store, gas station and café, about 1.5 km away. There is an emergency phone nearby. For Carmanah Walbran Provincial Park keep left up the hill. At Km 9, cross the Caycuse River bridge to a T-Junction. Turn right onto Rosander Main and follow the signs. This part of the route to the park is usually the roughest and best suited for a high-slung vehicle or truck.

The logging road switchbacks up Mount Rosander to great views of Nitinat Lake, the coast and Pacific Ocean. Rosander Main runs south, through a series of regrowing cutblocks separated by pocket old growth forest, and then eventually swings east to the park parking lot. This point is 37.5 km from the Nitinat Junction.

CAUTIONS

- Getting to Carmanah Walbran Provincial Park involves travel along gravel logging roads. Loaded logging trucks and industrial traffic may be frequent. Read Forest Road Travel on page 19 carefully. Sections of the backroads closer to the park are extremely rough and may not be suitable for all vehicles. A lack of logging activities results in less road maintenance. If you are unfamiliar with wilderness hiking or gravel backroading, go with someone who knows the area well.

- Hikers travel at their own risk. Hiking times are estimates only and will vary according to weather, trail conditions and a hiker's fitness level.

- Stay on marked trails and boardwalks to protect fragile vegetation. Visitors planning extended upstream forays should be in good shape and prepared for wilderness conditions.

- BC Parks warns, although park trails are passable, they are still extremely difficult to navigate. Sections of the trails are muddy and steep. Sturdy boots are recommended. BC Parks continues to work on trail and boardwalk improvements.

- Prolonged periods of heavy rainfall are frequent; go prepared for adverse conditions. Pack extra food, rain gear and warm clothing.

- Black bears and cougars may be encountered along park trails. These animals will normally avoid people, but they are unpredictable and potentially dangerous. See Hints and Cautions. Proceed with caution near grassy areas and berry patches and make noise to warn of your presence. Never approach or feed park wildlife. Closely supervise all children.

- Remember to boil, treat or filter all creek, lake and pump water.
- Cell phones may not work in all parts of the Nitinat or Carmanah Valley.

HIKE DESCRIPTIONS

Trailhead to Carmanah Creek Junction   Moderate/1.3 km, one way: From the trailhead near the parking lot the trail switchbacks steeply down to the valley floor and the Carmanah Creek Junction. Just before the junction is the Coast Tower, the first massive Sitka spruce hikers encounter. Allow about 25 minutes hiking time, one way. The hike back to the trailhead will take longer as it is mostly uphill.

Trailhead to Three Sisters Grove   Moderate/3.8 km, one way: From the trailhead hike to the Carmanah Creek Junction. Turn north (left) onto the Upper Valley Trail and head 2.5 km upstream to the Three Sisters Grove. This grove features three mammoth spruce trees all growing in the same place. Hiking time is approximately 1 hour, 10 minutes, one way.

Trailhead to Grunt's Grove   Strenuous/5.3 km, one way: Head down into the valley to the Carmanah Creek Junction. Swing left (north) to pass the Three Sisters Grove and continue upstream another 1.5 km to Grunt's Grove, one of the park's designated gravel bar camping areas. Allow 1 hour, 45 minutes hiking time, one way.

Trailhead to August Creek   Strenuous/8.8 km, one way: Hike to the Carmanah Creek Junction and turn left (upstream) to pass Three Sisters Grove, Grunt's Grove and Paradise Pool, the latter a lure for many

CARMANAH WALBRAN PROVINCIAL PARK has 12 walk-in campsites located along the service road. There are tent pads, picnic tables, fire rings and seasonal pump water. Short-term vehicle camping is allowed in the parking lot. Walk-in wilderness camping is permitted at designated campsites in the valley. Use a portable camp stove and practise low-impact camping. Over the summer, camp on Carmanah Creek's gravel bars but be wary of quick-rising water levels in the creek. Heavy rains may also flood low-lying regions. Do not camp near the spruce groves.

Fires are permitted only in the fire rings at the park campsites above the valley along the service road and near the trailhead. Seasonal fire closures may apply. A Park Facility Operator's station is close to the trailhead. There are a few pit toilets along the trails. Contact BC Parks for more information and updates on seasonal self-registration fees and closures.

hikers. About 2 km upstream is August Creek, Carmanah Creek's largest tributary. Camping is permitted here. Allow at least 4 to 4.5 hours hiking time, one way. Trail maintenance ends at August Creek.

Trailhead to Heaven Grove and Randy Stoltmann Commemorative Grove

Moderate/ 3.9 km, one way: Hike to Carmanah Creek Junction, swing right (south) onto the Lower Valley Trail and follow the creek downstream. Heaven Tree, at Heaven Grove, is one of the valley's widest Sitka spruce, with a diameter of 3.5 m. Twenty minutes downstream, near a park information signpost, is the Randy Stoltmann Commemorative Grove. Downstream of this point park trails are closed for public safety reasons. Please observe any posted notices. Allow 1 hour, 15 minutes hiking time, one way.

WORTH NOTING

- Carmanah Walbran Provincial Park features several small lakes, river canyons and waterfalls. The Carmanah and Walbran valleys and their tributary watersheds are home to cougar, bear, elk and deer. Bird life includes hawks, eagles and marbled murrelets. The latter are robin-sized seabirds that nest in the old growth canopy between May and late July.
- The forests within Carmanah Valley and the Walbran Valley, to the east, consist of giant Sitka spruce, Douglas-fir, large western hemlock and twisted red cedar. Many of the cedar trees are over 1,000 years old. A few ancient veterans in the spruce groves reach heights of 95 m and are over 800 years old.
- Elevated viewing platforms provide safe, environmentally-friendly places at which to see the park's huge trees.
- There is no trail access from Carmanah Walbran Provincial Park to the West Coast Trail.
- BC Parks discourages hiking in the Walbran Valley. Only primitive routes exist and there are no facilities.

NEARBY

West Coast Trail   Strenuous/75 km, one way: The rugged West Coast Trail (WCT) stretches 75 km along Vancouver Island's spectacular west coast. Hike highlights include Nitinat Narrows, Tsusiat Falls and the perfect splendour of the ever-changing seascapes all along the remote coastal route. Originally constructed between Port Renfrew and Bamfield as a life saving trail for shipwrecked mariners, the WCT is part of the

Parks Canada's Pacific Rim National Park Reserve (PRNPR). The park's existence is largely due to the vision and determination of Robert Bruce Scott. An Australian native, Bruce Scott worked for the Pacific Cable Board, an employment that brought him to Barkley Sound and the Bamfield Station. In the early 1970s he convinced Jean Chretien (then a federal cabinet minister) to personally tour the region. Chretien, in turn, persuaded then Prime Minister, the Right Honourable Pierre Trudeau, to visit, and ultimately preserve the area as a national park.

The WCT is suited for fit, well equipped, experienced hikers. Parks Canada does not recommend children under 12 hike the trail. Natural dangers include torrential rains, fierce winds, chilling fog, heavy surf, extra high tides and the threat of tsunami. High tides regularly inundate and, for a time, sever parts of the WCT. Accurate knowledge of daily tidal fluctuations is essential for camping and hiking safety. Pertinent information is available from the Canadian Hydrographic Service at www.waterlevels.gc.ca.

Along the trail expect rough, uneven ground, protruding roots and branches, thick underbrush, muddy sections, waterholes, blowdown, slippery boardwalks, wooden steps and bridges in varying states of repair. Hikers will encounter boulder-strewn beaches, rocky shorelines, impassable headlands, steep, rickety ladders and cable car creek crossings. Some creeks and rivers must be forded. Despite all its challenges, or perhaps because of them, the WCT is one of the world's most-treasured wilderness hiking destinations. Allow 6 to 8 days to hike the WCT.

The PRNPR's West Coast Trail Preparation Guide, now more than 12 pages, is a lot to absorb. Required Park Use Permits—overnight and day-use—are issued at the WCT Information Centres, located at Gordon River at Port Renfrew (south end) and Pachena Bay (north end) near Bamfield. These are the only authorized WCT starting points. Both are sanctioned exit points, as is Nitinat Lake. Access or exit anywhere else is not permitted, except in cases of emergency.

WCT fees include the Overnight Use Permit plus the cost of 2 ferry crossings; one at Gordon River, the other at Nitinat Narrows. Tack on a reservation fee in the peak season (June 15th to September 15th) as Parks Canada limits the number of daily hiking starts. A bonus of getting a reservation is the complementary waterproof Parks Canada WCT Map. A handful of trail permits will be issued on a daily standby basis. Long waitlists may ensue and there is no guarantee your hike will begin on your anticipated departure date. For public safety the trail is closed from October 1st to April 30th.

Over the years many books have been written about the West Coast Trail. Readers are directed to *Hiking Trail 2*'s Suggested Reading listing on page 235 for some recent titles. For complete details on current hiking regulations and cautions, camping hints, pre-trip preparations, registration, Park Use Permits, the mandatory orientation session (approximately 1.5 hours), current fees and reservation policies, transportation options to the trailheads and equipment requirements contact the PRNPR at www.pc.gc.ca/pn-np/bc/pacificrim.

Cape Beale Headlands, Bamfield   Strenuous/3.5 km, one way: One of the Pacific Rim National Park Reserve's (PRNPR) more intriguing hiking areas is situated near Bamfield's Cape Beale, gateway to Barkley Sound. The *Topaltos Bay Trail* and the *Keeha Beach Trail* stretch 3.5 km from Bamfield to two surf-lashed west coast beaches. Accurate tidal information is crucial when exploring these coastal regions. For the first 1.5 km, both trails share the same route until they branch apart at a signposted junction.

En route to the beaches are mudholes, slippery bridges, quagmires like the Kichha Lake slough, fallen trees, deadfall, thick salal and a few steep hills. Trail improvements are minimal. Flooding is common in low-lying areas, swampy terrain and near tidal flats. During wet weather the trails are prone to standing water and extensive muddy sections. Rubber boots are the suggested footgear. Despite the tough slog required to reach the secluded, sandy beaches, these trails appeal to many experienced hikers.

Access is in Bamfield, along South Bamfield Road. Park at the designated area about 400 m from the road's end. Please do not block driveways. In good weather, allow 2 hours hiking time, one way. A Park Use Permit is required and hikers must register at the Pachena Bay West Coast Trail Information Centre, 5 km from Bamfield. More details are available from the PRNPR at www.pc.gc.ca/pn-np/bc/pacificrim.

ADDITIONAL INFORMATION

www.for.gov.bc.ca/dsi (BC Forest Service South Island District)
www.env.gov.bc.ca/bcparks (BC Parks)
www.westernforest.com/wiwag (West Islands Woodlands Community Advisory Group)
Refer to NTS 92C/10 and 92C/15 (1:50,000)

APPENDIX

Vancouver Island Trails Information Society

The Vancouver Island Trails Information Society (VITIS) is a non-profit society dedicated to providing accurate information to the public about parks and trails on Vancouver Island. The object of the society is to increase the interest of the general public in the outdoors and in hiking, by publishing information relating to these activities.

The first edition of *Hiking Trails I, Victoria and Vicinity*, was published in 1972, followed by *Hiking Trails II, Southeastern Vancouver Island* in 1973 and *Hiking Trails III, North Vancouver Island, including Strathcona Park* in 1975. Originally the society was formed as the Outdoor Club of Victoria Trails Information Society under the direction and leadership of Editor, Jane Waddell Renaud. In 1993, to eliminate confusion, the society changed its name to the Vancouver Island Trails Information Society. Our society has an unbroken 38-year history of producing hiking trails books covering all of Vancouver Island. We also maintain an up-to-date web site with additional support and resource information. VITIS members are Eric Burkle, Betty Burroughs, Sheila Delaney, Joyce Folbigg, John W.E. Harris, Irm Houle and Grahame Ruxton. These volunteer members maintain the operation of the society and guide the production of the Hiking Trails books.

Information is gathered with the assistance of dedicated hikers and climbers who have contributed accurate descriptions of trail conditions, suggested corrections and pointed the way to new hiking destinations. We would also like to thank the many individuals, organizations and agencies noted in the Acknowledgements section who have provided helpful information.

For more information about VITIS
e-mail: trails@hikingtrailsbooks.com or visit
website: www.hikingtrailsbooks.com
telephone: 250-474-5043 or toll free 1-866-598-0003
fax: 250-474-4577 or toll free 1-888-258-4213

VITIS has confidence in the reliability of information about the hiking trails and backcountry routes presented in this volume as of publication date. However, the pace and scope of change makes uncertain the information regarding management agencies, organizational arrangement, the provision of services and maintenance of facilities. Any guidebook provides a snapshot of the terrain and the trails at a given point in time. Readers must be aware that there are regular changes in organizational structures, roles and capabilities of BC Parks and BC Forest Service, and of the ownership and tenure operation of various lands by timber companies.

This is important for access issues, but also, a greater reliance on "no trace" camping practices and "self maintenance" of the land is needed. Hikers are encouraged to check with the contacts suggested in the book before venturing where there are uncertainties. *Hikers are also encouraged to check our website for changes, and to report any discrepancies that they know about. See website and e-mail address on page 229.*

Reader Survey

We are always striving to improve our hiking books. In order to continue to produce the kind of book you want, we would like to get a better understanding of our readers. As well, we would also like your suggestions on how future editions can be improved in order to continue our successful 38-year history of publishing these books on a non-profit basis.

Thank you for your participation in this survey. In recognition of how important this is to us, we will periodically select a name from the responses received. The "winner" will receive a current edition of *Hiking Trails* of their choice. Please note that all responses are treated in confidence and that your e-mail address will not be shared with others. To participate in the survey, please go to our website at: www. hikingtrailsbooks.com/survey

Vancouver Island Spine

The "Vancouver Island Spine" is a project to build a single continuous trail from Victoria to Cape Scott, at the northern tip of the Island. It will traverse backcountry, sometimes mountainous, but periodically will approach villages and towns where hikers can resupply, get a meal or accommodations. The popularity of similar trails in the United States and Europe is an indication of the commercial and social advantages the Spine will bring to Vancouver Island. The VI Spine will increase tourism and local recreation dollars for communities currently searching for ways to diversify their economies.

While the route for VI Spine has not been finalized, there are about 188 km built or committed, and about 550 km still to complete. In the southern Island, the Spine will follow the Trans-Canada Trail, a non-motorized, multi-use connection from Victoria to Lake Cowichan. From there, the Spine will connect to Port Alberni, partly along the 1913 Canadian Northern Pacific Railway grade that still exists in places. North of Port Alberni VI Spine will follow the Log Train Trail in the valley to Hal Creek and then climb to the ridge of the Beaufort Range, where views both east and west will satisfy any hiker. After skirting Comox Lake to the east, the Spine will traverse a small part of Strathcona Park, where cyclists and horses are prohibited, but will avoid technical terrain where climbing skills are needed, and the heavy snowpack of higher ranges to the west. Farther north, the Spine will connect to the North Coast Trail (opened in 2008) and the coast trail to Cape Scott.

Local outdoor clubs have been asked to endorse the concept of VI Spine. Most of the regional districts have been contacted and are co-operating with the initial planning. The task force plans to have the route walked and located in detail by GPS. Construction is already progressing in some sections. South of Port Alberni, the "Runners" trail from Headquarters Bay to Francis Lake is now proceeding. The South connection from Langford to Shawnigan Lake is scheduled to start in 2010. There is still a long way to go.

Gil Parker

www.vispine.ca
vispine@vispine.ca

Information Sources

Enquiry BC provides toll-free calling to any provincial government office:

1-800-663-7867
(limited to calls within BC)

250-387-6121 (Greater Victoria)

Local hiking clubs and outdoor organizations. These groups offer regularly scheduled hikes and it is often possible to tag along. See the list below or check the Vancouver Island Trails Information Society (VITIS) website www.hikingtrailsbooks.com for more addresses and further information.

www.albernivalleyoutdoorclub.org
Alberni Valley Outdoor Club (AVOC)

www.accvi.ca
Alpine Club of Canada Vancouver Island Section (ACC)

www.comoxhiking.com
Comox District Mountaineering Club (CDMC)

www.mountainclubs.org
Federation of Mountain Clubs of BC (FMCBC)

www.islandmountainramblers.blogspot.com
Island Mountain Ramblers (Nanaimo)

www.justabunchahikers.ca
Port Alberni hiking group

www.ocv.ca
Outdoor Club of Victoria (OCV)

www.orcbc.ca
Outdoor Recreation Council of BC

www.clubtread.org
Victoria Club Tread

The following contacts are good sources of further information and, in many cases, offer detailed maps.

www.acrd.bc.ca
Alberni-Clayoquot Regional District

www.avcoc.com
Alberni Valley Chamber of Commerce

www.backroadmapbooks.com
Backroad Mapbooks

www.bcferries.com
BC Ferries

www.for.gov.bc.ca/dsi
BC Forest Service South Island District

www.env.gov.bc.ca/bcparks
BC Parks

www.waterlevels.gc.ca
Canadian Hydrographic Service

www.crd.bc.ca
Capital Regional District

www.nanaimo.ca
City of Nanaimo

www.cowichanlake.ca
Cowichan Lake District Chamber of Commerce

www.cvrd.bc.ca
Cowichan Valley Regional District

www.duncancc.bc.ca
Duncan Chamber of Commerce

www.pac.dfo-mpo.gc.ca
Fisheries and Oceans Canada

www.galianoclub.org
Galiano Club

www.galianoisland.com
Galiano Island Chamber of Commerce

www.pc.gc.ca/gulf
Gulf Islands National Park Reserve

www.islandhikes.com
Hiking Updates

www.weatheroffice.ec.gc.ca
Meteorological Service of Canada

www.morrell.bc.ca
Morrell Sanctuary Society

www.mountarrowsmith.org
Mount Arrowsmith Information

www.nalt.bc.ca
Nanaimo Area Land Trust

www.nanaimoharbourferry.com
Nanaimo Harbour Ferry

www.visitparksvillequalicumbeach.
com
Oceanside Tourism Association

www.pc.gc.ca/pn-np/bc/pacificrim
Pacific Rim National Park Reserve

www.pc.gc.ca
Parks Canada

www.sitesandtrailsbc.ca
Recreation Sites and Trails BC

www.rdn.bc.ca
Regional District of Nanaimo

www.ladysmith.ca
Town of Ladysmith

www.trailsbc.ca
or
www.tctrail.ca
Trans-Canada Trail

www.viha.ca/mho
Vancouver Island Health Authority

www.hikingtrailsbooks.com
Vancouver Island Trails Information
Society

www.westernforest.com/wiwag
West Islands Woodlands Community
Advisory Group

www.wildpacifictrail.com
Wild Pacific Trail

Search and Rescue

Call out for Search and Rescue
emergencies is done by telephoning
911. Local Search and Rescue
Organizations will only respond
through the "lead organizations",
namely the RCMP and BC
Ambulance. The Joint Rescue
Coordination Centre (military) is
involved in air and marine rescue,
again through the RCMP. More
information on Search and Rescue
groups and how to make donations
is available through the British
Columbia Search and Rescue
Association at www.bcsara.com.
No phone numbers are given to avoid
unfiltered call outs.

Alberni Valley Rescue Squad

Arrowsmith Search and Rescue
(Qualicum Beach)
kenneden@telus.net
www.asar.ca

British Columbia Cave Rescue

Comox Valley Ground Search
and Rescue
comoxvalleysar@yahoo.ca
www.cvgsar.com

Cowichan Search and Rescue
www.cowsar.org

Gabriola Island Search and Rescue

Ladysmith Search and Rescue

Lake Cowichan Search and Rescue

Mayne Island Search and Rescue

Nanaimo Search and Rescue
Organization

Pender Island Search and Rescue

Saltspring Island Search and Rescue

Acknowledgements

For this Ninth Edition of *Hiking Trails 2*, dedicated hikers, walkers, climbers and others have provided accurate descriptions of trail conditions, offered detailed trip accounts, suggested corrections, and pointed the way to new hiking destinations. Many people have gone to considerable trouble in offering their valued help. The BC Forest Service, BC Parks, Capital Regional District, Parks Canada, Regional District of Nanaimo, area logging companies, Tourist InfoCentres and various municipal, regional and other government agencies all contributed to the updates.

Numerous individuals went out of their way to ensure that map and text queries were answered correctly. Their efforts made this revision a lot easier. Special thanks to Joan Michel at the Regional District of Nanaimo and Quagger at islandhikes.com. Barb Baker provided key information pertaining to many Port Alberni trails. Peter Rothermel offered invaluable assistance and suggestions for trails and routes in the Mount Arrowsmith area. To them and any others whose help has not been acknowledged in these pages, extended thanks.

Thanks to: Jim Bisakowski at BookDesign.ca for deciphering my map revisions and for creating the newer maps; Frances Hunter at Beacon Hill Communications Group for her expertise and timely assistance; Gil Parker, editor of *Hiking Trails 3*, for his contributions.

And of course, thanks to the Vancouver Island Trails Information Society Editorial Committee: Eric Burkle, Betty Burroughs, Sheila Delaney, Joyce Folbigg, John W. E. Harris, Irm Houle and Grahame Ruxton.

Richard K. Blier

Suggested Reading

The books and publications listed below are a random selection of the many titles available to further enhance your Vancouver Island hiking adventures. Some titles may be out of print but will show up from time to time in second hand bookshops and online.

Adventuring Around Vancouver Island by Sue Lebrecht & Susan Noppe

Alberni Valley Trail Guide by the Alberni Environmental Coalition

Amphibians & Reptiles of British Columbia by Matsuda, Greens & Gregory

Aware of the Mountain, Mountaineering as Yoga by Gil Parker

Backroad Mapbook Vol. 5 Vancouver Island by Mussio Ventures

50 Best Dog Walks/Hikes Around Victoria by Leo Buijs

Best Dog Walks on Vancouver Island by Leo Buijs

Beyond Nootka: A Historical Perspective of Vancouver Island Mountains by Lindsay Elms

Birder's Guide to Vancouver Island: A Walking Guide to Bird Watching Sites by Keith Taylor

Birds of Coastal British Columbia by Nancy Baron & John Acorn

Birds of Victoria by Robin Bovey, Wayne Campbell & Bryan Gates

Blisters and Bliss, A Trekker's Guide to Vancouver Island's West Coast Trail by David Foster & Wayne Aitken

British Columbia Coast Names by John T. Walbran

Butterflies of British Columbia by John Acorn

Coastal Hikes by Philip Stone

Coast Mountain Men, Mountaineering Stories from the West Coast by Gil Parker

Coastal Wildflowers of the Pacific Northwest by Elizabeth L. Horn

Common Seashore Creatures of the Pacific Northwest by J. Duane Sept

Cowichan, Duncan, Chemainus, Ladysmith and Region by Georgina Montgomery

Cowichan Valley Tourist Map and Street Guide by Davenport Maps

Encyclopedia of Raincoast Place Names by Andrew Scott

Essential Wilderness Navigator: How to Find Your Way in the Great Outdoors by David Seidman

Explore Our Parks and Trails by the City of Nanaimo

Fishing Mapbook Vancouver Island by Mussio Ventures

Geology of Southern Vancouver Island by Chris Yorath

Hiking Adventures With Children: Southern Vancouver Island and the Olympic Peninsula by Kari Jones & Sachiko Kiyooka

Hiking on the Edge: West Coast Trail – Juan de Fuca Trail by Ian Gill & David Nunuk

Hiking the Ancient Forests of British Columbia and Washington by Randy Stoltmann

Hiking the Gulf Islands, An Outdoors Guide to BC's Enchanted Islands by Charles Kahn

Hiking the West Coast of Vancouver Island by Tim Leadem

Hiking the West Coast Trail South to North/North to South: A Pocket Guide by Tim Leadem

Hiking Trails 1: Victoria and Vicinity by Richard K. Blier

Hiking Trails 3: Northern Vancouver Island including Strathcona Park by Gil Parker

Hiking Vancouver Island by Shannon & Lisa Cowan

Island Adventures by Richard K. Blier

Island Alpine: A Guide to the Mountains of Strathcona Park and Vancouver Island by Philip Stone

Island Backroads: An Outdoors Guide to Vancouver Island by Richard K. Blier

Juan de Fuca Marine Trail by Matthew Payne & Adam Vaselevich

Kayaking Vancouver Island by Gary Backlund & Paul Grey

Nature Walks Around Victoria by Helen Lansdowne

Leave No Trace: A Guide to the New Wilderness Etiquette by Annette McGivney

More Island Adventures by Richard K. Blier

Mosses, Lichens & Ferns of Northwest North America by Vitt, Marsh & Bovey

Mushrooms of Northwest North America by Helene Schalkwijk-Barensen

Nanaimo/Qualicum/Parksville Tourist Map & Street Guide by Davenport Maps

Native Trees of British Columbia by Halter & Turner

Outdoor Safety and Survival in British Columbia's Backcountry by Mike Nash

Pacific Coast Fern Finder by Glenn Keaton

Pacific Coast Bird Finder: A Manual for Identifying 61 Common Birds of the Pacific Coast by Roger Ledere

Plants of Coastal British Columbia by Jim Pojar & Andy Mackinnon

Plants of the Gulf Islands and San Juan Islands and Southern Vancouver Island by Colin Varner

Regional Parks & Trails Guide by the Regional District of Nanaimo

Seashells and Shellfish of the Pacific Northwest, A Field Guide by Rick M. Harbo

Some Common Mosses of British Columbia by W.B. Schofield

South Vancouver Island Street Guide and Recreation Atlas by Davenport Maps

Tourist Map & Street Guide to Nanaimo, Qualicum/Parksville by Davenport Maps

Trans Canada Trail British Columbia by Bruce Obee

Vancouver Island Outdoor Recreation Guide by John Kimantas

Vancouver Island Shores by Linda Colbeck

Victoria-Nanaimo Nature Walks, the Easy Guide by John Henigman

Unknown Island by Ian Smith

West Coast Trail by Wolfgang Winterhoff and Outdoor Guidebooks

West Coast Trail: One Step at a Time by Robert J. Bannon

West Coast Trail Waterproof Map by International Travel Maps

Where to see Wildlife on Vancouver Island by Kim Goldberg

Wild Coast, A Kayaking, Hiking and Recreation Guide for North and West Vancouver Island by John Kimantas

Wild Coast 3, A Kayaking, Hiking and Recreation Guide for B.C.'s South Coast and East Vancouver Island by John Kimantas

Index

About the Editor

Outdoor writer, photographer, hiker and angler, **Richard K. Blier**, has explored Vancouver Island's trails, backroads, lakes, coastlines, parks and  campsites for over three decades. He is author of three backroad guidebooks: *Island Backroads* (Orca Book Publishers, 1998); *More Island Adventures* (Orca Book Publishers, 1993); *Island Adventures* (Orca Book Publishers, 1989). He also revised and edited *Hiking Trails II* (Seventh Edition, 1993 and Eighth Edition, 2000) *Hiking Trails III* (Ninth Edition, 2002) and *Hiking Trails 1* (Thirteenth Edition, 2007) for the Vancouver Island Trails Information Society. Mr. Blier is a regular contributor to *Island Fisherman* magazine. His Vancouver Island backroads feature stories have appeared in *BC Outdoors Sports Fishing* magazine and *The Islander, Times Colonist*. His photos have appeared in newspapers, magazines and other books. Please visit *Backroad Adventures on Vancouver Island* at www.members.shaw.ca/richardblier.

Also in this series:

Hiking Trails I
Victoria & Vicinity

Hiking Trails 3
Northern Vancouver
Island

*Published by Vancouver
Island Trails Information
Society and distributed
by Orca Book Publishers*

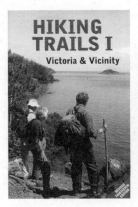

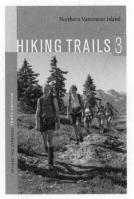